ARCHAEOLOGIES OF
THE GREEK PAST

Social memory – the shared remembrances of group experience – creates shared identity, and provides people with both an image of their past and a design for their future. But how are we to conceive the memories of past peoples such as, for example, the ancient Greeks? This book makes a strong case for the use of archaeology, particularly the evidence of landscape and of monuments, to trace patterns in commemoration and forgetfulness. Three detailed case studies (early Roman Greece, Hellenistic and Roman Crete, and Messenia in Archaic to Hellenistic times) focus on societies undergoing different types of social transformation. Material evidence allows us to observe how groups responded to these challenges, and how they made different uses of the past, in the past.

SUSAN E. ALCOCK is Professor of Classical Archaeology and Classics and Arthur F. Thurnau Professor at the University of Michigan and Adjunct Curator at the Kelsey Museum of Archaeology. She obtained her doctorate from the University of Cambridge and subsequently taught archaeology and classics at the University of Reading. She is the author of *Graecia Capta: The Landscapes of Roman Greece* (1993) and editor of *Placing the Gods: Sanctuaries and Sacred Space in Ancient Greece* (1994, with R. G. Osborne), *The Early Roman Empire in the East* (1997), *Pausanias: Travel and Memory in Roman Greece* (2001, with J. Cherry and J. Elsner), and *Empires: Perspectives from Archaeology and History* (2001, with T. D'Altroy, K. Morrison, and C. Sinopoli). Professor Alcock was recently awarded a MacArthur Fellowship by the John D. and Catherine T. MacArthur Foundation and has also been recognized with the Henry Russel award by the University of Michigan, as a Distinguished Faculty Member by the Michigan Association of Governing Boards, and with the Excellence in Undergraduate Teaching Award by the Archaeological Institute of America. She is on the editorial boards of the *Journal of Archaeological Research, Journal of Social Archaeology*, and *Archaeological Dialogues* and the monograph series Greek Culture in the Roman World, Topics in Contemporary Archaeology, and Cambridge World Archaeology, all published by Cambridge University Press.

THE W. B. STANFORD MEMORIAL LECTURES

This lecture series was established by public subscription,
to honour the memory of William Bedell Stanford,
Regius Professor of Greek in Trinity College, Dublin,
from 1940 to 1980, and Chancellor of the University of
Dublin from 1982 to 1984.

ARCHAEOLOGIES OF THE GREEK PAST

Landscape, Monuments, and Memories

SUSAN E. ALCOCK

Professor of Classical Archaeology and Classics,
The University of Michigan

CAMBRIDGE
UNIVERSITY PRESS

CAMBRIDGE UNIVERSITY PRESS
Cambridge, New York, Melbourne, Madrid, Cape Town, Singapore,
São Paulo, Delhi, Dubai, Tokyo

Cambridge University Press
The Edinburgh Building, Cambridge CB2 8RU, UK

Published in the United States of America by Cambridge University Press, New York

www.cambridge.org
Information on this title: www.cambridge.org/9780521890007

© Cambridge University Press 2002

First published 2002

A catalogue record for this publication is available from the British Library

ISBN 978-0-521-81355-6 Hardback
ISBN 978-0-521-89000-7 Paperback

Transferred to digital printing 2009

For
MOUNT TOM
and
FENWAY PARK

CONTENTS

ILLUSTRATIONS

PREFACE

Fittingly enough for a piece of writing about memory, this book stands as the end product of two acts of commemoration. In 1998 I was given the honor of delivering the Stanford Memorial Lectures, established by public subscription to honor the memory of William Bedell Stanford, at Trinity College, Dublin. There I first publicly explored the relationship of archaeology and social memory, focusing on case studies concerned with the Greeks under Roman rule and the Messenians under Spartan domination; chapters 1, 2, and 4 of the present volume are expanded and revised versions of those Dublin lectures. A year later, I gave the Seventh Ian Sanders Memorial Lecture in Classical Archaeology at the University of Sheffield. In honor of Sanders himself, a pioneer of historic Cretan studies, I turned to the commemorative landscapes of Hellenistic and Roman Crete; chapter 3 is a revised version of my lecture in Sheffield.

My curiosity about archaeology and memory, however, predated those two invitations. An obsession with memory has marked the closing decades of the twentieth century (in other words, my own adult life time); and near the turn of the millennium, when these lectures were delivered, the subject had become almost impossible to avoid, both within the academy and beyond. I remember first wondering about social memory and the Greeks when, while working with Peter Callaghan at Knossos on Crete in the 1980s, I heard about the discovery of Roman-period votives in the venerable – and, as I had conceived it, almost wholly prehistoric – Idaian Cave on Crete (discussed here in chapter 3). Research on regional developments in Roman Greece (considered a land "obsessed with its past") and fieldwork in Messenia (an excellent example of a "people without history") only prodded me further into wondering about what people in Greece, or indeed anywhere, remembered, and why, and how.

I met some people along the way who, directly or indirectly, fostered my ruminations about "the uses of the past in the past," and who provided me with the ammunition I have chosen to attack the subject. At the University of Cambridge, John F. Cherry and Anthony M. Snodgrass taught me about regional survey, and thus about landscape studies; here I have attempted to extend their convictions about the validity and power of survey evidence into the domain of commemorative behavior. At the University of Reading, my colleague Richard Bradley taught me to think about monuments and especially the "afterlife" of monuments, and demonstrated how to interpret them with panache. Combining the elements of landscape and monuments offers us not only an illuminating, but – I believe – an *indispensable* means by which to explore social memory in antiquity.

But make no mistake: this is not an easy endeavor. Memory's "fragile power" (in Schacter's phrase) resists easy conclusions or ready closure, however desirable these may often seem (Schacter 1996: 1–13). At an early stage of research I remember being heartened by the acknowledgments in Patrick Geary's book, *Phantoms of Remembrance: Memory and Oblivion at the End of the First Millennium*. There he quoted an anonymous reviewer's opinion of his proposed project:

> Historians from their earliest training are warned against arguments from silence, but Patrick Geary is proposing to study the sounds of medieval silences. But whatever the song affirms, silences remain silent. How can one study what people in the past forgot? . . . He wants to write on "structures of forgetting." My counsel to him would be: forget it.
>
> (Geary 1994: xiii–xiv)

But Geary persevered, and – for better or worse – so have I.

I would like to express my gratitude to the faculty and students of Trinity College, Dublin – especially Kathleen Coleman and Brian McGing – for their helpful comments on my Stanford Lectures and for their kind hospitality. Similar thanks must go to the Ian Sanders Memorial Lecture Committee and to my audience in Sheffield, with special acknowledgment to Paul Halstead, John Barrett, and John Moreland. Bettina Bergmann, Paul Cartledge, Kathleen Coleman, Jaś Elsner, Christopher Jones, Nino Luraghi, Robin Osborne, and Josephine Shaya have read all or parts of the book and offered much needed advice, as did an anonymous reviewer for Cambridge University Press. I must, as always, single out John F. Cherry for his unerring eye and unwavering grammatical sense. Some of the empirical data and theoretical approaches were also tried out on audiences at the American Anthropological Association and at the Wenner-Gren Foundation for Anthropological Research Symposium, "Imperial Designs: Comparative Dynamics of Early

Empires" (Alcock 2000; 2001b). Finally, I would also like to acknowledge the guidance of participants (particularly Hélène Lipstadt) in the workshop on "Monuments and Memory," sponsored by the Ford Foundation and held at the Department of the Classics, Harvard University, as well as the participants of my graduate seminar, "The Archaeology of the Second Sophistic," taught at Harvard during a term there as visiting professor in 2001.

Translations of Pausanias are taken from Frazer (1898a) with some modifications; the passage of Thucydides on p. 157 is from *Assassins of Memory* by Pierre Vidal-Naquet (© Columbia University Press. Reprinted with the permission of the publisher). Translations of other authors are as noted or my own. Robin Meador-Woodruff (Kelsey Museum of Archaeology, University of Michigan) and John Donaldson (Museum of Classical Archaeology, University of Cambridge) were instrumental in acquiring certain images; David L. Stone (Boston University) and Paul Jaronski (University of Michigan Photo Services) produced several of the illustrations. Work on this book was greatly assisted by my Arthur F. Thurnau Professorship at the University of Michigan.

ABBREVIATIONS

AAA	*Athens Annals of Archaeology*
AJA	*American Journal of Archaeology*
AJP	*American Journal of Philology*
ANRW	*Aufstieg und Niedergang der römischen Welt*
AR	*Archaeological Reports*
ArchDelt	*Archaiologikon Deltion*
ASAtene	*Annuario della Scuola archeologica di Atene e delle Missioni italiane in Oriente*
BCH	*Bulletin de correspondance hellénique*
BSA	*Annual of the British School at Athens*
CP	*Classical Philology*
EntrHardt	*Entretiens Hardt*
HSCP	*Harvard Studies in Classical Philology*
ICr	*Inscriptiones Creticae*
IG	*Inscriptiones Graecae*
JHS	*Journal of Hellenic Studies*
JRA	*Journal of Roman Archaeology*
JRS	*Journal of Roman Studies*
PastPres	*Past and Present*
PCPS	*Proceedings of the Cambridge Philological Society*
SEG	*Supplementum Epigraphicum Graecum*
TAPA	*Transactions of the American Philological Association*

ARCHAEOLOGIES
OF MEMORY

Memory – what a strange thing it is!
(Bachelard 1964: 9)

The present is "haunted" by the past and the past is modeled,
invented, reinvented, and reconstructed by the present.
(Assmann 1997: 9)

... memory is a process, not a thing ...
(Olick and Robbins 1998: 122)

This book is about something difficult to define, something troublesome
to pin down, and in which not everyone entirely believes. It is also about
something vital to our understanding of the ancient world. People derive
identity from shared remembrance – from social memory – which in turn
provides them with an image of their past and a design for their future.[1]
What people remember of the past fashions their sense of community and
determines their allies, enemies, and actions; they will argue over it and kill
for it. Social memory is manifestly a mighty force, but also a fugitive one.
Memories overlap and compete; over time they change or are eradicated;
people forget.

As this chapter will demonstrate, it is hard enough to follow the muta-
bilities of memory in the present day; so, inevitably, the problems are all the
more compounded for long-gone times. How to study a present "haunted"

1. Fentress and Wickham define social memory as "an expression of collective experience: social
memory identifies a group, giving it a sense of its past and defining its aspirations for the future"
(1992: 25). Olick and Robbins define memory studies as "a general rubric for inquiry into the
varieties of forms through which we are shaped by the past, conscious and unconscious, public
and private, material and communicative, consensual and challenged" (1998: 112). A closely
related concept is Assmann's "cultural memory," summed up tersely by Jonker as "the sum of the
memories which a society needs to emulate its past and from which it derives its identity": Jonker
1995: 30; Assmann delimits four spheres – mimetic memory, material memory, communicative
memory, and cultural memory – with the first three entering into the space created by the fourth:
Assmann 1992: 21, 48–66. Some recent general reviews of social memory include Bourguet
et al. 1990; Connerton 1989; Fara and Patterson 1998; Klein 2000, esp. 134–38; Lowenthal 1985:
193–210; Olick and Robbins 1998; Roth 1994.

by the past, when even that present lies far removed from us in time, leaving only fragments behind? How are we to conceive the memories of past peoples such as, for example, the ancient Greeks? Two academic strategies have evolved to deal with such questions. The first has been simply to relieve dead populations of the burden of their past, proceeding to analyze and assess their activities as if they had no memories at all. The second has been solely to rely on surviving documentary evidence when attempting to recover what societies valued and recalled. Neither strategy is satisfactory – the first based on an arrogant and unsound premise, the second on a severely limited view of what constitutes relevant data.

This book proposes another way forward by espousing the cause of archaeology, in particular the evidence it affords of monuments and landscapes. In archaeology the term "matrix" defines the material in which artifacts are embedded and supported; I shall argue here that memories are similarly embedded and supported within a material framework. To examine that framework is to expand the range of commemorative practices and impulses we can actually recognize and study, giving back to peoples in the past – if only ever partially – some of the vigor of their remembrances.

To make my argument, I will consider three specific case studies, each set in a different time period and with a different geographical scope. They are, however, related analyses, for each revolves around peoples at a time of especial stress and transformation (notably the impact of military conquest and annexation), and each employs archaeological evidence to trace responses to those challenges. To begin, however, I want to explore in somewhat more detail the nature of social memory and the present state of its study. The role of archaeology in this endeavor also requires clarification, detailing just which categories of material culture are most helpful in approaching anything as intangible and frangible as memory. At the chapter's conclusion, I introduce the three studies in which we will explore remembrance of things past – in the past.

SIX SHORT STORIES ABOUT SOCIAL MEMORY

I find talking in the abstract about social memory a rather arid discourse for such a dynamic subject. To that end, six short stories are here told that delineate the power and complexity of remembering. Myriad tales could have been invoked, but I deliberately chose the six to represent diverse contexts and approaches. The first vignette serves as a bridge to the principal focus of the book – ancient Greece – but the remainder are admittedly a geographically and temporally mixed bag. The short stories also display the mélange of means through which memory is sustained (including ritual performances, archival documentation, oral traditions, ethnographic testimony, and physical mementoes) – or erased – as well as a variety of scholarly styles. The cumulative impact of these short stories makes a variety of points essential to my argument, and these will be reviewed after the stories have been told.

Stripping the Parthenon

The story of the Greek Revolution against Turkish dominion – its enthusiastic European backing, its heroic indigenous leadership – has been recounted many times. Memories of past freedom stirred all parties involved; the invocations most frequently recorded called upon the classical age and, in particular, upon the liberty ensured by the Persian Wars. Innumerable quotations come to mind; Byron musing at Marathon "that Greece might still be free," or Alexander Ypsilantis proclaiming:

> Let us recollect, brave and generous Greeks, the liberty of the classic land of Greece; the battles of Marathon and Thermopylae; let us combat upon the tombs of our ancestors who, to leave us free, fought and died. The blood of our tyrants is dear to the shades . . . above all, to those of Miltiades, Themistocles, Leonidas and the three hundred who massacred so many times their number of the innumerable army of the barbarous Persians – the hour is come to destroy their successors, more barbarous, and still more detestable. Let us do this or perish. To arms then, my friends, your country calls you.

Pressure to locate the source of Greek identity in that particular, classic epoch continued in the wake of statehood – a choice externally urged by the influential "Philhellenes" of Europe and by the geopolitical situation of the young nation. Today, the history, art, and culture of the High Classical age still dominate global conceptions of what is truly significant about Greek history.

Also demanding recognition within this modern nation, however, are divergent patterns of commemoration, versions of Greek cultural origins that refused to forget the centuries intervening between Pericles and Kolokotronis. Advocates remember and speak for the heritage of Byzantium, and for indigenous developments in the country, even under Turkish rule. The title *Romiós* (or Romeic), derived ultimately from "Roman," has been used to sum up this stance, which (such is the authoritative power of the "Hellenist" image) has often been conceived in pejorative terms. The co-existence of these distinct memorial positions, and the contestations between them, have been

Fig. 1.1 Aquatint of the Athenian Acropolis, published in *Views in Greece, from Drawings by Edward Dodwell* (1821). A Turkish mosque would have stood within the Parthenon at this time, but that fact seems discreetly veiled.

remarked in many spheres – in poetry, in politics, in folklore, in music, above all in language.[2] But they could also be visible to the eye.

An aquatint published in 1821 (the very year of Revolution) by the British traveler Edward Dodwell helps to make the point (Fig. 1.1). That is indeed the Parthenon on the Athenian Acropolis, but here it stands side-by-side and surrounded by dwellings, religious structures, fortifications, and monuments belonging to quite distinct historical epochs – a palimpsest of construction and experience. For viewers and passers-by, elements within this collection would stimulate memories of different episodes, gods, or heroes; they would activate remembrance of different moments in the past. The continuing physical juxtaposition in Greece of churches and temples, Byzantine mosaics and

2. For a scholarly study of "Hellenist" and "Romeic" conceptions, as manifest particularly in folklore studies, Herzfeld 1982. Patrick Leigh Fermor was once told by a Greek friend that (in some uses) "Romiós" represented "our dirty linen" – or, in Leigh Fermor's words, "the helplessness of subjection and the strands of Turkish custom which . . . wove themselves into the web of Greek life." Fermor discusses the "Helleno-Romaic dilemma" at length in *Roumeli*, creating a list with sixty-four diverging characteristics and preferences. The last of these contrasts the Dome of St. Sophia with the columns of the Parthenon (1966: 96–147, quotation at 100). The Ypsilantis proclamation is quoted in full in St. Clair 1972: 23; out of a vast bibliography, see also Brewer 2001; Tsigakou 1981: 21–62.

Fig. 1.2 Twentieth-century view of the Athenian Acropolis.

Classical statues, allows both Hellenist and Romeic conceptions of the past to persist, and persistently to contend with each other.

That only remains true, however, if the structures themselves are allowed to survive. These observations cast new light upon a well-documented phenomenon: the stripping of the Athenian Acropolis over the course of the nineteenth century. Medieval and early modern monuments and structures – the Turkish mosque within the Parthenon, parts of the Ducal Palace, the Frankish Tower – were all demolished, with little record kept of their "destruction."[3] Left behind is a polished limestone surface on which stand scattered edifices and monuments dating almost exclusively to the classic "golden age" (Fig. 1.2). Explanations for these actions are numerous, complex, and deeply bound up with the emergence of Greek national identity and the *Megali Idea*, and with the imperatives of western cultural (not least touristic) expectations. The appearance of the present-day Acropolis must also be taken, however, as the result of a battle over social memory; it represents a struggle for control over a highly memorable space. The loser, characteristically, becomes invisible.

3. For an overview of this "destruction," McNeal 1991. A similar pairing of illustrations, as in Figs. 1.1 and 1.2 here, is employed in Schneider and Höcker 1990: 11.

The Camisard rebellion

In the early eighteenth century, Louis XIV, the Sun King, revoked the Edict of Nantes and outlawed Protestantism. Local enforcement of this central edict led, in the Cévennes mountains of southern France, to desperate revolt. Whipped up by Messianic exhortations and waging guerrilla-style warfare, the Camisards (as they are known) for a short time beat back the Royalist troops before being crushed. Over 250 years later, the historian Philippe Joutard discovered that the people of the Cévennes were still happy to talk about this Camisard rebellion. They described its leaders and heroes (one evocatively nicknamed "Roland," after the hero of the medieval narrative, *The Song of Roland*), as well as the course of various clashes; in particular they could identify geographical locales associated with the revolt, not least the refuge caves of the Camisards. To some extent these communal memories were fed by historical accounts and by formal monuments; on the other hand, such honors were late in coming – the rebels were widely condemned until a nineteenth-century Romantic reappraisal. Moreover, the fact that many of the anecdotes revolve around minor events – a particular skirmish, the exploits of a familial ancestor – points to the work of long-term oral tradition, rooted in strong memories of specific places.

These stories – some academically verifiable, some not – all work to the same end: "that of constituting the Protestant community's identification of itself as a community of resistance, which is partly backed up by and partly creates a tradition of resistance that has continued to exist in the area until today." The paradigmatic eighteenth-century outbreak invades and shapes remembrance of other historical events which become "camisardized," as James Fentress and Chris Wickham put it in their 1992 book *Social Memory*. Other groups at moments of opposition (notoriously the French Resistance of World War II) are cast very much in the Camisard mold, while men or events which fail to fit this pattern (even such "greats" as Napoleon or World War I) are disregarded – much to the horror of more conventional nationalist historians. This commemorative structure guides the region's ongoing political stance: steadfastly in favor of opposition, in favor of resistance.

Relative stability of population clearly contributed to this deep-running pattern of social memory; by contrast, neighboring areas, more transformed by processes of industrialization, possess far sketchier notions about the uprising. As the people of the Cévennes themselves become increasingly mobile, the detail of Camisard memories, and their inherent power, is also becoming attenuated.[4]

***

4. Fentress and Wickham 1992: 92–99, quotation at 93.

Digging Sargon

In the successive and competing dynasties and empires of ancient Mesopotamia, regimes continually invoked memories of their predecessors, using them to create and promulgate structures of political identity. A principal stimulus for these shared memories, Gerdien Jonker has argued, was the physical trace of the past in the present-day landscape: old cities, old walls, old temples, old statues – in other words, the material framework of the past in the present (termed, after Halbwachs [see below, pp. 24–25], the *cadre matériel*). While this led to a complicated "topography of remembrance," the most powerful commemorative magnet was late third-millennium BC Akkad and its legendary rulers Sargon and Naram-Sin. This "Akkad orientation" offered a legacy of centralized rule and state strength, in contrast to which names and events lacking such ingredients fell into "the black holes that recur in reconstructions of Mesopotamian memory patterns."

As the centuries passed, however, invoking the necessary *cadre matériel* became harder and harder to do, as the Mesopotamian landscape was profoundly rewritten, with new structures and features threatening or erasing those older traces. Yet Assyrian and Babylonian rulers of the first millennium BC still desired connections back in time, not least to the now distant days of Akkad. Kings thus turned philologist, reading (as one inscription claims for the seventh-century BC ruler Ashurbanipal) "the obscure Akkadian which is difficult to master. I inspected stone inscriptions from before the flood on which the dynasties had stamped their seal." Babylonian rulers, with monumental ruins in their territories, took an even more direct approach, purposefully digging at Akkad, at Ur, at Sippar, and elsewhere. Excavated discoveries were carefully recorded, resulting in texts oddly reminiscent of modern museum records: "Copy of a baked tile from the ruins of Ur. The work of Amar-Sin, king of Ur...Nabu-shuma-idinna...examined it and copied it for further surveying."

Not only did Mesopotamian kings practice excavation but, in a good cause, they would even salt their sites. Nineteenth-century AD excavations at Sippar discovered a container under the floor of the Ebabbar (the "White House"), abode of Shamash, god of the sun. In it were found building inscriptions of Nabonidus, last of the Babylonian kings (556–539 BC), together with a strangely shaped stone tablet (the "cruciform monument"; Fig. 1.3). Nabonidus, in recording his restoration of the Ebabbar, claimed to be building on the very foundations of Sargon the Great himself; there he discovered an inscription of Naram-Sin unseen by any other monarch, the king himself calculated, for 3200 years. This, the cruciform monument, bore Naram-Sin's

Fig. 1.3 The "cruciform monument" from the temple of Shamash at Sippar.

"original" regulations for the Shamash temple. Nabonidus implemented these rules, which seemed to come – in every sense – straight from the past, before reburying Naram-Sin's message with accounts of his own activity. A statue was also found in the old foundations, unequivocally identified by Nabonidus as an image of the great Sargon although the king noted "half of its head had broken off and it had disintegrated so that he did not find its face." The statue too was restored to a cultic function.

The strategy here is clear. Nabonidus sought, as a Babylonian king in an era of Assyrian decline, to claim the mantle of Akkad and thus of universal empire. If the necessary *cadre matériel* to summon up the necessary memories had vanished, then it was necessary to rediscover it. Nor should this be taken as an isolated royal fantasy. Through their engagement in ritual activity along lines laid down millennia before, broader communities came to see themselves as part of an ongoing chain of activity, anchored back in a hallowed time. Yet these links to the past, and the authority and pride they channeled, emerged only in carefully predetermined situations. As Jonker stresses, not all aspects of the past were equally important: not just any old excavation, in any old place, finding any old artifacts would do. The targets selected and the "chosen interpretation depended on the identity of the community that did the digging." The statue's face may have been missing, but Nabonidus none the less knew he had found Sargon.[5]

Neolithic gatherings

The prehistoric monuments of Britain are almost preternaturally long-lived. One example, Hambledon Hill in Dorset, is a local landscape inscribed with Neolithic long mounds, Bronze Age barrows, an Iron Age hillfort, and Anglo-Saxon burials; it has been documented as a notable regional landmark in accounts of the English Civil Wars, in the writings of Thomas Hardy, and in modern parish records (Fig. 1.4). Throughout this remarkable span of occupation, each period, in its own way, recognized its predecessors: earthworks respect earthworks, present-day archaeologists carefully disentangle the site's stages of activity.

5. Jonker 1995, quotations at 68, 156, 155, 170, 174. Another chest, this one dating to the ninth century BC, was also found (just below that of Nabonidus) in the nineteenth-century excavations of the Ebabbar temple. It too contained inscriptions and a cult relief of the god. Eleventh-century invasion had eradicated the cult of Shamash from Sippar; the "discovery" of this image, it was said, allowed new statues to be made and the cult renewed with honor. The king Nabu-apla-iddina then buried the relief "to prevent such a loss occurring again" (p. 163). Nabonidus must have been aware of this other casket, but makes no mention of it; his discoveries are turned to a different purpose. For other archaeological acts of Nabonidus, Schnapp 1996: 13–19, 31. For deliberate mutilation of another image of "Sargon": Nylander 1980.

Fig. 1.4 Aerial view of Hambledon Hill, Child Okeford, Dorset.

For the generations alive during the earlier British Neolithic (the fourth millennium BC), monumental complexes such as Hambledon Hill appear to have served as points in the landscape for the intermittent meeting of a population that was otherwise for the most part dispersed. Such gatherings allowed bonds of recognition and kinship to form, defining a larger social world for these small and scattered groups. Meeting at monuments provided contexts for exchange and feasting, for display and competition. These rituals and conversations provided the space necessary for the communication and consolidation of shared memories: "Within and around these arenas, it was possible to renew a sense of the collective, to mediate conflicts between lineages and confirm distinctions within groups... more often than not, these practices drew upon the past, the past of earlier generations and the past of ancestral time." To return again and again to the same places, over the decades and over the centuries, affirmed collective traditions and common respect for the past.

Such interpretations, of course, are based upon the results of detailed archaeological work, upon the assessment of artifact provenience, of human skeletal and faunal remains, of the changing shape and size of the monument as a whole. In his book *Ancestral Geographies of the Neolithic*, Mark Edmonds has tried to move beyond such ostensibly objective reportage, writing in a deliberately emic, empathetic vein to convey the human atmosphere of such Neolithic gatherings:

> Before the sun had set, all would gather again . . . Within talk of what would happen, most knew that the night was important because it was almost the last . . . Most trades had been concluded, and there was agreement among many on rights of access. Spring would see new calves and help with new ventures, confirmation of bonds that had been recognised in the circle. With help and good fortune, there would be no conflict when the land was reborn.
>
> The old ones watched. They had made the pattern many times and looked on as it was formed again. Each time it seemed that a new element was added, a twist in the tale. It was never repeated exactly . . . There was always a chance that the pattern would be lost. That was why they watched. The dead held the circle together and everything else in its place.

The "old ones" imagined by Edmonds were prescient about change and the possibility of change. Over the course of the Neolithic, gathering places were continually reworked and their practices recast. The increasing proximity of settlements and elaborate burials to the enclosures, for example, suggests the growing promotion of more sectional or familial interests, whose own readings of the past presumably now competed with those of the collective. Neolithic monuments follow a variety of subsequent trajectories, but some at least (including Hambledon Hill) ended violently. There, oak outworks were burnt, rubble filled its ditches, bodies were left for scavenging animals, the site – for a time – was abandoned. Whatever specific forces lay behind this destruction, they must in part reflect a rejection of a dominant pattern of memories, the weight of invested tradition, contained by Hambledon Hill.[6]

The Rock War of Kalymnos

In 1935, the women of the Greek island of Kalymnos clashed with Italian *carabinieri*, fighting as a group ("shouting, hooting, resembling a human ocean")

---

6. Edmonds 1999, quotations at 134, 131–32.

with their bare hands, and – in the final encounter – with rocks. The Italians occupied the island at this time, but the specific catalyst to violence was a perceived threat to the Greek Orthodox Church, a fear that the Italians wished to place it under the control of the Pope. The women's opposition lasted for three days, ending when a man, against their wishes, joined the fray with a slingshot and was killed. All in all, this *Petropolemos* ("Rock War") was no small affair, but "the largest and most violent protest that the Italians faced during their thirty-year rule over the Dodecanese."

The *Petropolemos* is today remembered in several fashions, as David Sutton observes in his study of Kalymnos, *Memories Cast in Stone*. Older participant women speak of it proudly in everyday conversation, emphasizing its collective nature and reveling in the memory of their strength. In some forms of official discourse, such as newspaper accounts, the "Holy Rock War" is invoked whenever new threats to traditional Kalymnian religion, such as prosyletization by Jehovah's Witnesses, appear on the scene. Male memories, by contrast, tend to be more guarded and less frequently proffered; those that do find expression downplay the women's efforts, as compared to the parts played by the murdered slingshotter or by a vocal Orthodox priest, Papa Tsougranis. An accompanying shift of emphasis, moving the event from its local context to more national significance, was also witnessed by Sutton in an annual commemorative ceremony in 1993:

> This celebration involved the typical elements of a Kalymnian historical celebration: the presence of the political and religious dignitaries of the island (almost exclusively men), the playing of the Greek national anthem by the local philharmonic band, and the laying of the wreath by the mayor of Kalymnos on the bust of the priest, Papa Tsougranis . . . In the audience of approximately 200 people, only a few were old enough to have participated in the Rock War. The schoolteacher's speech emphasized how the Rock War was one of many similar acts of resistance to foreign tyranny in Greek *national* history No longer an outstanding act of collective resistance on the part of unarmed women, the Rock War had become, in his account, an example of Kalymnos living up to the ideals of a united Greece.

In this version of events, the schoolteacher's keynote speech mentioned the women only once, and then he described them as swept into resistance by the leadership of Papa Tsougranis.

How to remember the "Rock War" of less than a century ago, when women took to the streets and fought in the center of their community, is clearly problematic in Kalymnian society. The "human ocean" of their struggle is "preserved in the memories and writings of a few, disputed by others, and for the rest . . . assimilated to the canons of legitimate history." As time and the generation of participants passes, its memory will not be reinforced in the living community and may ultimately disappear, outside the realm of academic accounts.[7]

Pecos Pueblo

The Pueblo Revolt of the American Southwest – "the first American revolution" – was a successful, if short-lived, rebellion. In 1680, an alliance of native villages temporarily drove the Spanish conqueror from their lands. Harsh levels of economic exploitation and determined missionary efforts to extirpate "idolatrous practices" underlay the formation of this ultimately shaky Pueblo coalition. Much aided by its internal dissensions, the Spanish under Diego de Vargas would return only a dozen years later, although completion of the *reconquista* would take some time.

The inhabitants of the Tano pueblo at Pecos, numbering about 2000 in 1680, participated vigorously in this revolt; the "fury of the Pecos" helped spearhead the siege of nearby Santa Fe and led to the slaughter of friars and settlers. But they fought in other ways as well, burning and leveling the monumental church (Nuestra Señora de los Ángeles de Pecos) which the Spanish had built within their pueblo in the 1620s. They then established a new kiva on the very grounds of the church's *convento* (rectory), with its entrance in full view of the now-ruined church (Fig. 1.5).[8] Kivas, subterranean circular chambers, were traditional spaces for religious ceremonials and other gatherings integral to pueblo society; not surprisingly, they became conspicuous points of contestation between indigenous peoples and Spanish missionaries. Kivas in several pueblos were visibly terminated through Christian activity; Alfred Kidder, the foremost early excavator of Pecos, noted that of the ten kivas in use at the beginning of the mission period, eight would either be stripped of their roofs or filled with garbage.

The symbolic juxtaposition of forsaken church and reasserted kiva would seem to point to an absolute and unified rejection of Christianity and of the Spanish by the Pecos community. Documentary sources, however, provide a somewhat different picture. It is attested that the pueblo's native governor warned the Spanish of the coming revolt. Pecos Pueblo emerged as an early

7. Sutton 1998, quotations at 89, 87, 93–94 (original emphasis), 95.
8. The kiva was placed in the *convento*'s corral; bedrock formations on site may well have prevented its establishment in an even more defiant location, such as the cloister: Hayes 1974: 33.

Fig. 1.5 The entrance to the post-rebellion kiva at Pecos Pueblo. In the background stand the foundations of the church destroyed in the Pueblo Revolt and its subsequent monumental replacement.

and firm ally of de Vargas in his campaign of recovery, although this split the community: dissidents either fled elsewhere or, in some cases, were actually executed by village authorities. The stamping out of one tradition and the reestablishment of another, so apparently clear in the site's architectural sequence, only partially reflects the decisions taken by the pueblo and masks its internal conflicts. The later construction of a new church on the ruins of the old, and the backfilling of the post-rebellion kiva, no doubt equally mask disagreement about right tradition and wrong memory.[9]

*

9. Hayes 1974; Sando 1979; Schroeder 1979; Simmons 1979. For other examples of symbolic "superposition" of monuments around the time of the revolt, Hayes 1974: 32–33. On the Pueblo Revolt, see Knaut 1995; Wilcox 2001. For later historic and present-day ethnic contestations, see Gonzales-Berry and Maciel 2000; Levine 1999.

I said at the beginning of this chapter that not everyone believes in social memory; even some believers are uncomfortable with certain aspects of the concept. A central concern is the straddle that must be made between individual reminiscences and their collective expression: how does a "society" remember? Amos Funkenstein (and many others) says "it" cannot: "consciousness and memory can only be realized by an individual who acts, is aware, and remembers. Just as a nation cannot eat or dance, neither can it speak or remember. Remembering is a mental act, and therefore it is absolutely and completely personal." A great fear arises that social memory offers a back door to re-creating essentialized categories ("collective," "people," "folk") of the very sort archaeologists, historians, and anthropologists have long sought to escape. In its more extreme forms, a denial of the individual can seem implicit, which leaves "the individual a sort of automaton, passively obeying the interiorized collective will."[10] These are serious methodological issues, made even more vexing by the fact that quite how individuals "remember" is not yet fully understood.

On the other hand, it is impossible to deny that social groups do share common memories (if not in lockstep and not to the exclusion of all else), and that those memories do powerfully inflect group perceptions and actions. The frameworks through which that shared shaping of remembrance takes place will be further discussed below (pp. 28–32). One other way to square this circle is to admit the existence of numerous "memory communities," with different sets of mnemonic practices, at work at any one time. The short stories illustrate this well, from the regional limits of the Cévennes, to the gendered remembrances of the Rock War, to the internal divisions of Pecos Pueblo. Memory communities are far from fixed or all-consuming entities, even when they encompass the "imagined communities" of national traditions or the bonding passions of ethnic groups. Other bodies – cities, institutions, regional associations, labor unions, and families – are also legitimate bearers of memory, and individuals are clearly capable of participating in more than one of these domains. This insistence on multiplicity avoids the danger of reifying some monolithic, mystical group mind.[11]

10. Quotations from Funkenstein 1993: 6; Fentress and Wickham 1992: ix, who compensate in part by using the term "social memory" rather than "collective memory." Touching on this point, from varying critical stances, see Gedi and Elam 1996 (who consider collective memory a "myth"); Klein 2000; Young 1993: xi. Olick and Robbins term the study of social memory a "nonparadigmatic, transdisciplinary, centerless enterprise," yet still end their review by saying "Sociology...cannot afford to forget memory" (1998: 105, 134). On recent advances in the "archaeology of the individual," see Meskell 1996; 1999; Tarlow 1997.
11. Halbwachs 1925. On national memories: Anderson 1991; James 1997; Kammen 1991; Olick and Robbins 1998: 116–19; see also references in n. 21. The term "memory community" is borrowed

What we are talking about, instead, is a plurality of concurrent, possibly conflicting, and potentially competing memories available to peoples at any given time. Dominant versions of the past obviously do exist (such as the traditions of the modern-day nation-state), but even these never stand alone. Subversive "counter-memories," chiefly belonging to a society's disempowered or deviant branches, forcibly challenge master narratives; in other cases, memory communities co-exist peacefully, if not always comfortably; in still other cases, they may operate in happy ignorance of each other.[12] So in the six stories above, we see different degrees of tension or contestation. Friction is averted with silence on Kalymnos, where men and women rarely confront each other about just what happened under Italian occupation. The people of the Cévennes preserved their Camisard memories, if at the expense of things the rest of France found more worthy of remembrance; in Greece the virtues of "Hellenist" and "Romeic" positions have been alternately promoted in both scholarly and popular culture. Memories came in more explosive conflict at Hambledon Hill, as well as at Pecos Pueblo, where choices about which past to acknowledge and which future to pursue were burnt and hammered into the site and where even a tiny community could further divide itself.

The story line, in each of these cases, is noticeably dynamic. Neolithic enclosures were constantly reworked over the generations; the destruction of Hambledon Hill represented its "death" in one incarnation, before it moved on to assume other meanings. Nabonidus, lacking the required link to a specific past, created his own version of Babylonia's relationship to ancient Akkad; the monuments of Pecos rise and fall. These observations raise a fundamental point: people may well represent their memories as constant and immutable (and firmly believe them to be so), yet – to return to Jan Assmann's quote at the chapter's head – "the past is modeled, invented, reinvented, and reconstructed by the present." Forgetfulness is as pivotal to this process as remembrance.[13] The medieval and Turkish Acropolis is gone; the inhabitants of the Cévennes region are beginning to forget the Camisards, as others have already done. As the older women of Kalymnos die, common knowledge of their saga goes with them. It is no longer in anyone's interests – political, economic, personal – to remember. These stories can never be

from Burke (1989), who patterns it on Stanley Fish's "interpretive communities" – subcultures within which criteria for judgment are implicitly or explicitly understood.

12. Davis and Starn 1989; Wickham 1994: 276; Zerubavel 1995: 10–11. On counter-memories: Foucault 1977: 139–64, though the term is currently little employed; given the inherent tensions in remembrance, it would be "redundant" (Klein 2000: 146, n. 6). For a famous debate about negotiation of "the present in the past": Appadurai 1981; Bloch 1977; see also Schudson 1992.

13. On forgetting: Battaglia 1992; Carsten 1995; Taylor 1993.

entirely lost, captured ("cast in stone") as they have now been by historians and anthropologists. But in the absence of such interventions, many former channels of memory have surely been erased beyond reconstruction, or even imagination.

This potential malleability of memory, coupled with its galvanic emotional charge, makes it too powerful, and too volatile, a forcefield to ignore. We are familiar with the politics of memory, not least in Northern Ireland, the former Yugoslavia, and the Middle East, places where conflicting, equally strongly affirmed, accounts of the past are sent into battle, much as people are. Yet the politics of remembrance were equally operative in the British Neolithic, in first-millennium BC Mesopotamia, or in seventeenth-century New Mexico. Memories often cluster around particular paradigmatic events (what Assmann terms "constellative myths") or around particular charismatic figures. The Camisard Rebellion and the Persian Wars fall in the first category, Sargon and Leonidas in the second; like lightning rods, they drew energy to select versions of the past.[14] Conversely, amnesias – be they encouraged by the male-dominated discourse of Kalymnos or enforced through the back-filled kivas of the pueblos – likewise play a part in creating a "correct past." But who makes those decisions? Or, as Peter Burke put it: "It is important to ask the question, who wants whom to remember what, and why? Whose version of the past is recorded and preserved?"[15]

An obvious aspect of memory politics is the manipulation of the past by rulers or ruling elites. As Jacques Le Goff states flatly, "To make themselves the master of memory and forgetfulness is one of the great preoccupations of the classes, groups, and individuals who have dominated and continue to dominate historical societies."[16] Authoritative pronouncements formed one part of this process, such as when Nabonidus "reminded" his people of their historic link to Akkad. But material acts also created "masters of memory," as with the encroachment of elaborate family burials onto Hambledon Hill, or with the stripping of the Acropolis to fit a philhellenic, externally acceptable image of nationhood.

14. Assmann 1997: 7; Fentress and Wickham 1992: 92–114. Schwartz (1982: 290) uses the phrase "charismatic epoch," another example of which is the Greek Civil War (Collard 1989). Other charismatic figures include the hero *caciques* (hereditary chiefs) of the colonial peoples of the Columbian Andes (Rappaport 1998: 31–41), the Madagascar ruler Andrianampoini-Merina (Larson 1999), and the Messenian hero Aristomenes (see chapter 4).
15. Burke 1989: 107. See also Davis and Starn 1989: 2.
16. Le Goff 1992: 54. Foucault put it this way: "If one controls people's memory, one controls their dynamism . . . It is vital to have possession of this memory, to control it, administer it, tell it what it must contain": quoted in Baker 1985: 134. See also Alonso 1988; Duby and Lardreau 1980; Geary 1994: 3–9, 12; Gillis 1994b; Wachtel 1990.

Elite commemorative choices are ultimately – inevitably – going to prove most visible and effective; it is their version of the past that, most frequently, will be "recorded and preserved." Having admitted that, however, other possible answers do exist to Burke's questions. As he himself remarks:

> Given the multiplicity of social identities, and the co-existence of rival memories, alternative memories (family memories, local memories, class memories, national memories, and so on), it is surely more fruitful to think in pluralistic terms about the uses of memories to different social groups, who may well have different views about what is significant or "worthy of memory."[17]

Attempts to determine (and to agree on) what is "worthy of memory," of course, are where things get sticky. It is not an accident that so many of my short stories revolve around episodes of contestation, resistance, and violence.

I said earlier that the short stories were also intended to illustrate the various means by which memories travel and can be traced. "*How* societies remember" is a vastly complex matter. Here I merely outline some of the principal components of that process; each will reappear in action in the book's case studies. To begin, we can name ritual and ritual performances; the cult activities prescribed by Nabonidus and the gatherings at Hambledon Hill were what activated links to the past. Often related to ritual is the viewing of artistic representations, another means of conjuring recollection.[18] Crucial perhaps above all is the working of oral tradition, many of the characteristics of which (hardly surprisingly) echo those associated with social memory. Students of oral lore stress its selective, often anachronistic nature; its embeddedness as a "social product"; its structural amnesias; its political and contingent nature. With the "technological miracle" of writing (to quote Jan Vansina), such evanescent traditions can be permanently recorded, irrevocably affecting the flow and character of available information.[19] Writing (or other modern modes of capturing material) preserves stories that may

17. Burke 1989: 107.
18. For a general overview of "how societies remember": Connerton 1989. On artistic imagery: Grütter 1997; Küchler and Melion 1991. A related issue, not taken up here, is Aby Warburg's conception of "social memory" in his study of artworks as repositories of history, and of the recurrence and meaning of motifs and gestures in western art: Gombrich 1970.
19. Vansina 1985: 199; 1980; 1985; see also Bohannan 1952; Henige 1982; Tonkin 1995. For ancient Greece, and for further references and discussion, see Thomas 1989; 1992. The concept of dynamic homeostasis – in which traditions are perfectly congruent with their society at any given point in time – is obviously relevant here: Goody and Watt 1968; for a partial critique, Vansina 1985: 120–23.

otherwise be lost, such as those of the women of Kalymnos. In all cases, however, someone must first consider them "worthy of memory."

All these elements make up the normal arsenal of those broaching the subject of social memory. One additional source, however, can be identified. In each story, the physical world and tangible objects prompted and guided the course of memory; each possessed strong material correlates. Formally constituted memorials are part of this picture, from the belated monuments to Camisard heroes to the bust of Papa Tsougranis. But people of the Cévennes could also identify with confidence the battlefields and refuge caves of a Camisard topography; Mesopotamian dynasts worried about the disappearance of an ancient and valuable material record to the point of digging it up; monumental building testifies to Neolithic community and Pueblo confusion. In other cases, as on the Athenian Acropolis, things must be destroyed. In short, there is a strong *materiality* to these memories, and that provides archaeology with a space in which to work.

QUESTIONS OF MEMORY

"Welcome to the memory industry" runs the slightly sour beginning of a recent article. Twentieth-century crises (from the Holocaust to the rise of multi-culturalism), capped by the turn of the millennium, have for the past few decades fueled an intense absorption with memory in all manner of guises: social, individual, animal, autobiographical, psychological, physiological. The subject's intersection of humanistic and scientific perspectives, of the political and personal, makes it highly appealing; everyone has something to offer and much to say.[20] The appearance of yet *another* book with memory in the title would thus seem to carry the proverbial coals to Newcastle. I defend this enterprise on two grounds. First, while archaeologists are beginning to recognize the unique power of their data, specifically *archaeological* research into the dynamics of social memory remains by and large at a relatively early stage. And second, modern obsessions with memory revolve chiefly around the modern; this book pushes that inquiry back to the ancient Mediterranean world.

Inevitably, however, the broader scholarship that swirls around this topic has directly impacted my own treatment. One chief defining characteristic of that scholarship is a focus on "Disturbing memories," to cite the title of the

20. Memory industry: Klein 2000: 127; warnings of "burn out" have begun to appear: Confino 1997; see also Chippindale 1993: 33–35; Maier 1993. On other archaeological studies, see nn. 46–47; Alcock and Van Dyke, in prep.; Hall 2001.

first of the 1996 Darwin College Lectures (on "Memory") at the University of Cambridge. Trauma – loss, dispossession, moments of crisis, death – is an inexorable magnet for attention, as are the threatened subaltern memories of the colonized or oppressed.[21] Heroes or martyrs of resistance are standard charismatic figures; glorious defeats provide fertile ground for constellative myths. More rarely do happy moments appear the focus for collective remembrance: "Only that which does not cease to hurt remains in memory."[22]

It has been shrewdly argued that this very "boom" in memory studies is trauma-derived: "academics speak incessantly of memory because our epoch has been uniquely structured by trauma."[23] The most fraught of our memorial controversies turn on just how to commemorate victims of war or of genocide. How to remember the Holocaust is a particularly unceasing zone of debate, especially as the last generations of survivors pass on. Communities have been torn apart merely by discussing the design of Holocaust monuments.[24] War memorials too prove perennially divisive; the Vietnam Veterans Memorial may be the most prominent recent example of a monument's angry reception, but it is far from an isolated instance.[25] Other, still burning issues revolve around past shameful episodes or historical injustices, such as the legacy of fascism or the iniquitous treatment of indigenous peoples.[26]

Also considered "disturbing" are perceived contemporary changes in the way we remember, and relate ourselves to, the past. Authentic memory is

21. Sennett 1998; see also Olick and Robbins 1998: 107–8. A range of illustrative studies (appearing since the mid-1980s) include Abercrombie 1998; Bahloul 1996; Borofsky 1987; Darian-Smith and Hamilton 1994; Davis and Starn 1989; Gurahian 1990; Hall 1998; Healy 1997; Hutton 1994: 102; Rappaport 1998; Silverblatt 1988; Slyomovics 1998.
22. Nietzsche, quoted in Huyssen 1994: 9. Or one could quote Walter Benjamin (1965: 255): "To articulate the past historically does not mean to recognize it 'The way it really was' (Ranke). It means to seize hold of a memory as it flashes up at a moment of danger." The link of change and trauma, remembering and forgetting, is also central to Anderson's conception of the "imagined communities" of nationality: "All profound changes of consciousness, by their very nature, bring with them characteristic amnesias. Out of such oblivions, in specific historical circumstances, spring narratives" (1991: 204).
23. Klein 2000: 138–42 with references, quotation at 138; Olick and Robbins 1998: 119–20.
24. Out of a vast body of writings: Friedlander 1993; Koonz 1994; LaCapra 1994; 1998; Lappin 1999; Linenthal 1995; Olick and Levy 1997; Roth 1995; Vidal-Naquet 1992. On monuments: see Young 1993; 1994b. For new technologies of remembering the Shoah, see the website of the United States Holocaust Memorial Museum (www.ushmm.org/).
25. Hass 1998; Lin 1995. Controversies still rage over the ongoing modification of that memorial's site, as well as over the commemorative landscape of Washington, DC as a whole: note, for example, the uproar over the planned World War II memorial on the Mall. The Enola Gay controversy could also be cited: Linenthal and Engelhardt 1996. On war memorials generally: Azaryahu 1993; Borg 1991; Davies 1993; Harbison 1991: 64–66; Rowlands 1993: 146; Winter and Sivan 1999; and papers by Laqueur, Piehler, Savage, and Sherman in Gillis 1994a. An especially vibrant literature revolves around the memorialization of World War I: Lipstadt 1999; Tarlow 1997; Winter 1995.
26. See, for example, Barkan 2000.

dead, some would argue, necessitating its paradoxical prefabrication through the deliberate creation of designated "sites of memory" (*lieux de mémoire* in Pierre Nora's phrase). The work of Nora and his school has provoked an ongoing dispute over the extent to which post-modernism has seen the end of a tradition of memory.

> *Lieux de mémoire* are fundamentally vestiges, the ultimate embodiments of a commemorative consciousness that survives in a history which, having renounced memory, cries out for it. The notion has emerged because society has banished ritual. It is a notion produced, defined, established, constructed, decreed, and maintained by the artifice and desire of a society fundamentally absorbed by its own transformation and renewal. By its very nature that society values the new over the old, youth over age, the future over the past. Museums, archives, cemeteries, collections, festivals, anniversaries, treaties, depositions, monuments, sanctuaries, private associations – these are relics of another era, illusions of eternity.[27]

Lieux de mémoire (which, for Nora, range far beyond material places or things) serve as select relics, as enduring elements of a memorial heritage. Technological transformations foster such developments, as the "quick-time" circulation of information piles on ever more relentlessly and as the pace of remembrance is forced. Nora's arguments patently spill over into the realm of "heritage industries" and of archaeological display: for example, in outcries over site presentation and museum exhibitions, and their alleged production of a prepackaged, controlled, and sanitized past.[28]

These modern anxieties provide one influential backdrop to my study. They are certainly quite alien to the majority of calmer, more theoretical treatments of memory in the classical world. Ruling the roost there, of course, is the rhetorical and forensic *ars memoriae*, the famed "art of memory" with its extensive post-classical afterlife. This "art" (whose genealogy stretches back to the Archaic poet Simonides, but which is best described by Cicero

27. Nora 1996: 6; for the full scope of his project, see Nora 1997; 1996–98. Frederic Jameson voices related sentiments, discussing "one major theme: namely the disappearance of a sense of history, the way in which our entire contemporary social system has little by little begun to lose its capacity to retain its own past, has begun to live in a perpetual present and in a perpetual change that obliterates traditions of the kind which all earlier social formations have had in one way or another to preserve" (1985: 125); he designates the post-modern "as an attempt to think the present historically in an age that has forgotten how to think historically in the first place" (1991: ix). See also Assmann 1996; Huyssen 1995. For Nora, and many others, the sundered relationship of history and memory is a central issue for debate, but one that shall, by and large, be bypassed here.
28. Out of a vast literature on "who owns the past" and the heritage industry: e.g., Baker 1988; Chippindale *et al.* 1990; Kirschenblatt-Gimblett 1998; Layton 1994; Lowenthal 1997.

and Quintilian) drew on explicitly material mnemonic techniques. Places and images (*loci* and *imagines*) – "linked one to the other like dancers hand in hand" (Quintilian, *Institutio Oratoria* 11.2.21) – were associated with points necessary for building and delivering a successful rhetorical performance. Imaginary walks through houses or streets would thus prompt Roman orators to the right thought in the right order, much to the admiration of both contemporary observers and later scholars:

> The word "mnemotechnics" hardly conveys what the artificial memory of Cicero may have been like, as it moved among the buildings of ancient Rome, *seeing* the places, *seeing* the images stored on the places, with a piercing inner vision which immediately brought to his lips the thoughts and words of his speech.[29]

Such phenomenal feats of memory were politic and advisable in the competitive atmosphere which characterized Roman elite interaction.

Apart from the *ars memoriae*, the classical world made one other principal contribution to the field of memory studies. From the writings of philosophers and theologians from Aristotle to Saint Augustine emerged one long-lived conception of how memory operated: a static model of recollection, in which elements could be retrieved pristine (if with some effort) from the "depository" or "storehouse" of the human mind. That reassuringly stable construction, founded in part on the authoritative classical canon, was only finally and unceremoniously exploded in the later nineteenth and twentieth centuries, as recognition swelled of memory's dynamism and "unreliability."[30]

The study of ancient memory is expanding these days, for example with the techniques of the *ars memoriae* turned on issues of artistic style and social display, or with detailed discussion of the "logistics" of memory, such as the creation and transmission of books.[31] The fact is, however, that the subject of *social* memory (in the senses outlined earlier) remains relatively neglected in the classical world. Egypt and the Near East have been analyzed by the work of

29. Yates 1966: 1–26, quote at 4 (original emphasis); C. Edwards 1996: 29–30; Small 1997: 81–137; Vasaly 1993: 88–130; see also Haverkamp and Lachmann 1991. Fabian (1983: 111–13) asserts a link between such mnemotechnic aids and the development of the modern discipline of anthropology.
30. On classical conceptions of memory: Carruthers 1990; Coleman 1992; Farrell 1997; Yates 1966. Parallel understandings, in which memory was "crafted," always ran side-by-side with the "storage" model; for medieval versions of the *ars memoriae*, employing Noah's Ark or a seraph's wing feathers, see Carruthers and Ziolkowski (forthcoming). For one schematic review of the early history of memory, Olick and Robbins 1998: 112–14.
31. Art historical studies: Bergmann 1994; Elsner 1995: 76–80. Memory "logistics": Small 1997. For a general review, Small and Tatum 1995.

Assmann and his circle; Roman emphasis on *monumenta* and *mos maiorum* has drawn scholarly fire as well, if not always precisely targeted on social memory *per se*.[32] Left underrepresented are the memories of ancient Greece.

Taken at face value, such an assertion no doubt seems strange, if not actually false. That the Hellenes were a memorious people has never been in doubt, and their mythic self-conceptions and histories have been endlessly examined and emulated. Relevant issues, such as studies of oral tradition, could be cited as exploring the "uses of the past in the past," as could particular topics of archaeological analysis – for example, the practice of Geometric and Archaic hero or tomb cult. Nevertheless, I stick to my argument. Few students of Greek antiquity have yet to approach social memory within specific historical contexts, or to consider it as a dynamic expression of collective experience, as a point of likely internal contestation, as a consequential element in decisions about present and future.[33] My argument, then, is that it is time explicitly to recognize and tackle this phenomenon – but that does leave us with the question of how to proceed.

A PHYSICAL SETTING FOR REMEMBRANCE

Literary and epigraphic evidence has borne the brunt of reconstructing ancient attitudes to the past, and nothing can, or should, dislodge such sources from their place in this analysis. Yet *sole* dependence on them, as remarked earlier, carries with it certain decided hazards. Such texts best illustrate dominant commemorative narratives, and it is rare for them to offer alternative versions or a glimpse into the potential range of counter-memories. Distinctions of status, faction, or gender become blurred; variations (regional or civic, urban or rural) can easily be lost. Male, elite, and urban perspectives, almost inevitably, pronounced upon what was deemed "worthy of memory." The result is a filtered set of memories left for our consideration.

If people in the past were "more integrated and whole than we fragmented moderns," such a filter might not seem to pose much of a problem.[34] But I don't concur with that beguiling assumption; nor is it supported by the stories

---

32. Assmann 1988; 1992: 167–228; 1995; Assmann and Hölscher 1988; Assmann *et al.* 1983; Jonker 1995. Some recent relevant Roman studies include Beard 1987; Davies 2000; C. Edwards 1996: 27–43; Favro 1993; Jaeger 1997: 94–131; Koortbojian 1995; Moreau 1994; Small 1997: 230–35; Wiseman 1986.
33. Recent research is moving rapidly in this direction; for a handful of examples, see Antonaccio 1994; Cartledge 1997: 18–35; Foxhall 1995; Gehrke 2001; Higbie 1997; Osborne 1996. On oral tradition, Thomas 1989; 1992, with additional references; see also Finley 1965. Hero and tomb cult: Antonaccio 1995; Morris 1988; Whitley 1988. For the rubric "uses of the past in the past," see Bradley and Williams 1998.
34. Ortner 1995: 174, who does not accept this premise.

told earlier. Of course, one is here walking a fine line. As Matt Matsuda warns, "'memory' has too often become another analytic vocabulary to impose on the past; the point should be to re-historicize memory and see how it is so inextricably *part* of that past." The inhabitants of the ancient Mediterranean were not living with or through the "acceleration of history" (in Nora's phrase) or in the wake of the Holocaust.[35] The problems of modern memory cannot be shipped back to them wholesale. But that does not mean the pendulum can swing entirely in the other direction, to erase the presence and power of the past from their lives. Nor is there any justification for assuming that social memory "back then" somehow formed an automatically simpler and more homogeneous whole. A *spectrum* of memories, in the past as in the present, should be anticipated and sought.

This leaves us with the pressing issue of how to expand our grasp of that spectrum, moving beyond the ambit of the textual sources. At this point we can turn to the figure of the French sociologist Maurice Halbwachs. In social memory studies it is *de rigeur* to speak of Halbwachs, who inaugurated the field in writings such as *Les cadres sociaux de la mémoire* (first published 1925) and *Mémoire collective* (1950). There he articulated many of the central theses thus far discussed in this chapter: memory's inherently "social" nature, its multiplicity, its dynamism. Over the course of his career (he died at Buchenwald), Halbwachs undertook an eclectic range of sociological studies, and was also an associate of the early *Annales* historians, but unquestionably it is his work on memory that keeps his own name alive.[36] Later scholars have found much to criticize in Halbwachs's formulations, not least his Durkheimian emphasis on the collective nature of remembrance at the expense of the individual, and his rigorous separation of "history" from "memory."[37] Such criticism merely reflects his importance, however, and for all the flaws, his work remains fundamental.

For our purposes, what is most crucial is Halbwachs's repeated insistence on the physical setting of remembrance. He returns again and again to the way

---

35. Matsuda 1996: 16, original emphasis; Nora 1996: 1. Nora would certainly argue for the richness of memory in "peasant culture," but that has not played into discussion of the ancient world. For a broader discussion of peasant memory: Fentress and Wickham 1992: 87–114.
36. Halbwachs 1925; 1950. For evaluations of the man and his thinking: Halbwachs 1992; Sennett 1998; Slyomovics 1998: xi–xii; Wachtel 1990: 5–8; and Hutton 1993: 73–90, where additional references are provided. Halbwachs was not completely alone in advancing such arguments; the first psychologist to emphasize the social dimensions of memory, arguing that memory was never "out of context," was Frederick Bartlett (1932).
37. Critiques and extensions of Halbwachs: Baker 1985: 156–59; Connerton 1989: 36–40; Funkenstein 1993: 7–9; Geary 1994: 9–16; Gedi and Elam 1996; Irwin-Zarecki 1994; Jonker 1995: 16–26; Namer 2000; Wickham 1994: 276–77; Zerubavel 1995: 4–5. On "invention": Hobsbawm and Ranger 1983.

in which memory is localized in objects and in places, not least in the material framework of the past in the present (his *cadre matériel*): "The memory of groups contains many truths, notions, ideas, and general propositions ... But if a truth is to be settled in the memory of a group it needs to be presented in the concrete form of an event, of a personality, or of a locality."[38] He also recognized, however, that contingent circumstance affected perceptions of this framework, allowing for commemorative adaptation over time. This interplay of durability and dynamism is best exemplified in his study *La topographie légendaire des évangiles en terre sainte: étude de mémoire collective* (1941). Halbwachs there traced the shifting topography of the Holy Land over a long time-span, from the generations immediately following the life of Jesus until the Christian Crusader reconquest.

In this analysis, places and monuments linked ("accurately" or not) to Jesus and early Christianity can be seen to appear, disappear, and move about in space, depending on the exigencies of the particular historical moment. Thus, in speaking of Christianity's early days of persecution and alienation from both mainstream Jewish and Roman society, Halbwachs contended that the group turned to its own immediate past and to places imbued with its own memories:

> Christian thought contrasted sharply with the outlook of the surrounding groups in the midst of which it tried to organized itself. Its beliefs were drastically opposed to Jewish and pagan belief systems because of its different conceptions of life and society ... This collective representation was construed without the help of any pagan elements, or of aspects of life in Jerusalem. How could such a memory continue if it failed to attach itself to some points in the terrain? These places were just as real in the present as in the past. With their assistance the life of Jesus, whatever its supernatural aspects, could be represented in a world of images that were by no means hallucinatory, but on the contrary familiar, accepted by everybody, and taken for granted in the normal course of contemporary life.[39]

By contrast, Christians of later periods would lay increasing doctrinal stress on Christ's Passion and thus on Jerusalem as the "theater" for those all-important events (such as the place of his crucifixion on Golgotha, Fig. 1.6). The Galilean landscape, where Christ dwelt and taught for most of his earthly existence, proceeded to lose much of its commemorative force. Also

38. Halbwachs 1992: 200 (1941: 159, in the original French edition).
39. Halbwachs 1992: 202 (1941: 161).

Fig. 1.6 Photograph of "Golgotha" taken by G. R. Swain in 1920. Swain added his own commentary on the remembrance of this place; the entry in his photo journal reads: "Palestine. Jerusalem. The place outside the present wall of the city supposed by some to be Golgotha, from the somewhat fanciful resemblance of the ledge to the eyes of a skull. Really the place has been a quarry, and doubtless much changed since the time of Christ."

compelling is Halbwachs's recognition of the vulnerability of monuments; he notes how the investment of memories in select places and things offered a ready target for attack, in the case of the early Christians as elsewhere:

> It may well be that enemies of emergent Christianity tried to deface these places and to destroy signs that could help to recognize them. Legend has it that an emperor ordered the planting of a sacred wood dedicated to pagan deities on the site of Calvary so as to prevent the Christians from gathering there. This is like the behavior of a government that, in an attempt to maintain order in a previously rebellious city, destroys the

centers of an uprising or the seat of revolutionary battles by constructing large avenues or huge public edifices to wipe out any memories that threaten its reputation.[40]

The subject of *La topographie légendaire des évangiles en terre sainte* was neither the historical life of Jesus, nor any single subsequent period, but rather the diachronic history of the Holy Land as it was *remembered* – its "mnemohistory" in Assmann's terminology.[41] But with his stress on the tangible world – monuments, tombs, shrines, streets (notably the via Dolorosa), ruins, even old stones reused within new houses – Halbwachs sketches out what is almost a kind of "mnemoarchaeology." Through it, each age constructs its own topography of remembrance: "in each period the collective Christian memory adapts its recollections of the details of Christ's life and of the places where they occurred to the contemporary exigencies of Christianity, to its needs and aspirations."[42] Nowhere in Halbwachs are the resultant multiple versions of the Holy Land, dependent as they are on contemporary "needs and aspirations," treated in any pejorative sense as "fictions."

This tolerance of "invention," and its acceptance as a legitimate object of study, has obviously been widely adopted. His stress on the materiality of memory is another legacy, as the present torrent of literature on modern monuments, mementoes, and other "sites of memory" signally attests. Subsequent research in such fields as psychology and phenomenology has served only to support and refine that link of object or place and remembrance – a relationship which can of course be traced back ultimately to the Roman *ars memoriae* and its *loci* and *imagines*.[43]

If we follow the general approach pioneered by Halbwachs, it becomes possible to think formally in terms of an *archaeology of memory*. Metaphor, in any case, tends to bind these two concepts together: after all, we speak casually of "burying memories," or of "digging down" to recover them.[44] But

---

40. Halbwachs 1992: 202–3 (1941: 161–62). See also Roth 1997. A classical parallel might be the olive tree produced on the Acropolis by Athena to lay claim to her eponymous city; burnt in the Persian sack of 480 BC, it was miraculously renewed (Pausanias 1.27.2). Alterations on the nineteenth-century Acropolis could also be remembered in this context.
41. Assmann 1997: 8–17. For a different discussion of encounters with the Holy Land's "landscape of belief," see Davis 1996; compare also Murphy-O'Connor 1998.
42. Halbwachs 1992: 234 (1941: 205). See also Dagron 1984.
43. E.g. Casey 1987: 181–215; 1993; Neisser 1989; Tilley 1994: 26–29; and the references in nn. 29–31. On the concept of "environmental memory," Quantrill 1974.
44. Schama (1995: 16), in *Landscape and Memory*, evokes such metaphors: "My own burrows through time only follow, of course, where many other conscientious moles have already dug." One could also remember Sigmund Freud's famous analogy between the city of Rome and the human mind in "Civilisation and its discontents" (1985): 257–58, discussed in a classical context by C. Edwards 1996: 27–43.

perhaps there is more than metaphor at stake here, more vested in the hard data of archaeology.

MONUMENTS, LANDSCAPES, AND MEMORIES

Various expansive phrases – physical setting, material milieu, *cadre matériel* – serve to remind us that memories can dwell anywhere. Within these broad frameworks, however, there is one useful and very basic distinction worth making, and that is between *monuments* and *landscape*. Both will be deployed in the course of the book's detailed case studies.

Monuments – that is, places, structures, or objects deliberately designed, or later agreed, to provoke memories – will no doubt initially seem the more straightforward category for analysis. Cenotaphs, columns, tombs, trees, statues, weapons, votives, obelisks, inscriptions, unworked stones, henges, tumuli: any list of potential monuments is bound to be long and will differ from culture to culture. In all cases, however, the "link between past, present and future is made through their materiality. Objects of a durable kind assert their own memories, their own forms of commentary and therefore come to possess their own personal trajectories."[45] These enduring entities have been designated as one form of "inscribed" memorial practice, favoring a conservative transmission of cultural information. "Incorporated" practice, by contrast, tends to involve "performative ceremonies which generate bodily sensory and emotional experiences, resulting in habitual memory being sedimented in the body."[46] Without question, inscribed practices are far more visible to the archaeologist, and thus dominate much of the discussion in the following chapters. On the other hand, inscribed and incorporated forms of commemoration are far from mutually exclusive, and rituals and ceremonies (often played out in monumental settings) played a central role in the Greek memorial enterprise.

By their very nature, monuments appear eminently stable things, landmarks and bulwarks of continuity. Yet the commemorative activities that surround them, and the interpretations placed upon them, can vary remarkably over time, even as the monument itself remains relatively unchanged. Stonehenge and Masada – one a constructed monument, the other the site of

---

45. Rowlands 1993: 144. See also Bradley 1993; Edmonds 1999: 134–49; Lowenthal 1985; Tatum 1995a. Texts and iconography are considered to be other forms of "inscribed" practice.
46. Hamilakis 1998: 117. In some cultures, incorporation can involve the deliberate loss or destruction of a "monument," such as the *malangan* sculptures of New Ireland, Papua New Guinea (Küchler 1987; 1993; Tilley 1999: 59–61). On inscribed and incorporated practices: Connerton 1989; Rowlands 1993.

Fig. 1.7 Special medal struck by the Israeli government to commemorate events at Masada.
The camp of the Roman besiegers lies at the foot of the distinctively shaped plateau; the legend
states: "We shall remain free men."

a momentous event – are two familiar, but still impressive, examples of such
revolutions in meaning. Apart from its undoubted range of prehistoric functions, since medieval times Stonehenge has passed from being a lair of magic to
a locality conserved by the National Trust, from a connubial present from a
certain Mr. Chubb to Mrs. Chubb to a World Heritage Site. Over the course
of the twentieth century alone, Masada has passed from relative neglect
to a nation's proud emblem, with interpretive emphasis shifting from the
defenders' mass suicide to their heroic sacrifice (Fig. 1.7). As Richard Bradley
reminds us: "Monuments may stay the same when societies change. Like
archaeologists today, people in the past would have been forced to engage
in acts of interpretation, and that very process can tell us something of their
shifting preconceptions."[47]

Stonehenge and Masada, without doubt, act as common symbols in
British and Israeli society, respectively, yet both are also repeatedly invoked in
bitterly divisive political battles, battles which directly implicate the practice
and presentation of archaeology. Spectacular though they be, in this dimension they are hardly unique, for all monuments allow divided memories.
Even when faced with the most apparently concrete and unambiguous of
memorials, the temptation to oversimplify its message must be resisted: "A
monumental work, like a musical one . . . has a *horizon of meanings*: a specific

47. Bradley 1993: 91. On Stonehenge: Bender 1992, quote at 266; Bradley 1998: 91–100; Chippindale
    1994. On Masada: Ben-Yehuda 1995; Yadin 1966; Zerubavel 1994; 1995. Sacré-Cœur in Paris
    has also been analyzed in this fashion: Harvey 1979; Loyer 1992.

or indefinite multiplicity of meanings, a shifting hierarchy in which now one, now another meaning comes momentarily to the fore, by means of – and for the sake of – a particular action."[48] To put it another way, different audiences – with their own expectations, needs, or knowledge – bring different experiences to bear on the viewing of any monument. Memorial objects and monumental spaces thus take on an inescapably dialogical quality, resisting uniform readings even for a single point in time, let alone across the ages.[49]

As Halbwachs recognized in *La topographie légendaire des évangiles en terre sainte*, monuments are both sensitive and vulnerable indicators. Their construction, renovation, or outright eradication – the molding of Hambledon Hill, the renovation of the Ebabbar of Shamash, the "clean up" of the Acropolis – declares a firm intent to alter the course of commemoration. Yet interpretation of such acts is never unambiguous, as the reconfigurations of Pecos Pueblo remind us. Indeed, for supposed bulwarks of memory, monuments are actually quite slippery things, suggesting two steps be taken to control their testimony. First, a monument must, as far as possible, be resituated in the historical context relevant to a particular analysis of its meaning. And second, generous allowance must always be made for the possibility of alternative readings and layers of dissonance in a monument's reception, even if they cannot always be fully recognized or recovered.

Monuments, of course, live within a wider matrix of human activity; they are set within a landscape. Landscape, a capacious and currently much utilized concept, contains a multitude of meanings, all of which revolve around human experience, perception and modification of the world. Landscape thus embraces the physical environment, patterns of settlement, boundaries and frontiers, fields, cities, natural features, monuments, pathways, holy places, wilderness, and much much more. The concept also frequently foregrounds the profound affective ties between people and their emotional "sense of place." While memory is not always directly discussed as part of this phenomenon, it can never be far removed, bound up as it is with a community's longitudinal relationship to a particular locale.[50]

Landscape, of necessity, presupposes a fairly sweeping scale of analysis (what is not part of a landscape?). Nor can it be assumed that a landscape is any

48. Lefebvre 1991: 222 (original emphasis); Barrett *et al.* 1991: 6–8; Bradley 1987; 1993; Lowenthal 1985: 243. "Popular negotiations over memory were more like an endless conversation than a simple vote on a proposition": Thelen 1989: 1127.
49. On this dialogical quality in Holocaust memorials: Huyssen 1994: 15; Young 1993; 1994a: 21, 37.
50. On "place": Basso and Feld 1996; see also Appadurai 1988; Black *et al.* 1989; Borofsky 1987; Casey 1993; Hayden 1995; Hirsch and O'Hanlon 1995; Morphy 1993; Rodman 1992; Rosaldo 1988.

more "fixed" in meaning than a monument. In recent years, anthropologists, archaeologists, landscape historians, and scholars in several other disciplines besides have come to acknowledge "the contingency, temporality and fluidity of ancient landscapes" and of the variable ways in which they were perceived and understood over time.[51] Landscapes may thus appear sprawling and intractable things, but they are just as essential to my analysis as the more localized monuments. Human landscapes provide the broad physical framework that shaped communal experience; disturbance or dispossession would strike at memories invested in the places to which people became attached, in the places where they dwelled, worked, and worshipped. Examples of such disturbance (and we shall see all of them later on in the book) include the forced restructuring of settlement or landholding patterns, the creation of exiles, and the denial of traditional rites in traditional places.[52] Stability in a landscape might enable, if not ensure, the maintenance of memories (as was the case among the people of the Cévennes); radical disjunctures would make their transmission that much harder, or ultimately even impossible.

Tracking the lives and afterlives of monuments, then, might testify most immediately to alterations in what was deemed commendable to remember or wise to forget. Landscape analysis reveals conditions favorable for memory's conservation or loss, or for the prompting of new memorial traditions or interpretations. At this juncture, there is one very straightforward point that needs to be made. The types of data called for here – monuments, settlement patterns, tombs, urban centers, sanctuaries, and so on – involve standard, well-established categories for archaeological exploration, categories long investigated and mined for the answers to other scholarly questions. An archaeological approach to the study of social memory requires, it would seem, not so much fresh objectives for additional future fieldwork as the redeployment of evidence often already in hand.

The chapters that follow are designed to illustrate this point. Most of the data used in them, certainly, are not particularly "new." On the other hand, they do help us tackle some questions not previously considered in quite this way:

51. Brady and Ashmore 1999: 125. For a selection of recent landscape studies, see Ashmore and Knapp 1999; Bender 1993; Hirsch and O'Hanlon 1995; Ingold 1993; Schama 1995; Tilley 1994 and the papers in *Archaeological Dialogues* 4 (1997).
52. For example, on dispossession and the creation of exiles, Slyomovics 1998: 82–168; on the disturbance of traditional Orange Order parade routes in Northern Ireland: Jarman 1993. The words of Lefebvre are apposite here: "The analysis of *any space* brings us up against the dialectical relationship between demand and command, along with all its attendant questions: 'Who?,' 'For whom?,' 'By whose agency?,' 'Why and how?'" (1991: 116, my emphasis). Such questions obviously run in parallel to the questions posed earlier by Burke (p. 17): "who wants whom to remember what, and why? Whose version of the past is recorded and preserved?"

What did people choose to remember, and commemorate, of their past?

What was forgotten, and at whose behest?

Who formulated and promulgated the dominant commemorative narratives, and how effectively were other versions of the past masked or erased?

How many alternative, and possibly competitive, memory communities can be discerned at work?

Turning with enthusiasm to the use of material evidence does not, magically, make these critical questions easy to answer. But it does provide a very real amplification of the spectrum of memories we can detect, and it does return a greater degree of the original force of social memory to long-gone societies. This involves, not least, conceding the possibility of sharp disagreements about the past in the past for – as the following chapters demonstrate – disturbing memories are far from a modern preserve.

ACHAIA, CRETE, AND MESSENIA

Analysis of social memory in fully prehistoric contexts is certainly far from impossible, as a number of pioneering studies from Europe amply demonstrate.[53] The focus in each of chapters 2–4, none the less, is on situations for which some sort of narrative framework exists, no matter how sketchy or flawed it may be. Just as important is the fact that each boasts a wide range of archaeological data, including the results of excavations at urban centers or sanctuaries, mortuary studies, architectural or art-historical analyses, and so on. Results from regional survey projects are another crucial element, for reasons which should be apparent given the foregoing discussion of landscape.

Equally important in determining my case studies were the particular circumstances engaging the societies chosen. For while social memory is *never* inert or static, manipulation of the past is most pronounced at times of marked social, religious or political change: that, certainly, is what each of the short stories at this chapter's outset suggests. The following chapters thus deal with periods characterized by various forms of transformation, including outright conquest. We will see processes of annexation, exploitation, negotiation, colonization, accommodation, dispossession, resistance, and consolidation – all carrying with them the need for reconfigurations of memory. The case studies operate on fairly lengthy time-scales, reflecting the unavoidable constraints of many archaeological data; in all cases, they examine developments over the course of decades, if not over centuries. This is, of course, far from ideal, and

---

53. Among the many recent studies of prehistoric monuments: Bradley 1998; Edmonds 1999; Thomas 1993; papers in Bradley 1990 and Bradley and Williams 1998.

finer-grain distinctions and commemorative variations are thus no doubt lost; but that is not sufficient reason to abandon the analysis.

Chapters follow a reverse chronological order and a contracting geographical scope. The early Roman imperial epoch on the mainland of Greece forms the principal subject of chapter 2; chapter 3 compares the Hellenistic and Roman periods on the island of Crete; chapter 4 examines Messenia, the southwestern corner of the Greek Peloponnese, in Archaic through Hellenistic times. Each chapter traces a slightly different course in its exploration of social memory, with variable scales of analysis and divergent bodies of evidence. All three studies, however, do share some essential characteristics. As just noted, each chapter takes as its *point de départ* a particular social crux – be it imperial annexation, internal dissension, or local exploitation. Each involves discussion of the wider landscape, as well as of individual monuments and monumental complexes. Each attempts to recover different strands of memory and different memory communities at work, and to outline overlapping or competing versions of the past. The political vulnerability of these societies should not cozen us into expecting fewer or less dogged contestations over the past; any "impulse to sanitize the internal politics of the dominated must be understood as fundamentally romantic."[54]

Finally, each chapter engages with concerns and queries generated by earlier scholarship, reconsidering them now through the particular lens of social memory. For example, it is well known that the Greeks of the early Roman empire were magnificently obsessed with their past. Yet this conspicuous phenomenon has too often been written off as a hapless form of "mere nostalgia," instead of being appreciated as an active cultural strategy on the part of an unusual subject population. Likewise, Crete's golden age has always been defined as that of its Bronze Age "Minoan" culture, with its palaces, labyrinths, and bull games; and so, for tourists and scholars alike (at least until quite recently), this fascination has largely precluded much serious interest in what happened later. What goes missing from such a reconstruction is the fact that the historic inhabitants of the island possessed their own decided and dynamic views about the uses of the Cretan past. Finally, there is the controversy of how to write Messenian "history," given the region's silence in thrall to the Spartan state. Thinking instead about how the Messenians constructed identity through local memories, both under external rule and following liberation, bypasses that conundrum and, to some extent, rescues the Messenians from an oblivion that long outlasted Spartan domination.

54. Ortner 1995: 179.

Attention to past scholarly attitudes – which invariably determine the nature of inquiry into these regions and periods – raises one final essential point, to be underlined in one last short story. In his book, *Phantoms of Memory: Memory and Oblivion at the End of the First Millennium*, Patrick Geary hammers away at the unwelcome but inescapable fact that everything we have to study and to analyze – everything we weave into our own narratives of the past – is itself the product of previous ponderings, selections, and rejections. In eleventh-century Europe, memory specialists such as monks shaped and patted tradition to fit the necessary present, occluding or obliterating insignificant or inconvenient memories. Individuals were thus forgotten, charters destroyed, archives only partially recopied. Old things of little use were, in the words of one monk, "buried with reverence," leaving behind at best only trace phantoms of unwanted memory.[55] Such selectivity is not unique to early medieval Europe; nor is the degree to which such inexorable (and often irreversible) filtering affects what is left behind. Geary does not exempt himself or other modern scholars from this process, wondering if they too are not phantoms of remembrance:

> intent on creating our own versions of the past and hoping that our creation will be so successful in selecting, suppressing, and manipulating our data that the evidence of our subjective intervention, like that of our eleventh-century predecessors, will vanish before the eyes of our audience, present and future.[56]

If one sits back and thinks about it, the consequences of such memorial winnowing are staggering. Nor can archaeology be expected somehow to turn back or subvert this process completely. Monuments and landscapes, like texts, can be invented, rewritten, and erased; archaeologists, like historians, are not innocent of "subjective intervention."[57] It remains true, however,

55. Geary 1994: 8. The full quote, from the early eleventh-century monk Arnold of Regensburg, is even more direct: "Not only is it proper for the new things to change the old ones, but even, if the old ones are disordered, they should be entirely thrown away, or if, however, they conform to the proper order of things but are of little use, they should be buried with reverence." This is reminiscent of Jonker's warning about the "topography of remembrance" in ancient Mesopotamia, where the targets chosen for investigation and the "chosen interpretation depended on the identity of the community that did the digging": Jonker 1995: 174.
56. Geary 1994: 181.
57. Fentress and Wickham 1992: 5–6. See also Foxhall (1995: 146), who addresses this specifically in relation to monuments: "we attach our own origin in 'western civilization' to an image of Greece which they left us almost on purpose. The criteria for selection reflect the concerns of the dominant elite for perpetuating themselves. When we look back at the past of the Greeks or of ourselves, it is easy to forget that the meaning and significance of events and persons have been rearranged for us in this way."

that material evidence can help us watch for phantoms of otherwise invisible memory, and thus can prevent over-easy acceptance of overly tidy versions of the past. Otherwise we must accept this ongoing massaging of memory, and our own complicity in it, and do the best we can. Eric Hobsbawm adopted a memorably fluid metaphor: "We swim in the past as fish do in water, and cannot escape from it. But our modes of living and moving in this medium require analysis and discussion."[58] The material framework of monuments and of landscapes volunteers one means of navigation in these uncertain waters.

58. Hobsbawm 1972: 17.

2

OLD GREECE
WITHIN THE EMPIRE

> Nostalgia, they say, is an exercise in grammar wherein you find the
> present tense and the past perfect (Whitmer 1993: 267).[1]

Empires mess with people's minds. That simple statement covers a multitude
of complicated developments, many of which directly impact the sphere of
social memory. The victorious power's own sense of history is transformed
to reflect success and its consequences, while central authorities reinscribe
provincial memories in order either to undercut opposition or to encourage compliance. Still more commemorative changes emerge in reaction and
response from within the subject populations themselves.[2] In a plural imperial world, the questions – "Who wants whom to remember what, and why?
Whose version of the past is recorded and preserved?" – become increasingly
tangled.

"Old Greece," the Roman province of Achaia, is a wonderful place to engage with these issues (Fig. 2.1). The province in its early imperial incarnation
(for our purposes here, the period from roughly the first century BC to the
early third century AD) until recently received comparatively little scholarly
attention. The reasons for that relative neglect are not far to seek. In the study
of Greek history and archaeology, the key period – the commemorative high
point – was for a very long time the High Classical epoch: that is, roughly,
the fifth and fourth centuries BC, the floruit of the independent Greek polis.
As Geary observed regarding his medieval "phantoms of memory," scholarly
choices and interventions are not always innocently made; in the case of classical Greece, as we have seen, so much was invested – in terms of western
cultural hegemony, in terms of European geopolitics – that the pressure to
focus on the "right" era was correspondingly insistent (pp. 3–5). Investigation
of other periods, when Greece was not free or when other political regimes

---

1. Quoted by Cherry 2001: 247. I would like to thank John Cherry for sharing this nugget.
2. For recent works on transformations in Rome itself: Habinek and Schiesaro 1997; Nicolet 1988;
   North 1993; Woolf 2001. On other empires: Hall 1998; Hill 1988; Mignolo 1992; Miller 1991;
   Silverblatt 1988; Yates 2001.

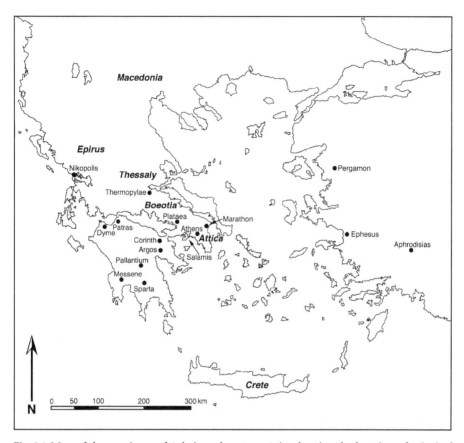

Fig. 2.1 Map of the provinces of Achaia and western Asia, showing the location of principal places mentioned in the text.

held sway, was thus discouraged; the paradox of "Roman Greece" would be especially suspect to a world-view venerating (as quite separate entities) "the glory that was Greece, the grandeur that was Rome."[3]

This particular form of scholarly astigmatism has often slid into outright disdain for the Greeks under Roman rule: an undoubtedly cultured, but in-effectual, people; competitive, but to no good purpose; a sycophantic bunch, invoking ancestral virtues in no way their own. A more moderate formulation envisages the Greeks of the eastern empire as calmly withdrawing from the world stage, passing the torch of leadership to the successor state of Rome. Achaia, in this view, becomes a kind of quiet backwater, still culturally potent

3. One measure of neglect is the chronological gap between Finley 1857 (second edition) and the next book-length study of the Roman province of Achaia, Alcock 1993; mention must be made, however, of Larsen's (1938) extensive study of the province. On biases in classical archaeology: McNeal 1991; Morris 1994. For such attitudes in anthropological perspective: Herzfeld 1987.

and thereby insulated from the ruder shocks of conquest seen elsewhere. "Old Greece," awash with satisfying retrospective memories, lived on on its laurels in a kind of museal twilight.[4] In either reconstruction, the vitality of a glorious past (one that lay, by the second century AD, at a distance of some six or seven centuries) overwhelms and sadly highlights the deficiencies of the present.

To be fair, of course, the classicists who espoused such opinions were, to a greater or lesser extent, merely following what others, and their perceived betters, had said before them. Authoritative Roman sources, for example, frequently display a similar ambivalence: respectful of past greatness, dismissive of present-day *Graeculi* ("Greeklings"). Examples abound; one fairly typical example is a pardon granted by Julius Caesar to an Athens with a record of picking the losing side: "How many times will the reputation of your ancestors save you from utter self-destruction?" (Appian, *Bella Civilia* 2.88). Even more influential was the preserved body of what was said and written by the Greeks themselves; the term Second Sophistic has frequently been applied to this early imperial literary and rhetorical production. Witnessed there is a fascination, at times even an obsession, with the past – but a past with a particular shape. More recent imperial and Hellenistic events and individuals are largely occluded; what shines forth most brilliantly is the Classical age.

This phenomenon appears in numerous guises which have been elsewhere well reviewed. Very briefly, the "Second Sophistic" takes its name from a conscious connection drawn by the late second-/early third-century AD author Philostratus between a "first" (fifth-century) sophistic florescence and a "second" incarnation, usually dated to *c.* AD 50–250. These sophists repeatedly, and repetitively, spoke to set topics drawn predominantly from fifth- or fourth-century BC history: fathers of the Marathon dead praising their sons; Xenophon refusing to survive Socrates; Demosthenes swearing he did not take the bribe of fifty talents, and so on. In showy epideictic displays, the new sophists used a purist, old-fashioned form of Attic Greek unlike the language common in everyday use.[5] Classicizing trends extended into other fields as well: calendars, forms of measurement, personal and geographical nomenclature, administrative terminology, epigraphic letter forms, art and

4. Alcock 1993: 1–3 for earlier literature, including Jones 1963. Concern with such reconstructions has been voiced before: e.g., Bowie 1974; Mitchell 1984.
5. Philostratus, *Vitae Sophistarum* 481. For general works touching on the Second Sophistic: Anderson 1993; Bowersock 1969; 1974; Brunt 1994; Millar 1969: esp. 12–14; Reardon 1984; Saïd 1991; Swain 1996. On linguistic purism, where "language functioned as a badge of elite identity": Swain 1996: 27–64, quote at 64; Schmitz 1997: 67–96. On the sophists themselves: Bowie 1982; Bowersock 1969: 58; Crawford 1978; Reardon 1984: 38–39; Schmitz 1997: 160–231.

architecture, and more.[6] Such backward-looking practices were far from un-precedented in earlier Greek self-perception and self-presentation, but their marked *intensification* characterized the early imperial period.

No wonder, then, that later scholarship followed the path that it did, molded as it was by ancient testimony and by its own imperatives. That leaves us with the problem, however, that the commemorative decisions taken in early imperial times – this "nostalgia" if you will – have been sanctioned as both understandable and natural: indeed, as the obvious thing to do given the circumstances. In other words, the attitudes of the Romans, and the predilec-tions of the Greeks, have been accepted at face value and not as something requiring critical assessment. Instead, it must first be asked *why* the Greek past became – for both parties – such a vital term of engagement. And second, what happened to the range of Greek memory communities and their re-membrances, as their land was converted into the very different framework of a Roman province?

This chapter begins by analyzing the power of the Hellenic past and by arguing that its early Roman deployment was no artless or inevitable devel-opment. Next, it proceeds to explore four different topics, each of which relies upon different types of data and each of which offers a different means to nuance the age's commemorative complexities. First comes the evidence of the Achaian landscape, where we will examine how far memories invested in a particular way of life and a particular social framework were disturbed, as well as how far Roman interventions worked to rewrite local histories. Second, we will turn to a specific memorial space, the urban center of the Athenian Agora. That the Agora experienced major renovations in early Roman times is hardly a revelation, but the precise political meaning and emotional impact of those changes has been much disputed. This chapter suggests that, depending upon the audience, several meanings and varied impacts are to be expected, as the Agora contained and expressed more than one commemorative message.

The third study turns to rituals and places associated with the immensely powerful events of the fifth-century BC Persian Wars. Around this constella-tive myth, a multiplicity of often competing memories gathered, with battles such as Marathon or Thermopylae serving as both bond and barrier be-tween Greeks and Romans. Finally, the issue of commemorative mobility and mutability, seen everywhere in the chapter, is further addressed, in partic-ular through the recognition of new forms of hybrid memory. Examples of

---

6. Bowie 1974, esp. 197–203. See also Macready and Thompson 1987. The point should be made that the eclipse of the Hellenistic period, while impressive, was never complete, nor was the present inevitably viewed with dire pessimism: for one reevaluation of Pausanias, see Arafat 1996.

monumental spaces and memorial rituals from elsewhere in the Greek east are here considered, to begin the necessary process of moving this analysis beyond the borders of Achaia.

RELIANCE ON THE PAST

The provincial actors most visible, through textual and archaeological evidence, are the prominent, urban-based elite families of the Greek east. Individuals in such families shouldered much of the imperial burden: tax collection, maintenance of public order, organization of civic and imperial cult. Through a combination of their political authority and economic capability, these would also have been the premier decision-makers when it came to the celebration of regional or civic memories.

The question thus becomes why these elite families (most effectively, their adult male members) intensified their reliance on the classical past, and why they made it manifest in the ways already noted. Various explanations have been proffered, all of which are rooted, to a greater or lesser extent, in the fact of Roman conquest and the resulting change in Greek political status. Modern analysts of the situation assume the change to have been a blow, leading to dissatisfaction with the present-day and thus preoccupation with a preferred past. Bowie expresses it thus: "For a Greek, the paradeigmatic political animal, the contemporary balance of politics was profoundly unsatisfactory. This is what led orators to declaim on the happier days of Marathon and Salamis and historians to forget the period after Alexander."[7] Bowie's fundamental contention – that Greek interest in the past was tied directly to their situation in the present – is difficult to dismiss; certainly it conforms to models both of social memory and of oral tradition in which the past is continually refracted through the present.

Once beyond that basic point, however, dissensions quickly arise, largely thanks to disagreements about the nature and worth of nostalgia – a term used here not in its strict etymological sense (of a "painful desire to return"), but to mean the contemplation of a preferred past from the standpoint of an altered present. Indulgence in nostalgia evokes a range of responses, often hostile or condescending; in this particular case it has been stigmatized as the cultural weakness of a defeated people or as a kind of escapist amnesia: "If the present is unsatisfactory, it *is* tempting to rummage around in the past, to see what you can find to preserve self-respect."[8] In the wake of more sophisticated memory

7. Bowie 1974: 184.
8. Reardon 1984: 39–40 (original emphasis); see also Van Groningen 1965. For a review of other negative verdicts on the Second Sophistic: Anderson 1993: 240–46; Gleason 1995: xvii–xx.

studies, reversions to the past (such as nostalgia, archaism, or classicism) are no longer thus perceived. Far from automatically being deemed negative or at best neutral developments, today they are investigated as active strategies of self-assertion, even of resistance to external interference.[9]

It is no longer possible then either to pity the poor Greeks or to treat their attitudes to the past as epiphenomenal concerns. Instead, those attitudes emerge as central to personal self-definition and social ascendancy; as Simon Swain puts it: "we are really dealing with a feeling of great political importance touching on the sources of power and rights to exercise it. We are concerned, in short, with the culture-political identity the Greek elite now adopted."[10] In such an interpretation, care for the past became the especial province of the Greek elite, notably the *pepaideumenoi*: the educated men from whose ranks the vast majority of authors and sophists were drawn, who provided the principal patrons and students, and who made up the most informed audiences.

"Nostalgia" could offer such men a bulwark against many challenges. Roman rule encouraged new economic and status distinctions within the eastern provinces; the subtleties of certain practices, such as Atticizing rhetorical displays on recherché topics, allowed the elite to define themselves clearly against hoi polloi. Rhetorical "star turns" impressed the populace: "By this kind of dramatization, enhanced by all the charms of symbolic violence, the gap between the educated and uneducated came to seem in no way arbitrary, but the result of a nearly biological superiority." Such public displays also allowed for a kind of intra-elite competition, which none the less posed no genuine threat to internal class interests at a time when bonds between these families were expanding and multiplying. Finally, *paideia* rooted in the classical age, together with issues of personal presentation, took on additional importance in an imperial setting: "efforts to articulate and formalize an empire-wide code of elite deportment might be welcomed by provincial aristocrats who suddenly found themselves faced with a wider world."[11] Certain forms of knowledge and behavior became markers of group identity and

---

9. Geary 1994: 8; O'Brien and Rosebery 1991; Pocock 1962; S. Stewart 1984; K. Stewart 1988; Thelen 1989: 1125–26. "Symbols of the 'past,' mythically infused with timelessness ... attain particular effectiveness during periods of intensive social change when communities have to drop their heaviest cultural anchors in order to resist the currents of transformation": Cohen 1985: 102.

10. Swain 1996: 6. Impatience with past attitudes is becoming increasingly clear; as Jones (1996b: 462) puts it: "the question of whether second- and third-century sophists were expressing 'dissatisfaction with the political situation of the present' is overdue for retirement." On the *pepaideumenoi*, see Andrei 1984; D. Edwards 1996: 28–33; Galli 2001; Millar 1993; Quass 1982.

11. Gleason 1995, quotations at xxi and xxv; see also Schmitz 1997: 97–135. On growing economic distinctions in the Greek provinces: Alcock 1993: 85–92; Briscoe 1974; Cartledge and Spawforth 1989: 162; Ste. Croix 1981, esp. 523–29.

guarantors of mutual acceptance, just as "the classics" would play a similar role in demarcating the ruling classes of other, later empires. Along various axes defining relationships among Greeks themselves, then, the past served as a reservoir of elite-controlled power. For Swain, this speaks to a sense of special confidence among these "rightful inheritors of the classical world."[12]

It is clear, however, that more was involved here than an internal means of social categorization and validation. The past also offered resources for negotiation with imperial authorities, not least by providing an arena in which Greeks could distinguish themselves *vis-à-vis* their Roman rulers, much in the manner of Greeks setting themselves in contrast to barbarian cultures in other periods. Yet the Hellenic past also offered what Millar has termed "a frame of reference or a channel of communication," thanks to a strong (if not always uncontroversial) philhellenic streak at work in cultured Roman circles.[13] Generals, governors, and emperors alike acknowledged and paid homage to antique Greek achievement. In a frequently quoted letter, Pliny wrote to a colleague (possibly Sextus Quintilius Valerius Varus Maximus) who was on his way to act as *corrector* (overseer) to the free cities of Achaia:

> I know you need no telling, but affection urges me to remind you to keep in mind and put into practice what you already know . . . Remember that you have been sent to the province of Achaia, to the genuine and pure Greece, where culture and literature, and fruitful agriculture too, are thought to have begun . . . Respect their gods, their founders and the titles they bear, respect their ancient glory and their very age, which in man commands our regard, in cities our reverence. Give heed to their antiquity, their great deeds, and the legends of their past. Do not take away from anyone's rank, independence or even pride, but always keep before you that this is the land which provided us with justice and gave us laws, not after conquest but at our entreaty; that it is to Athens you go and Sparta you rule, and to snatch from them the name and shadow of freedom, which is all they have left, would be an act of cruelty, ignorance and barbarism . . . Remember what each city once was, without sneering because it has ceased to be so . . .   (Pliny, *Epistles* 8.24.1–5)

Division between glorious past/unworthy present is here very apparent, but so too is the relationship between the two, and the former's ongoing ability to influence the latter. As shall be seen, antiquity (well argued) could overcome

12. Swain 1996: 8.
13. Millar 1969: 12. The obviously relevant issue of Hellenism in Rome will not be considered in any detail here; for recent discussions: Guldager Bilde *et al.* 1993; Pollitt 1986: 150–63; Wallace-Hadrill 1990; 1998; Zanker 1988.

contempt; in many instances the fate of Greek cities under Roman rule could be radically affected by the past histories they could invoke.

We must be careful about carrying the cosiness of philhellenic goodwill too far. As the need for such a prompt by Pliny suggests, respect for the *Graeculi* was not always forthcoming. Nor were the Greeks alone in their concern for keeping ethnic categories clear; their cultural distinctions, rooted in the deeds of ancient forebears, did not earn them superiority in all, and even more essential, domains. One analysis of the Latin vocabulary applied to Greeks makes this point:

> The people that they judged culturally superior, but also (and without doubt precisely for that reason) morally inferior, inspired in them a complex mixture of attraction and repulsion. The stereotypes which made up their vision of Greece were ... the most contrasting they could imagine to their own characteristic national values of *fides, uirtus, pietas, grauitas.*[14]

Pliny's emphasis – that the past glories of the Greeks alone are what earn them respect in the present – also resonates well with what Renato Rosaldo, in modern contexts, has termed "imperialist nostalgia."

> Imperialist nostalgia revolves around a paradox: A person kills somebody, and then mourns the victim. In a more attenuated form, somebody deliberately alters a form of life, and then regrets that things have not remained as they were prior to the intervention ... In any of these versions, imperialist nostalgia uses a pose of "innocent yearning" both to capture people's imaginations and to conceal its complicity with often brutal domination.

Romans' admiration for the Greek past should not mask their "often brutal domination" of the Greek present, nor wipe away the "crocodile tears of the Roman patrician who reproduced the grandeurs of the very Greece that his country had humiliated."[15] The decision to cater to such imperial desires is, of course, a long way from the decision to honor one's own past, for one's own purposes. Whatever else we make of the Greek turn to nostalgia, we must perceive this continual push and pull of pressures both internal and external.

We can also see, despite the complexities of this highly ambiguous relationship, the force of memory at work. This brief reappraisal of Greek reliance on a select past, however, has been almost entirely dependent upon textual

14. Dubuisson 1991: 334. Contrast, for example, the frequent favors done to the city of Athens with the attack of Cn. Calpurnius Piso upon its citizens "whom he called Athenians no longer," but rather the earth's dregs (Tacitus, *Annals* 2.55.1). For Roman philhellenism and its converse: Ferrary 1988: 497–526; Petrochilos 1974; Rawson 1985: 3–18, esp. 10–13; Wardman 1976.
15. Rosaldo 1989a: 69–70; Eco 1986: 39. See also Rosaldo 1989b, esp. 107–10.

sources. In the rest of this chapter, the evidence of landscapes and monuments is added to that documentary base. The goal, as outlined in chapter 1, is to gain some broader sense of the varieties of memory communities and of commemorative choices present within this imperial society. Such evidence can also shed light on Rome's treatment of Greece, and how far philhellenism actually "protected" the people of Achaia. We can begin with this question and with the landscape of Roman Greece.

CHANGES IN THE LAND

Images of Old Greece as a quiet backwater somehow insulated from imperial expansion crumble rapidly when confronted with the evidence of recent regional investigations. It is now apparent that numerous aspects of Achaia's human environment were altered, destroyed, moved – or at very least recast in a new social and political atmosphere. I have examined these developments elsewhere, but with very different sets of questions in mind. Yet if (as argued in chapter 1) established patterns of social memory are linked to the existing framework of landscape, then changes in one raise the possibility of changes in the other. Memories may be maintained, but that will require work; alternatively, new forms of remembrance might be forged over time.

The boundaries of the Roman province of Achaia were more or less conterminous with those of the modern nation-state of Greece, minus the island of Crete and the northern regions of Thessaly and Macedonia (Fig. 2.1). Although transformations are everywhere visible, no uniform picture can be drawn of this small province's treatment in the early years of Roman control. The fate of Athens was unlike that of Corinth, that of Boeotia unlike Lakonia; some cities and regions thrived, others declined; differences between the west and the east of the province have been posited. This diversity makes a nonsense of the idea of a passive Achaian countryside; it also reveals the indisputable – if not ubiquitous – part played by Roman intervention in rewriting the Achaian landscape.

Roman rewrites

While this is not the place for a comprehensive review of Roman actions in Greece, a few of the high points must be noted: not least warfare, resettled populations, colonization, reallocation of land, and symbolic displacement of cult and cult images. The last two centuries BC witnessed frequent military activity in the region, which reached its violent heights during the Civil Wars

of the first century BC – Actium, of course, was fought just off the penin-
sula's west coast. Throughout these various conflicts, certain zones – Epirus,
Boeotia – were harder hit than others; cities were destroyed or maimed, not
least Corinth in 146 BC, while Athens itself suffered a particularly vicious
sack by Sulla in 87/86 BC.[16] Over this same time span, Romans and Italians
began to acquire land in various parts of the mainland and islands, either as
aristocratic absentee landlords or as actual residents; communities of foreign
negotiatores, the businessmen known as *Rhomaioi*, played an active part in the
civic and religious life of places such as Messene in Messenia or Thespiai in
Boeotia. With growing *de facto* control of the territory came bolder transpo-
sitions and impositions, including land grants or population resettlements.
Pompey, for example, relocated "most of" more than 20,000 Cilician pirates
at Dyme in the northwestern Peloponnese.[17] The province's formal creation
probably took place only around 27 BC, but patterns of Roman intervention
were long established by that time.

Most striking, perhaps, was the institution of Roman colonies, chief
among them Corinth (Colonia Laus Julia Corinthiensis) and Patras (Colonia
Aroe Augusta Patrensis), founded by Julius Caesar and Augustus respectively.
Augustus also created the *civitas foederata* (allied city) of Nikopolis, a "Victory
City" to commemorate the site of his watershed naval triumph at Actium.[18]
None of these foundations was a neatly bounded, unobtrusive entity; rather,
their tentacles extended in all directions and over often substantial distances.
People and resources were reassigned to the new centers: for example, the
residents of Aetolia were coerced into residence at Nikopolis, and natural
resources (such as a lake near Aetolian Kalydon) assigned to the *Rhomaioi* of
Patras (Fig. 2.2). Not surprisingly, new regional settlement hierarchies (and
thus political and social hierarchies) emerged, led by the imperially favored
cities whose satellites now included formerly independent communities.

Of all these Achaian colonial changes, two particular developments can
be highlighted. First, it has only recently been acknowledged that their hinterlands were formally surveyed and new land divisions made, even though
this was standard practice for Roman colonies elsewhere. Recognition of
Achaian centuriation was long retarded by prevailing scholarly paradigms,

16. Epirus: Ziolkowski 1986; Boeotia: Fossey 1988; Athens: Hoff 1997. For a general survey, see
 Alcock 1993: 8–24, 129–45.
17. Plutarch, *Pompey* 28.4. On *negotiatores* generally, see Alcock 1993: 75–77; Hatzfeld 1919; Wilson
 1966. Messene: Giovannini 1978: 115–22; Thespiai: Jones 1970.
18. Dyme and Buthrotum were the two other Achaian colonies. Only a few recent references, with
 earlier bibliography, will be given here. Buthrotum: Bergemann 1998; Corinth: Engels 1990;
 Williams 1987; Dyme and Patras: Rizakis 1997; Nikopolis: Murray and Petsas 1989; Purcell
 1987.

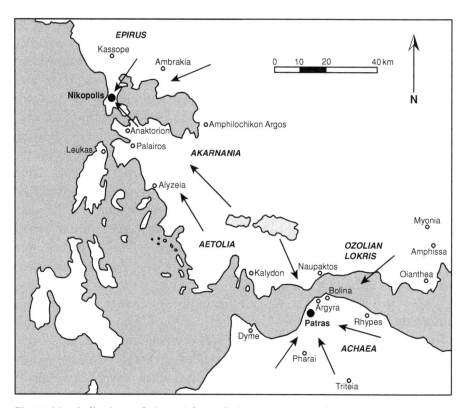

Fig. 2.2 Map indicating early imperial population movement and resource displacement in western Greece.

which trustingly assumed both Roman respect for Greek civic integrity and Roman contempt for Greek agricultural potential. Yet fairly obvious traces of such activity can be detected at places like Dyme, Nikopolis, and Corinth (Fig. 2.3). Such reallocation of the land testifies to severe disruptions not only in tenure, but in attachment to particular properties on the part of individuals and of communities. Land division was a pragmatic economic step, but one that simultaneously packed a substantial symbolic punch through its fundamental reordering of territory.[19]

The second development is the phenomenon of displaced cults, in which the divine images of either newly defunct or dispossessed communities were transferred to more successful centers, be it to imperial foundations or to Rome itself. Cult statues and temples, and thus cult, were moved, for example, from Aetolia to Nikopolis and Patras – most famously in the case of the Kalydonian Artemis Laphria. Roman artistic connoisseurship is usually invoked in this context, yet the movement (or eradication) of monuments

19. Doukellis 1988; 1990; 1994; Rizakis 1997: 26–28; Romano 1994; 2000. On the social impact of such reinscription of the landscape, see Purcell 1990.

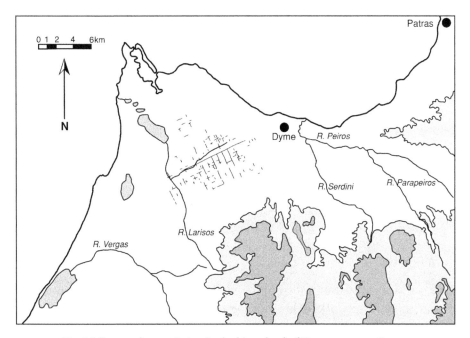

Fig. 2.3 Traces of centuriation in the hinterland of Dyme, western Greece.

has other potent meanings. Halbwachs spoke to this vulnerability in relation to Golgotha in the Holy Land; the priests of Pecos had good reason to require the abandonment of ritual kivas. As Henri Lefebvre observed: "Small wonder that from time immemorial conquerors and revolutionaries eager to destroy a society should so often have sought to do so by burning or razing that society's monuments. Sometimes, it is true, they contrive to redirect them to their own advantage."[20] Cult displacement appears an example of one such redirection, retraining as it did regional loyalties and rerouting attention toward new imperial centers of gravity. What these tactics engendered was a forced reconfiguration of the cultic landscape and of ritual practices.

All of these readjustments could simply be viewed as the normal provincial calibrations which follow conquest: building celebratory cities, stabilizing

20. Lefebvre 1991: 221. Several examples are known from Greece, summarized in Alcock 1993: 175–80; see also Ferrary 1988: 573–88. On Artemis Laphria, Pausanias 7.18.8–9. At least in the times of the Punic Wars, cult displacement was perceived as a controversial and potentially dangerous strategy. Plutarch commented that Marcellus was popular with the people of Rome "because he had adorned the city with beautiful objects that had all the charms of Grecian grace and symmetry; but Fabius Maximus, who neither touched nor brought away anything of this kind from Tarentum, when he had taken it, was more approved by the older men. He carried off the money and valuables, but forbade the statues to be moved; adding, as it is commonly related, 'Let us leave to the Tarentines these offended gods.' They blamed Marcellus, first for placing the city in an invidious position, as it seemed now to celebrate victories and lead processions of triumph, not only over men, but also over the gods as captives" (Plutarch, *Marcellus* 21, trans. Dryden [1962]).

troubled areas, encouraging depressed zones. Yet these undertakings and their consequences, as they recast the Achaian landscape, also affected patterns of living, worshipping, and remembering. Through a mixture of intention and accident, the topographic and symbolic settings of life were radically transformed, if in some areas more than in others. Almost nothing speaks directly to the reactions or emotions of the peoples affected, but the second-century AD traveler Pausanias records at least one resistant strain:

> A hundred and twenty furlongs from Delphi is Amphissa, the largest and most famous city of the Locrians. But the people reckon themselves Aetolians, being ashamed of the name of Ozolians, and their contention derives a certain probability from the fact that when the Roman Emperor turned the Aetolians out of house and home in order to gather them into his new city of Nikopolis, the bulk of the population withdrew to Amphissa.   (Pausanias 10.38.4)

This is a rare glimpse of noncompliant behavior, behavior notably grounded in remembered networks of kinship. Despite our lack of evidence, this episode is unlikely to have been unique.

Local shifts

If Roman intervention is responsible for certain alterations in the Greek land-scape, still others can be traced to the more indirect influences of imperial annexation. Various long-term trends have been identified and elsewhere discussed in detail:

> the relative abandonment of the countryside, especially by small proprietors, with a corresponding decline in rural cult activity;
> shifts in land ownership in favor of the wealthy and a new willingness to mark their presence in the landscape;
> the demise of certain smaller poleis as they lacked the economic underpin-nings (or the glorious history) to compete and to survive.

The first two trends have been argued chiefly through the evidence of archaeological survey, employing the results of numerous regional projects; the latter instead relies principally upon textual evidence, notably the *Periegesis* of Pausanias, with archaeological confirmation obtained where possible.

As far as our sample allows, the basic evidence for the first of these phenomena suggests that it was more or less consistent throughout the province.[21]

21. See Alcock 1993 and 1997 for evidence and discussion of these developments. Some regional variations are beginning to appear, for example in the zone around Patras (Rizakis 1997) and in Messenia (Alcock *et al.*, in prep. and see pp. 165–66).

Admittedly its dating, in most survey results, is attributable roughly to the Hellenistic and early Roman periods (c. fourth century BC to third century AD), but it is reasonable to assume some degree of causal link with the impact of Rome. New factors in provincial society – central taxation, growing reliance on elite patronage, the need for various economic and social "safety nets" – would encourage movement away from isolated dwelling and heavy investment in the rural landscape and toward life in cities or other larger settlements. While the majority of the Greek population was always urban-based, this is none the less a material shift in orientation, and it resulted in a very different organization of the countryside.

Rural ritual in part mirrors this shift in settlement. Archaeological evidence, again calling on survey results, testifies to the cessation of much rural cult activity during the Hellenistic and early Roman periods. This occurred not indiscriminately, but chiefly at small-scale shrines, places which would have been dear only to more restricted local audiences. By contrast, those rural sanctuaries that endured seem either to have been the largest, the oldest, or the most "charged" of cult places. These important survivors no doubt were supported by civic elites, leaving lesser cults (sponsored by lesser patrons) more vulnerable. Human and divine abandonment of the countryside intersect here, and together attest "to a major upheaval in the religious landscape, and thus to a radical restructuring of local allegiances and indeed emotions."[22] To that formulation could be added the radical restructuring of local memories.

The second development, the redistribution of landed resources in favor of the wealthy, is hardly surprising in a provincial setting and would have resulted in much the same disruptive effects as colonial centuriation. Also significant here is the way such properties were visually distinguished. In some places, conspicuous villas, bath structures, or tombs were erected, ostentatiously marking the rural landscape in a way not seen for centuries. Such elements may be more immediately apparent around the colonies of Corinth and Patras, but new rural expressions of wealth and status appear in other regions as well.[23]

Finally, Strabo and Pausanias (who wrote during the late first century BC/early first century AD and the mid-second century AD, respectively) report numerous cities as "in ruins." The pace of such civic demise was exaggerated, part and parcel of both ancient and modern rhetorical lamentations

---

22. Alcock 1994b, quote at 261; Jost 1985; Spawforth 1989.
23. The quintessential Achaian villas are those of Herodes Atticus: Faklaris 1990; on his building patronage, see Tobin 1997. For a recent study of Roman burial practices in Greece, see Rife 1999.

over Greek decline accompanying the loss of *eleutheria*. In Achaia, however, it
does appear that some, usually smaller and less "remarkable," communities
did go under. Even granted the benefits of the *pax Romana*, provincial taxation
would put new stresses on the polis unit, leading to disappearance, or – less
drastically – to synoecism, dependence on more successful neighbors, or the
formation of league associations. Protection from such pressures could come
from a by now unsurprising source. A city's antiquity could determine its fate
under Roman rule; much would depend on the histories, genealogies, and
mythologies it could summon to its aid.[24] The village of Pallantium in Arcadia
is an excellent instance of a place redeemed by the fame of its forebears:

> The plan of my work next requires of me to describe Pallantium, if there
> is anything notable there, and to explain why the Emperor Antoninus the
> First changed Pallantium from a village into a city, and granted it freedom
> and immunity from taxes. They say, then, that one Evander by name was
> the best of the Arcadians both in council and in war . . . and that having set
> out to found a colony at the head of a band of Arcadians from Pallantium,
> he built a city by the river Tiber. And that quarter of the present city of
> Rome which was inhabited by Evander and his Arcadian followers got the
> name of Pallantium in memory of the city of Arcadia; but in after time the
> name was changed by the omission of the letters L and N. It was for these
> reasons that privileges were conferred on Pallantium by the Emperor.
>
> (Pausanias 8.43.1–3)

All of the developments here briefly reviewed are indicative of the evolution of a new political geography within Achaia. In this context what must be
stressed is that the landscape of Old Greece underwent a compelling degree of
alteration and disruption. Signs of early imperial intervention, such as colonial foundations or displaced gods, are normally perceived and interpreted
from the "top down"; they are assessed from a central point of view. Another
approach, however, would be to adopt a more local perspective, and to accept
all this as evidence for a fundamental reworking, for good or ill, of the social
framework of people's lives. Given the emplacement of memories within the
landscape, it becomes necessary to accept that the channels and contexts for
their transmission and reinforcement were similarly disturbed. More detailed
local studies would reveal more of the precise course and chronology of these
disruptions, and perhaps of more specific local responses.

At a general level, what the backdrop of landscape both reveals and accen-
tuates is that this age was no unchanged "continuation" of its predecessors,

24. Alcock 1993: 129–71.

and that the memorial work of early Roman Greece required effort and inventiveness. Loyalties to the past were neither automatic nor inevitable; this is dramatically underlined if one considers the variety of options open at this juncture. Radically altered social and material frameworks can lead to reevaluation, even abandonment, of what was previously thought "memorable"; human mobility and economic development, for example, contributed to the lost memories of peoples neighboring the Cévennes. In a nearer Roman context, it has been argued that indigenous peoples of the western provinces adopted precisely such a "forgetful" path, with an apparent willingness to jettison large chunks of memory – including their history before the Romans came.[25] By contrast, the inhabitants of Achaia made the choice to stay aligned with a particular part of their own pre-conquest past, and to mobilize it aggressively. In the face of changes in the land, nostalgia became an energetic strategy, with tactics requiring new forms of commemoration and of commemorative space.

THE AGORA AS MEMORIAL SPACE

Ironically, one such "new" commemorative space was actually quite old. Today it is practically cliché, as Susan Walker has observed, to comment on how the composition of the Athenian Agora dramatically altered in the early years of Roman control. However familiar the story in outline, it is still a shock to compare a plan of the Agora in the fifth or fourth century, or even in the second century BC, to one of the second century AD (Figs. 2.4–2.5). To put it most simply, what had once been a relatively open (albeit increasingly framed) urban space was now filled with a diverse assortment of buildings and of monuments. One showpiece of this reconfiguration, to be further discussed below, was the wholesale transplantation of a complete temple and other architectural elements (dating to the fifth and fourth centuries BC) into the Agora's heart. It has been suggested that such "itinerant temples" (in Homer Thompson's phrase) were related to imperial cult celebrations; more certainly such movement of antique elements into a hallowed public space reflects yet another dimension of the age's classicism. Between the choice of transplanted materials, and the location embellished, the Agora has been taken as a superb architectural equivalent to the antiquarian tendencies of the Second Sophistic.[26]

25. Woolf (1996) traces this phenomenon in Gaul particularly.
26. Walker 1997: 67. For general reviews of the Agora's development: Camp 1986: 184–87; Shear 1981; Thompson and Wycherley 1972: 160–68; Walker 1997.

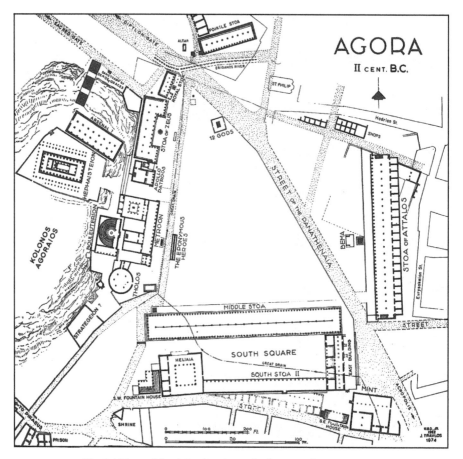

Fig. 2.4 Plan of the Athenian Agora in the second century BC.

Scholarly interpretations of this transformation, not surprisingly, tend to be governed by more general attitudes to the relationship of Greek and Roman. Shear, for example, works within the traditional paradigm of post-conquest loss and decline, believing the change:

> as clear a statement of the new ordering of the world as can be made through the medium of architecture. A conquered city had little need for democratic assemblies and a subject citizen little voice in the determination of his destiny ... it is almost as if ... the builders of the new era seem determined to obliterate that symbol of Athenian democracy, the market square itself, in order to reflect the vanished reality.[27]

How far, of course, the Agora was actually perceived as first and foremost a "symbol" of classical democracy is a fair question, but this remains an

27. Shear 1981: 361.

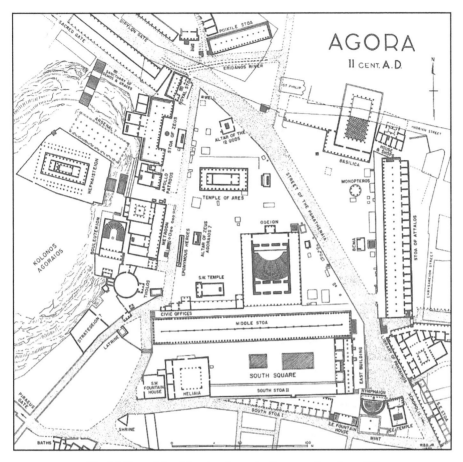

Fig. 2.5 Plan of the Athenian Agora in the second century AD.

influential treatment of the problem. While recognizing the compelling nature of such elegiac readings, Walker prefers to emphasize factors of centrally
driven change, notably Rome's transition from republic to empire. Musing
on this highlighting of the classical past (especially the itinerant temples), she
remarks: "The reason for creating, as it were, a sacred museum of religious art
and architecture at Athens may be sought in the role played by the classical
polis in Augustan moral propaganda, a role very clearly seen in the art and
architectural decoration of Augustan Rome."[28]

This broad political and ideological context is illuminating, yet such a
conception undoubtedly privileges a central perspective over more local views
and responses. The use of the term "museum" (which many have applied to the
imperial Agora) is also problematic, running the risk as it does of emphasizing

28. Walker 1997: 72; see also Felten 1983: 94–95; Spawforth 1997. Zanker (1988: 261–63) speaks of
    "moral rearmament."

old or elite elements at the expense of contemporary or lesser monuments, and thus skewing our appreciation of the space. The label "museum" also potentially underrepresents human participation in this space, which (while it did lose certain functions, as shall be seen) remained an active thoroughfare, a center for ritual activity, and a focus for civic business.[29] It is necessary to envision varied audiences, with varied goals and expectations, acting in and moving through this space (see below, pp. 64–71).

That observation in turn creates difficulties for treatments of the Roman-period Agora characterized by a museal emphasis on the classical elements alone. Isolation of "important" elements can take many forms, from setting things off with guide-ropes (as in museums) to using bold outlines (as on one published plan of the itinerant temples). Subtly or not so subtly, monuments can be separated from the wider matrix in which they actually stand. This archaeological myopia is not uncommon. About the "afterlife of monuments" in a European context, Bradley remarked:

> monuments feed off the associations, not only of places, but also of other monuments. Monuments are enhanced and rebuilt; they are reinterpreted and changed; and new constructions are created around old ones. We tend to lose that dimension of the archaeological record as we become immersed in chronological analysis.[30]

To understand how "monuments feed off associations," a more balanced reading of the space – and of its potential horizon of meanings – is necessary, one which examines not only old and transplanted, but expanded, renewed, and even new elements. The following review revolves around the Augustan and Julio-Claudian epoch, when much of the reconfiguration of this memorial space took place.

Itinerant temples

The rollcall of itinerant or "floating" structures includes one complete temple and assorted architectural pieces, all transferred from their original contexts

29. Another possible way to conceive of the Agora would be as a "memory theater," with buildings and images intended to conjure up specific and controlled memories of the past (Yates 1966: 129–72, 320–67). In the original sense of the term, such theaters were ornate Renaissance conceptions, deliberately fashioned (or at least designed) to serve as a "direct aid for the recall of the past" – a model which does not really fit the long-term development of the Agora. While an evocative phrase, conceiving of the Agora as a "memory theater" also de-emphasizes human activity in favor of a more passive viewing experience. For one suitable, excellent application of the concept in Roman art, see Bergmann 1994.
30. Bradley 1993: 129. The plan mentioned is Dinsmoor 1982: fig. 1, where the "floating temples" and other findspots are heavily outlined to emphasize their location. While this is visually helpful, it also militates against embedding the new elements in their wider context.

to the early imperial Agora. To judge from ceramic finds and masons' marks, this activity spans from the time of Augustus into the first half of the second century AD, with the bulk of it occurring toward the early end of that range.

Most astonishing was the move of the fifth-century BC Temple of Ares, the original location of which remains in question. Early suggestions included locales within Athens itself (the Areopagus or the site of the Market of Caesar and Augustus), but a move from the deme of Acharnai (where a cult of Ares and Athena was known) later came to be more widely accepted. While this would agree with the unquestioned harvesting of classical architectural components from other deme sites (e.g., Thorikos; Sounion), the evidence was never conclusive. Very recently the "footprint" of an appropriately sized temple has been located at Pallene in Attica, and this now appears to be gaining support as the temple's most likely place of origin – leaving open, however, the possibility that the altar (of fourth-century BC date) may still in fact have come from Acharnai.[31] This altar, set in a previously open zone east of the Temple of Apollo Patroös, lies on an axial alignment with the Odeion of Agrippa (see below, p. 63); the manner in which the Ares temple extends to the west, so as not to obscure the façade of the Odeion, similarly suggests a deliberate linkage of the two structures (Fig. 2.5). The temple's transfer probably followed the Odeion's construction, both falling within the Augustan era. Much time and care went into this effort, not least in demolishing and labeling the various elements, in avoiding damage in transit, and in preparing a sound foundation. The amount of labor involved in this enterprise makes an important general point: it is vital not to confuse reuse and reconstruction with doing things on the cheap.[32] Itinerancy, in other words, cannot be reduced to economizing.

The temple's dedication to Ares, a god never hugely popular in Greek civic cult, has inevitably led to hypotheses about its association with specifically Roman interests. Eastern tours by Gaius and Drusus Caesar – honored as the "new Ares" or the "new god Ares" – are cited, and connections posited to central building programs, such as the Mars Ultor temple in the Forum of

---

31. Dinsmoor 1940: 50–51; McAllister 1959: 64; Thompson and Wycherley 1972: 165. Hartswick (1990: 258–67) stresses the independent significance of the altar, which lies on alignment with both temple and Odeion; she traces the "Ares Borghese" type to the new cult statue created for the rededicated temple. See Spawforth 1997: 187–88 on *IG* II(2) 2953, an Athenian dedication "to Ares and Sebastos" from "the koinon of the Acharnians." On recent finds at Pallene: Barber 1999; *ArchDelt* 49 (1994 [1999]) Chr. 71–73; *AR* 46 (1999–2000) 17. Robin Osborne has reminded me that the temple at Pallene would, in the fifth century, have been dedicated to Athena Pallenis; Athena would thus, neatly, have been transformed by this move into Ares/Mars.

32. Dinsmoor 1940; Dinsmoor Jr. 1974: 236; McAllister 1959; Thompson 1952: 93; Thompson and Wycherley 1972: 162; Townsend 1955. The reconstruction involved use of a sima from the Sounion Poseidon temple as well.

Augustus. Whether any explicit link can be made (there seems to be no other evidence for formal cult to Gaius or Drusus in Athens), dedication of a temple to Ares/Mars patently bows in the direction of Roman preferences.[33] On the other hand, Pausanias tells us that in the second century AD the temple was crowded round with a variety of statues and images: Aphrodite, Ares, Athena, and Enyo stood within the structure; Heracles, Theseus, Apollo, Calades, and Pindar stood "round about" the temple; Harmodius and Aristogeiton were "not far off" (1.8.4–5). Notably absent, at least in Pausanias' account, are any imperial images. To his eyes, the Ares temple was a particularly congenial spot for Greek, and especially for Athenian, heroes to gather.[34]

Two other "new" temples, drawing in part on reused classical material, have been identified, one in the southwest and one in the southeast corners of the Agora (Fig. 2.5). Unlike the canonically Greek, peripteral design of the Ares temple, both took the form of prostyle podium structures. The Southwest Temple stood south of the Temple of Ares, opposite the Tholos and other venerable civic buildings; it included columns probably from a Doric-order building at the Attic deme site of Thorikos, as well as pieces from yet unidentified structures. The resulting "architectural patchwork" is dated by pottery to the Augustan age.[35] As its unassuming name suggests, no patron deity can here be named. Thompson believed that the "sudden and comparatively late appearance of so large a shrine... is perhaps most easily explained on the hypothesis that it was intended to house some imperial cult." A statue base found nearby, assimilating Livia Julia Augusta with Artemis Boulaia, may offer some support to this suggestion, but no unambiguous proof of the connection exists.[36] As for the Southeast Temple, according to the most recent reconstruction its façade employed columns from the Temple of Athena at Sounion. This transfer apparently took place in the first half

33. Bowersock 1984; Spawforth 1997: 186–88; see also Dinsmoor 1940: 49–50.
34. Also lacking in Pausanias, oddly enough, is any mention of the itinerant nature of this temple: "one might have expected him to be interested in the fact that the Temple of Ares was a Periclean building transferred to the middle of the Agora in comparatively recent times... but Pausanias has nothing to say of it": Thompson and Wycherley 1972: 205. Pausanias' account of the Agora, the best we have from antiquity, lies in Book I (3.1–17.1).
35. In general, Dinsmoor 1982, quote at p. 428. The Thorikos structure (sometimes referred to as a "stoa") is of unusual design; it seems to have been unfinished at the time of its dismantling; Dinsmoor 1982: 415 and n. 9, 425–28. A second "phase of destruction" took place in the nineteenth century AD, when parts of the building were looted for construction in the modern town of Laurion (*Ergon* 1996: 19–23; 1997: 23–24).
36. Thompson 1952: 90–91, quote at 91; Camp 1986: 186; Dinsmoor 1982: 437–38. On Artemis Boulaia: Oliver 1965. Dinsmoor (1982: 433–34) viewed the Southwest Temple "as part of an architecturally balanced design for the west side of the Agora along with the temple of Ares and the altar of Zeus Agoraios."

Fig. 2.6 Altar of Zeus Agoraios (?), Athenian Agora.

of the second century AD, or in other words, somewhat later than the other itinerant structures. The temple's position meant it "must have dominated the vista as one approached the Panathenaic Way" – at least until the subsequent construction of the neighboring Nymphaeum (Fig. 2.5). Found within the cella were fragments of a colossal (about 4 meters tall) Pentelic marble statue which represented a peplos-clad female in late fifth-century style; her identity (and that of any associates she may have had) remains unknown.[37]

Other smaller monuments also played a part in this novel form of refurbishment. South of the Temple of Ares, and just northeast of the monument to the Eponymous Heroes, stood the "handsomest altar found in the Agora," a fourth-century structure which appears precisely to fit a foundation cutting discovered on the Pnyx. This altar has been identified, if not with absolute confidence, as that of Zeus Agoraios (Fig. 2.6); masons' marks point to its redeployment in the first century BC or AD. Such an apparently charged political transfer did not go unnoticed: "it may not be coincidence that Zeus, whose special task it was to govern the political assemblies of the Athenians, should depart the Pnyx at just the time when Augustus is said to have curtailed

37. Thompson 1960: 339–43, quote at 339. Like its southwestern counterpart, this has been viewed as part of a wider program, with the "architectural expansion of the southeast part of the Agora along with the Library of Pantainos, the Nymphaion and the Southeast Stoa": Dinsmoor 1982: 431–33, quote at 433. On the cult statue and its giant pedestal (capable of supporting several colossi): Dinsmoor 1982: 435–37; Harrison 1960: 371–73; Thompson 1960: 339, 341.

sharply the powers of those same assemblies."[38] A fifth-century BC poros base, found in an Early Roman context in the Agora's northeast corner, possibly supported a monumental herm, as did another similar base noted near the Temple of Ares. Several "floating" Ionic columns complete this résumé of itinerant stuff; coming in two sizes, these have been characterized as "of the highest quality and finest workmanship." Neither the site of their original context, nor that of their imperial reuse, is known.[39]

Itinerancy, as already observed, can be taken as no mere exercise in civic cheese-paring. That would grossly underestimate the symbolic strength, and even potential hazard, of such reuse, especially in an atmosphere so infused with awareness of the past. Robbing one temple to furnish another did not always meet with approval. To cite an Italian comparison, the Roman censor Quintus Fulvius Flaccus stripped marble tiles off the temple of Juno Lacinia at Bruttium to adorn a shrine in Rome. The local people of Bruttium were too much in awe of Flaccus to prevent this act of sacrilege; the Senate felt no such compunction, but ordered the roof tiles returned and offerings of atonement made. As with the displacement of cult images from their original home, authority was on show and a new locale was benefited, but feelings of loss and resentment could also result.[40]

Renewals, expansions, and annexations

Impressive though they are, the reordering of the Agora involved far more than these itinerant elements. Venerable monuments still *in situ* were also subject to renovation and celebration, in some ways reminiscent of the homage of Mesopotamian dynasts to their own *cadre matériel*. One example is the Sanctuary of Aphrodite Ourania (Heavenly Aphrodite) at the northwestern corner of the Agora, west of the Stoa Poikile and not far from the Temple of Ares (Fig. 2.7). In Augustan times a new temple was set on axial alignment with an existing, Archaic-period altar to the goddess, probably dating to *c.* 500 BC. In this alignment, in its podium form and in its proportions (with deep porch and shallow cella), the excavators noted parallels with both the Southeast and Southwest temples, as well as with "contemporary temples of the Italian homeland and of Rome in particular." The structure simultaneously displays connections to older Athenian monuments, however, both through aspects of its decoration which relate to the north porch of the

---

38. Shear 1981: 365; see also Camp 1986: 186–87; Thompson and Wycherley 1972: 160–62.
39. Bases: Thompson 1952: 102. On the "floating columns": Camp 1986: 186; Thompson and Wycherley 1972: 166.
40. On the impiety of Flaccus, Livy 42.3. See above, pp. 46–47 and n. 20.

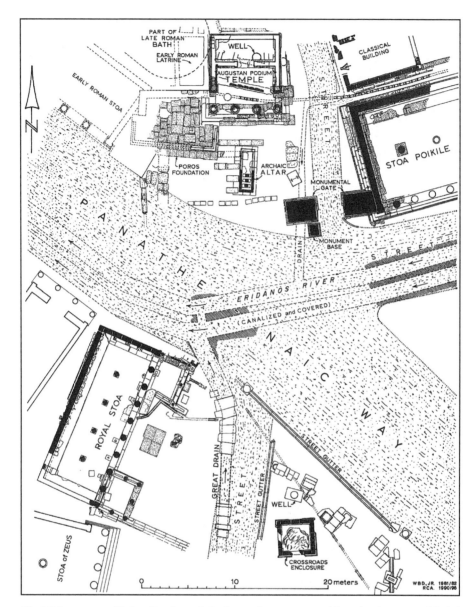

Fig. 2.7 Sanctuary of Aphrodite Ourania in the northwest corner of the Athenian Agora, labeled here as "Augustan podium temple." The Archaic altar lies in front.

Erechtheion and – most obviously – through its clear affiliation to the ancient altar of Aphrodite.[41]

41. Shear 1997: 498, on the temple in general, 495–507; Shear 1984: 33–40; Pausanias 1.14.7. On the altar of Aphrodite, Camp 1986: 56–57. Shear (1997: 507) suggests a close link between the Aphrodite Ourania temple, the temple of Roma and Augustus, and the Erechtheion; craftsmen became familar with the latter monument from repairing the damage done by Sulla's troops in 87/86 BC.

Still on the west side of the Agora, but at its southern end, the venerable civic structure of the Tholos also received care and attention. Badly damaged in the Sullan siege of 87/86 BC, it was repaired probably soon afterward. In Augustan times, it went on to receive a monumental entrance and, around the middle of the first century AD, a more elaborate style of flooring. In this same southwestern area, near the Tholos and the Strategeion and along the Agora's major western passageway, an old shrine likewise received a new façade, with a small Doric propylon attached to what may be the cult of the Athenian hero Strategos.[42]

As these examples already begin to demonstrate, any highlighting of the past, particularly the classical past, in the Agora must be balanced against clear signs of an imperial present. Renovated structures played a part in this infiltration. With no small trouble, an annex with a double cella was affixed to the later fifth-century Stoa of Zeus Eleutherios (Fig. 2.8). Most assign this work to the time either of Augustus or of Tiberius. While the specific attribution of this annex is not entirely certain, Thompson, not unreasonably, suggested an association with the imperial cult: "In view of its intrusion into one of the principal sanctuaries of Zeus in Athens and into a highly esteemed old building, the new cult must be assumed to have been of very considerable importance."[43]

Monuments were also "converted" to imperial use, a phenomenon seen elsewhere in Athens and throughout the province at large. For example, a tall monument topped by a bronze quadriga stood before the Stoa of Attalus. This conspicuous item, almost certainly dedicated originally to Attalus II and dating to the second century BC, was rededicated to the emperor Tiberius "in thanks for past favors and in lively anticipation of favors to come," as Eugene Vanderpool wryly put it. The monument's size and location (close by the Panathenaic Way) ensured it a prominent place on the urban skyline. Reassignments of this type were not solely confined to emperors: in the Athenian Prytaneion stood statues of Peace, Hestia, and Autolycus the pancratiast, together with likenesses of Miltiades and Themistocles which, according to Pausanias, "have had their titles changed to a Roman and a Thracian" (1.18.3).[44]

---

42. Tholos: Hoff 1997: 38; Thompson 1940: 56–57, 63–64, 136; Thompson and Wycherley 1972: 46. On the hero shrine: Lalonde 1980: 98; Thompson and Wycherley 1972: 73.
43. Thompson 1966, quote at 180; Spawforth 1997: 186 and n. 21; Thompson and Wycherley 1972: 102–3.
44. Vanderpool 1959, quote at 90. Rededications to famous generals include the Monument of Agrippa on the Acropolis (Dinsmoor 1920) and the column of Aemilius Paullus at Delphi (Plutarch, *Aemilius Paullus* 28); see Alcock 1993: 196–98. A statue of Orestes in the Argive Heraion

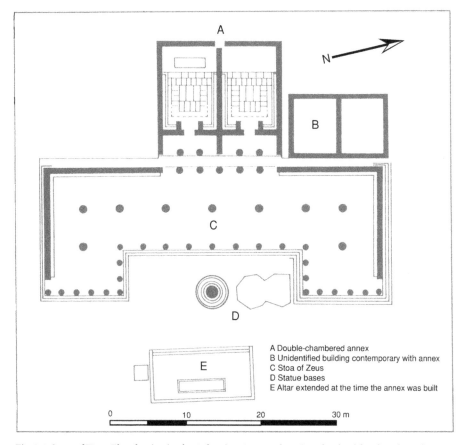

A Double-chambered annex
B Unidentified building contemporary with annex
C Stoa of Zeus
D Statue bases
E Altar extended at the time the annex was built

0   10   20   30 m

Fig. 2.8 Stoa of Zeus Eleutherios in the Athenian Agora, showing the double-chambered annex added in early imperial times.

New foundations and new views

Last to be considered is the introduction of entirely new structures into the Agora environment. The most important, the Market of Caesar and Augustus (the so-called Roman Agora), actually lay some 150 meters beyond the boundaries of its predecessor (Fig. 2.9). The majority of commercial activities once carried out within the ancient center were now transferred to this alternative space. Funds for this structure – a large porticoed enclosure, open to the sky, with monumental, decorated entrance – were provided by Roman authorities, with the market being completed *c.* 11–9 BC. Parallels for the expulsion

was renamed as Augustus: Pausanias 2.17.3. For a less exalted case, see Pausanias 8.9.9–10 on the statue of Podares in Mantinea. Cicero worried about being palmed off with a reused statue: *Epistulae ad Atticum* 6.1.26; see also Dio Chrysostom's *Rhodian Oration* (31.9, 141); Jones 1978a: 26–35, esp. 28–30.

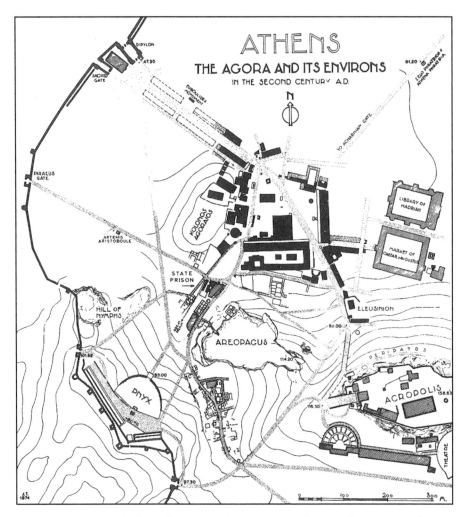

Fig. 2.9 General map of Athens, the Agora and its environs in the second century AD, showing the location of the Roman Agora (the Market of Caesar and Augustus).

of more mundane business from its former home, and the resultant intensification of that space's religious and sacral character, can be found elsewhere, not least in Rome itself. The discovery of altars, statues, and other dedications to the imperial family in the vicinity of the original Agora help to bear out this trend.[45]

45. For the Market of Caesar and Augustus: Camp 1986: 184; Hoff 1988; 1989b. For Augustan altars in the Agora: Benjamin and Raubitschek 1959; the names of later emperors would be added to these as time passed. For a possible imperial cult center near the Market, see Hoff 1994; 1996: 195–200. More generally on the changing nature of agora space: Felten 1983. Near the Market, in the northeastern corner of the Agora, was found another poorly understood structure of Augustan date; this was later incorporated by the Hadrianic basilica: Shear 1971: 261–65.

Fig. 2.10 Model of the Athenian Agora in the second century AD. The Odeion of Agrippa occupies the middle ground; to its right is the Temple of Ares. The Southeast and Southwest podium temples are also visible: the Southwest between the Odeion and the round structure of the Tholos; the Southeast at the bottom left of the model, next to the hemicycle of the Nymphaeum.

It is usually assumed that this dual shift in functions (the loss of political independence, the departure of commercial activities) allowed the Agora's "infilling." Undoubtedly the most impressive new structure was the multi-storied Odeion of Agrippa which – looming over and dwarfing all else (Fig. 2.10) – singlehandedly swallowed up much of the formerly open space at the Agora's southern end (Fig. 2.5). Its construction has been linked to an eastern tour made by Marcus Agrippa between 23 and 13 BC, and it was probably finished before the general's death in 12 BC. The Odeion was a large covered concert hall suitable for sophistic as well as musical performances; indeed, Philostratus describes epideictic displays in this very building. The glories of Athenian history were thus declaimed on historic ground, if not in a "genuinely" ancient structure.[46]

46. Philostratus, *Vitae Sophistarum* 2.5.4; 2.8.4; Camp 1986: 184, 194–96; Thompson 1987: 6–9; Thompson and Wycherley 1972: 111–14; Ward-Perkins 1981: 267–68. When the large unsupported roof span collapsed in the mid-second century AD, the building was remodeled and reworked, diminishing the capacity of the audience from about 1000 to about 500 people.

For one final "new foundation," a large rectangular foundation, found near the quadriga of Tiberius, can be named. This may be the bema supposedly built before the Stoa of Attalus by Roman generals in the first century BC. If this identification is correct, "it was a very solid structure, intended to be permanent." Homer Thompson and Frank Wycherley go on, however, to remark: "but... there is nothing to indicate that it ever had more than occasional use."[47] The notion of a Roman bema in the heart of Athens plainly evoked a certain squeamishness.

This review – while by no means a comprehensive catalogue of constructions, dedications, and developments – at very least moves beyond sole focus on itinerant, "classicizing" elements to provide a more holistic sense of the Agora's metamorphosis. Another helpful shift in perspective would be to advance beyond purely two-dimensional representations, to allow a better sense of how far various additions and renovations altered people's experience of the space (for some limited sense of this, see Fig. 2.10). Even its exterior frame, with greater emphasis on entrances and exits, was modified.[48] The prominent location of structures such as the Southeast Temple or the quadriga now topped by Tiberius, the dominating height of the Odeion, the reorganization and re-presentation of areas such as the southwest zone near the Tholos, the implantation of the Temple of Ares: all did much more than "fill space." Instead, they contributed to a dramatic transformation of a walk through the Agora. But that brings us to the question: how can we can move from recognizing such transformations and such new experiences, to understanding how this memorial space actually worked?

Memorial audiences

Why would people go to the Agora, and what would they do there? Some would be on their way to sacrifice at temples; others would call at buildings still active in civic administration; others would be sightseeing; still others would merely be passing through, on their way to the Market of Caesar and Augustus, to the Acropolis, or to ends known best to themselves. For the classical period, Millett identified some twenty-three attested activities, ranging from administration to dancing, gambling to religious practices, seeking publicity

---

47. Thompson and Wycherley 1972: 51–52. The bema is mentioned by Athenaeus (5.212e–f) in an episode involving an inflammatory, anti-Roman speech made by Athenion, a supporter of Mithridates in 88 BC.
48. Stoas newly lined the section of the Panathenaic Way between the Dipylon Gate and the Agora proper, and stone paving was placed on the Way itself as it climbed up toward the Acropolis: Thompson and Wycherley 1972: 108–9, 193.

to begging, picking up a prostitute to fetching water, collecting information to telling the time. There is no reason to believe these particular goings-on ceased in Roman times, although the export of commercial affairs, and the changed political nature of the community, would have somewhat reduced Millett's original list.[49] Moreover, the universe of people engaged in these affairs was now, if anything, expanded. Tourists, ephebes, priests, soldiers, citizens, emperors, slaves, Romans, Greeks, native Athenians, men, women: all these and countless more made up the audience of the Agora. They would each move through their own version of the space for their own purposes: to visit different monuments, to perform different rituals, to seek different services, and to enjoy different things.

This heterogeneity of performance stymies any hope of pinning down a singular reading of the Agora as memorial space – a faint hope at best, given the essential ambiguities predicted for monuments and monumental complexes. What *can* be done is to tease out some of the principal commemorative strands contained within the early imperial Agora. These, it will turn out, often overlap and sometimes contest each other, giving some sense of the complexity of the various memory communities welcomed into and served by this space.

One obvious place to begin, it might be thought, would be by identifying the agency behind the altered design of the Agora. Unfortunately, no easy answer presents itself. First of all, the foregoing review collapsed several decades into a synchronic picture of change. More importantly, the existence of one force behind all these moves seems highly unlikely, although a degree of central Roman intervention is difficult to dispute. Athens had patently fallen on hard financial times at the very end of the Republic, arguing for a condition of some dependency; the composition of aspects of the Agora (for example, alignments between the Temple of Ares and the Odeion of Agippa), not to mention the selection of Ares for veneration, similarly point in this direction.[50] The evidence is not sufficient, however, to justify the assumption that Roman direction and financial backing underlay *all* the developments noted. Epigraphic evidence from this period certainly attests to the active participation of Athenian notables in civic ceremonials or imperial cult

49. On "mixing it in the Agora," Millett 1998: 211–18, esp. 215–16, n. 25.
50. "One can attribute these developments, which gave the Agora something of the aspect of a Roman forum, to the patronage of the imperial family, to whom the Athenians showed their gratitude and homage by the installation of appropriate cults, with numerous altars and statues": Thompson and Wycherley 1972: 23. By contrast, cheaper work, such as the use of "second-hand" material in the modifications to the Stoa of Zeus Eleutherios, was attributed to civic initiatives. See also Thompson 1966; 1987.

activities.[51] Probably a mixture of imperial encouragement and local enterprise, as seen elsewhere in the Greek east, should be envisioned behind the reconfigured Agora. On one level, of course, the entire question is a bit of a red herring, for to establish who built, or who financed, a particular monument is only to begin the discussion of its commemorative significance.

Nevertheless, when starting to disentangle the different memorial audiences at work in the Agora, it still makes sense to begin with the new ruling authorities. The category "Romans," of course, hardly calls to mind an undifferentiated group, but embraces emperors, youthful students, generals, businessmen, art lovers, soldiers, and more. Walker and others, as already noted, attribute what happened in the Agora to wider currents in Augustan moral propaganda, seeing it as supportive of the "pious agenda" being established in Rome. Certainly many aspects – the embrace of Aphrodite and Ares (or Venus and Mars), the interpolation of the imperial cult, the axial alignments which echoed forum design, the splice of Greek to Roman history (later to be neatly summed up by Hadrian joining the line of Eponymous Heroes) – would have worked to make the Agora a welcoming and in some ways familiar space for visitors from Rome, one deliberately reminiscent of "home."[52] Yet a harsher element can also be traced here, a "rewriting" of the Agora akin to Roman interventions in the Achaian landscape. Shear's remark – "it is almost as if . . . the builders of the new era seem determined to obliterate that symbol of Athenian democracy, the market square itself" – cannot be taken as a complete explanation of the Agora's transformation. Yet a radical change in the topography of such a significant space (not least by creating a clear relationship between a peripteral marble temple and a vast structure built by a Roman general) demanded new forms of visual and emotional connection.

Beyond those general observations, the attitudes of one specific group of Roman citizens can be glimpsed through the writings of Cicero (an individual who would himself play multiple roles in the Greek east). This is the cadre of young aristocrats who visited Greece, and especially Athens, for periods of cultural study and philosophical reflection. In *De Finibus*, Cicero offers a dialogue among the members of such a company:

> When we reached the promenades of the Academy, which are so rightly famous, we had them all to ourselves, as we had wished. Then Piso said: "Whether it is a natural instinct or an illusion, I can't say; but one's

51. Geagan 1979a; 1979b; 1997; Spawforth 1997.
52. On the monument to the Eponymous Heroes: Shear 1970.

emotions are more strongly engaged by seeing the locales that tradition records to have been the favorite places of worthy men, more than by hearing about their deeds or by reading what they wrote. I am moved now in just this way. To my mind comes Plato, the first philosopher, so we are told, who customarily held discussions in this place; and indeed the nearby garden not only brings back his memory but seems to set the actual man before my eyes..."   (Cicero, *De Finibus* 5.1.1–2)

The young men go on to take turns enumerating their favorite highlights in an Athens filled with such physical reminders of eminent men, with each choice influenced by the individual's own particular philosophical or literary interests. Places selected in this fashion included the tomb of Pericles, the village of Sophocles, the garden of Plato, the beach of Demosthenes, and so on: as Lucius Cicero remarks: "there is no end to it in this city; wherever we walk, we set foot on historic ground" (*De Finibus* 5.2.5). Thus suitably identified, the greatness of these places, and of the men associated with them, are used to rouse the young Lucius to suitable emulation.

These particular visitors, at least as represented by Cicero, display a supremely "touristic" attitude to Athens, and to Achaia. Indifferent to more present-day activities or more local concerns – having the place to themselves as they had wished – the young men stand at the head of a long line of "travelers to be inspired by the idea of a Greece that no longer was."[53] From this perspective, the Agora, indeed the city at large, would indeed present itself as a kind of museum, a collection of monuments and images to be selectively rummaged through. Sentiments and memories would thus be enjoyably stimulated about a lost past: a past firmly severed from the present not least (in Rosaldo's framework of imperialist nostalgia) by the actions of the forebears of these young men.

Given the reliance on the past outlined earlier in the chapter, a parallel "pushing" of classical history and monuments on the part of the Athenian elite makes perfect sense. A showcase of Periclean art and architecture was very much in their interests, ensuring due admiration and respect, together with all the material advantages those could bring. The Agora, for example, provided a dignified setting for the reception of visiting luminaries, for example in the celebration of the Panathenaia or for initiation into the Eleusinian Mysteries. The temptation to write off such self-promotion as unworthy or vulgar must be strongly resisted. Created here instead was a theater of self-representation

---

53. Eisner 1991: 30; Spencer 1954: 48–54. This "power of place," of course, worked in Rome as well: Cicero, *De Finibus* 5.1.2. On Roman visitors and students in the city: Daly 1950; Habicht 1997; Jones 1978b.

in which notable Romans could be received, and perceived, more as partners than as conquerors.[54]

Design changes in the Agora did more, however, than foreground memories agreed to bring esteem and authority. Equally visible – in the ubiquitous juxtaposition of new and old shrines in new and old styles, of ancient gods and imperial images – was a close integration of the classical past with the contemporary present. For Greek and Roman alike (if in different ways and to different degrees), a journey through the Agora would not only maintain awareness of an Athenian heritage but would inculcate familiarity and acceptance of the new order. The monumental combinations of the Agora worked to harmonize local interests with those of the ruling power (and vice versa), teaching the values of mutual respect and of close identification between periphery and center (see below, pp. 88–89). The visible amalgam of past and present could accustom people to viewing Athens in particular as part (somewhat separate, but equal) of the Roman way of doing things: a foundation upon which the Panhellenion would later build.[55] Articulated by an alliance of central authorities and local elites, set forth in a central, public space, such a message would reach – if not necessarily convince – a wide audience.

This line of interpretation provides, of course, a relatively *compliant* version of Greek memories inspired by the Agora. Other readings can be offered which instead stress alternative, even resistant uses of the space, and of its classicism in particular. Just as aristocratic Romans created their own version of the city through the appropriation of certain elements and the neglect of others, so – for a very different group of people – the Agora might be perceived first and foremost as a "museum" of a proud civic history, a monument to a past that could not be invaded. The Agora, in this particular construction, truly belonged only to some; others could visit at best as tourists, welcome on restricted terms. An accent on antiquity, made manifest in the itinerant

54. Panathenaia: Neils 1992 (though with little on Roman times); Eleusinian Mysteries: Clinton 1989; 1997.
55. The Panhellenion, founded (or at very least strongly supported) by Hadrian, was a league of Greek cities drawn from all over the eastern Mediterranean. Its central headquarters, however, was established in or near Athens, possibly at Eleusis. Membership in the organization revolved around issues of descent, making genealogical relationships and affiliations – in other words issues of memory – central to its functioning. The Panhellenion deserves further study from this angle, not least to explore possible tensions between this emphasis on descent versus an emphasis on *paideia* as arbiters of "Greekness." The relative lack of specifically *archaeological* correlates for the league (the physical location of its meeting place, for example, has been widely sought but not found) leaves it beyond the bounds of this particular study. See Oliver 1951; 1970: 92–138; Spawforth and Walker 1985; 1986; most recently: Jones 1996a; 1999a; Lamberton 1997; Spawforth 1999; Weiss 2000.

temples, laid claim to enduring Hellenic uniqueness and guaranteed a sense of identity that could be imitated or envied, but never usurped. Such local self-regard, of course, would be most strongly articulated at Athens, the antique Hellenic city *par excellence*.[56]

Divergent and potentially competitive readings of the Agora were by no means limited to the two, themselves open-ended, categories of "Greeks" and "Romans." A range of "Greek" peoples would have moved to, or passed through, Athens in early imperial times; few would view its downtown in precisely the same way as that city's autochthonous inhabitants. No extant texts attest specifically to these different responses, but – once one gets past a genuine, if generic, philo-Atticism – such dissonances are certain. Whether an individual or group of people came to Athens from Asia Minor, or elsewhere in Old Greece, from another "antique" city (Ephesus) or an ancient enemy (Sparta), from a city said to have medized (Thebes) or a city that stood firm (Plataea), from a Hellenistic royal center (Pergamon) or from a Roman colony (Corinth): each experience would be filtered through and framed by distinct civic or regional histories, each marked by different relationships – cordial or hostile – to Athens. Comparing the experience of the Asian-born Pausanias in Achaia to that of a New Zealander of Scottish descent on tour in Scotland is fanciful – as Konstan (whose notion it is) admits – but it does provide some flavor of what was happening here.[57]

What distinguishes the Agora from the texts or the epideictic performances of the Second Sophistic is, of course, its genuine accessibility to all elements within society. If many of the refinements of the age (in language, literature, or rhetoric) were not widely shared, and indeed could be used to sharpen status distinctions, diverse populations were open to the commemorative messages of such a public complex. The *promotion* of nostalgia may have been largely in the hands of the elite, but – thanks to memorial spaces such as the Agora – its *experience* and its *interpretation* were not limited solely to that

56. "Admiration of the past went together with admiration of Athens": Bowie 1974: 195–203, quotation at 195; see also Henrichs 1995; Spawforth 1999: 352. One example of this more resistant classicism may be the protests raised over the practice of Roman-style games in the hallowed Theater of Dionysos, even though the theater was physically remodeled (by Tiberius Claudius Novius, reintroduced later as the "best of the Hellenes") to accommodate gladiatorial shows. Welch sets these protests "in the larger context of politically conservative Greek opposition to Roman rule and its rituals," see Welch 1999: 127–33, quotation at 132.

57. Konstan 2001; see also Elsner 1992. For Greeks from the Black Sea studying in Athens: Braund 1997: 134–35. On Roman distinctions of "Atticism" and "Asianism" in rhetoric: Swain 1996: 21–27, with bibliography. I would like to thank Christopher Jones for prompting my thoughts on the heterogeneity of the Greeks.

group.[58] In early imperial Achaia, the use of monuments and the development of places such as the Agora ensured that the demos remained witnesses and agents in remembering the past; this does not mean that they necessarily always discerned, or always followed, the commemorative narratives of the ruling classes.

This observation comes into special play if it is remembered that, apart from a spectrum of visitors (Greek and Roman alike) and from a thin stratum of elite residents, other people also lived in Athens and possessed a special relationship to its hallowed reputation. No first-hand testimony is available, but a modern-day analogy drawn from another Greek community "famous for its past" (Rethemnos in Crete) may offer some insight into their situation:

> Rethemnos is a lived place, and its people must deal with the realities of social existence. It is also a real topos, both in literature and in architectural history. The cultural topology imposes strains on the experience of physical and social place that a less visible and ideologically less interesting cultural conjuncture might have escaped. The residents of this ancient town certainly exploit the benefits of tourism, boast of their heritage and their monuments, and pride themselves on the literary attention that today exposes them to some, at least, of the pressure they encounter. Conversely, however, they want to get on with the comforting ordinariness of their everyday lives.[59]

The people of Athens, and no doubt other "notable" Greek towns such as Sparta, conceivably shared in some of these internal tensions, veering (depending on circumstances) between pride in their heritage, and resentment of the burdens it imposed.

The people of Rethemnos never resolve this tension, nor can their community history be boiled down into a single untroubled version. Michael Herzfeld in fact warns that "a shared rhetoric of the past, however official it may seem on the surface, can conceal multiple interpretations and experiences of time" and insists upon the investigation of "as many of the competing (and often submerged) authenticities as possible."[60] Such competing and hidden versions of the past are no less likely in the Athenian case, but they remain much harder to investigate. One source, the *Periegesis* of Pausanias, hints at such multiple experiences, not least by periodically offering different accounts

---

58. An alternative scenario would have been the development of a tightly controlled and restricted "high culture" of the sort argued in Baines and Yoffee 1998; for reconsideration of their arguments, see Brumfiel 2000 and the other papers in Richards and Van Buren 2000.
59. Herzfeld 1991: 258.　60. Herzfeld 1991: 15, 13.

of the same story. At one juncture, Pausanias outlines alternative Athenian foundation legends for the Agora shrine of Aphrodite Ourania:

> The image still existing in my time is of Parian marble, and is a work of Phidias. However, there is an Athenian deme, Athmonon, the inhabitants of which say that their sanctuary of the Heavenly Goddess was founded by Porphyrion, who reigned before Actaeus. *There are other stories which the people of the demes tell quite differently from the people of the capital.*
>
> (Pausanias 1.14.7, my emphasis)

This observation leads to the consideration of one final memory community: the residents of the territory encircling Athens, especially locations such as Sounion, Thorikos, or Pallene – the possible origin points for elements transplanted to the Agora. When a monument moves, most attention follows it to the new locale and to the new story it there tells. But such a shift has repercussions at the other end as well. For all that has been written about the "itinerant" elements in the Agora, little thought has been given to the absence left behind. Any possible sense of loss has been disregarded or downplayed, on the grounds that Attica is usually assumed to be gravely depopulated, and its cult sites neglected, at this time. This premise, however, has been challenged, and the allegedly parlous state of the Attic landscape – human and sacred – stands in need of significant modification.[61] That the removal of temples, altars, or parts of buildings would pass unnoticed or unfelt should not be taken for granted, and a diversity of responses can be imagined, whereby locals variously colluded in, deplored, or were indifferent to such actions.

Although these "competing (and often submerged) authenticities" – from memories constructed by imperial arbiters to those stolen from rural dwellers – have here been temporarily disaggregated, they were all simultaneously active and available within the Agora. No doubt things were even more complicated than the dynamics charted here. Excavation reports and Pausanias' *Periegesis* can provide only an incomplete sense of the space and its memorial prompts; factors such as individual family histories or gender distinctions have not been brought into the discussion. It is also true that perceptions would change with the passage of time, from a city feeling the "shock of the new" to generations for whom the reconfigured Agora would become a familiar entity.

---

61. On depopulation: Camp 1986: 187; Thompson and Wycherley 1972: 23, 160; cf. Alcock 1993: 194. On the early imperial restoration of sanctuaries in Attic territory, numbering up to some eighty in number: Culley 1975; 1977. The influence of Augustan moral legislation has been detected in this act: Culley 1977: 289.

The focus so far has been on the best-understood civic complex in Roman Greece, but precisely similar phenomena can be observed in other urban spaces and in major sanctuaries. An early imperial pattern of emphasizing civic history and mythic founders, for example, is to be seen in Achaia and elsewhere: for example, at Argos, Cyrene, Ephesus, and the cities of Bithynia.[62] As for Sparta:

> Until the time of the Herulian raid at least, the hub of the Roman city remained the agora, the civic centre of Sparta since at least the fifth century B.C. By the Antonine period, in a development paralleled elsewhere in Greece, notably at Athens, *this area had acquired the character almost of a museum*, crowded with statues of deities and famous Spartans and old tombs and sanctuaries, and dominated by its showpiece, the Persian Stoa, originally built from the spoils of Plataea and famous for the figures of defeated Persians which supported the facade. As well as offering attractions for cultural tourists, the agora served as the administrative centre of the Roman city, being flanked by the offices of the chief magistrates, the council-house of the gerontes, and the so-called Old Ephoreia.

Archaeological evidence, reviewed by Paul Cartledge and Anthony Spawforth, reports Roman-period renovations or repairs at other major Spartan monuments, such as the sanctuary of Artemis Orthia, the Round Building, and the so-called Altar of Lycurgus. Increased financial outlay on religious ceremonials to long-established civic cults, such as the Dioscuri and Tainaron Poseidon, also emerge from epigraphic data of the Augustan epoch.[63]

Emphasis on the past embraced the revival of ancient institutional practices and observances, including the famed, if poorly understood, rites for young men at the sanctuary of Artemis Orthia. Such developments were once treated dismissively: "The keeping up of ancient appearances was no more than a colorful stage setting for the benefit of visitors, particularly wealthy Romans, who would come to Sparta as to one of the most famous cities of Greek history."[64] As at Athens and elsewhere, such negative judgments are now being reconsidered. Cartledge and Spawforth lead the way, putting a more positive spin on the city's "image of tradition" and how it helped "this

62. For Argos: Amandry 1980; Piérart and Touchais 1996: 75–81. On monumental links between Danaos and Hadrian at Argos: Piérart 1999. For Ephesus: Rogers 1991; Walker 1997; for Cyrene, Walker 1997; for Bithynia, see Mitchell 1984; 1990.
63. Cartledge and Spawforth 1989: 127 (my emphasis). Building renovations: Cartledge and Spawforth 1989: 220–21. Ceremonials: Cartledge and Spawforth 1989: 99. For recent archaeological work in Sparta, see Cavanagh and Walker 1998. For Pausanias' description of the city: 1.10.2.
64. Oliva 1971: 318. On the *agoge* in its later incarnations, see Kennell 1995: 49–69 and *passim*.

otherwise fairly typical provincial Greek city to maintain a place in the world and allowed the Spartans to feel that they were still 'special.' "[65] The memorial spaces of Sparta could be "untangled" in a fashion much like the Athenian Agora; interesting topics to explore would be the role of aristocratic families (such as the Euryclids) in the control of civic commemoration; the numerous ties of fictive kinship (*syngeneia*) between the antique mother city of Sparta and a disparate scatter of communities; and the expression of popular forms of memory which still encouraged rivalries (now non-violent) with Athens or with the Messenians.[66] If one asked why the Spartans in Roman times would choose to renovate the Altar of Lycurgus, a range of "correct" answers (as we saw in Athens) should be anticipated.

Examination of the monumental centers of those classic rivals, Athens and Sparta, leads to the same end: it reveals the influences of those spaces upon the memories, and thus the convictions, of broad and cosmopolitan audiences. One way to reinforce the Athenian Agora's importance as a site of commemoration is simply to consider some of the roads *not* taken. The urban center could have been left more or less as it was following first-century BC conflicts – an open, somewhat banged-up space. Or, as commercial functions were shifted away from the area, the Agora could have become an unimportant passageway to more affluent civic sectors. Nothing immutably declared that this spot required restoration and embellishment.[67] Similar scenarios could be envisioned for the civic center of Roman Sparta. Instead, these urban places were transformed, at considerable effort and no small expense, with *in situ* monuments refurbished and others added to provoke "right memories" – though no absolute consensus would emerge on precisely what those were. As the product of strenuous cultural mythmaking, as the servant of a variety of agents and agenda, they are fascinating, and eerily familiar, spaces.

65. Cartledge and Spawforth 1989: 210. "In the Roman age the maintenance of venerable shrines and images and the performance of traditional rites of hereditary officiants within the context of an apparently ageless social structure helped to sustain the myth of an unchanging Sparta on which the prestige of the Roman city, as well as of individual families in the local élite, partly rested": Spawforth 1992b: 238.
66. On the Spartan "image of tradition," see Cartledge and Spawforth 1989: 190–211. On the Euryclids and their *dunasteia*: Bowersock 1961; Cartledge and Spawforth 1989: 97–104; Spawforth 1978. On *syngeneia* and Sparta: Spawforth and Walker 1986: 88–96. For ongoing rivalry with the Messenians, see chapter 4.
67. Nor did the Agora remain unchanged in the years following the Augustan and Julio-Claudian renovations; Hadrian, of course, did much to and for the city – not least dividing it into "Old" and "New" Athens: Boatwright 1983; 2000: 144–57; Kokkou 1971; Willers 1990. Ultimately, of course, the Agora does lose its civic prestige; for its later history, see Frantz 1988; Thompson and Wycherley 1972: 208–19. Bishop Synesios, in AD 398, wrote: "all that is left for us is to walk around and wonder at the Academy and the Lyceum and, by Zeus, the Poikile Stoa after which the philosophy of Chrysippos is named, now no longer many coloured; the proconsul took away the sanides to which Polygnotos of Thasos committed his art" (*Epistles* 135); see Camp 1986: 71.

PERSIAN WAR BLUES

> Cato's expeditions added no great matter to the Roman empire, which already was so great . . . but those of Aristides are the noblest, most splendid, and distinguished actions the Grecians ever did, the battles at Marathon, Salamis and Plataea.   (Plutarch, *Aristides and Cato Major, synkrisis* 5.1)

The Akkadian ruler Sargon and the Camisard rebellion were earlier identified as charismatic elements, inspiring rich clusters of memory for peoples far distant in time. The most potent "constellative myth" for the Greeks of the early empire involved events occurring some five centuries before Augustus: the desperate struggles of the Greeks, most spectacularly the Athenians and Spartans, to repel Persian invasion (Fig. 2.11). The enduring power of such myths can be wonderful indeed; we have already seen the Persian Wars invoked as rallying point and emotional focus in the nineteenth-century struggle for Greek independence (pp. 3–5).

Marathon, Thermopylae, Salamis, Plataea, Darius, Leonidas, Xerxes, Themistocles, Miltiades: as in the rhetoric of the War of Independence, all were names to conjure with in the rhetorical exercises and literary works of the early empire; their story provided a common thread of understanding and of interest across the Greek world. Numerous examples could be cited: one sophist, Ptolemy of Naucratis, was nicknamed "Marathon" because of his repeated invocation of that particular battle; the *Periegesis* of Pausanias is riddled with references to memorabilia, monuments, and moments from the time when Greeks withstood the barbarian. To remain with the two cities discussed so far, in Athens he enumerates many relevant dedications and structures, including a temple "of Good Fame, another offering from the spoils of the Medes who landed at Marathon" (1.14.5) and in the Stoa Poikile a painting of "the combatants at Marathon: the Boeotians of Plataea and all the men of Attica are closing with the barbarians" (1.15.3). Sparta contained statues, celebratory trophies, and associated sanctuaries; every year speeches were made over the tombs of Pausanias and Leonidas and games held "in which none but Spartans may compete" (3.14.1).[68]

Reverence for this conflict was not new in Roman times, but its appeal strengthened to the point of becoming a Persian War "mania."[69] This mania has often been taken as but the logical culmination of respect for the High

---

68. For Ptolemy of Naucratis: Philostratus, *Vitae Sophistarum* 595. On Pausanias and *ta Medika*: Alcock 1996, on Athens, pp. 251–52; on Sparta, p. 253. On the Marathon painting in the Stoa Poikile in Athens: Harrison 1972. The translation of Plutarch at the section's head is by Dryden (1962).
69. As Spawforth (1994b) calls it.

Fig. 2.11 Fifth-century BC cup tondo by the Triptolemus Painter, dating to shortly after the Persian Wars and depicting Greek victory over the trousered barbarian.

Classical age and of protection for Hellenism's antique purity. Yet, as in the case of the Athenian Agora, examination of the sites and rituals of the Persian Wars reveals a range of overlapping – sometimes harmonious, sometimes conflicting – commemorative practices and attitudes at work in early Roman Achaia.

Battlefield monuments, battlefield rituals

One reasonable place to start this review would be with monuments raised to the glorious dead. Pausanias, in combination with archaeological evidence, attests that Persian War testimonials were scattered across Achaia, but attention here will be trained on one particular type of monument.

War memorials, as maintained in chapter 1, are always "loaded" sites, but those erected on the very battlefields themselves convey a particular emotional charge. Such monuments "mark the site where the commemorated events took place and derive their sacredness from their locations; they proclaim that place to be a historical site and enhance its significance. They thus embody the 'myth of the place'."[70] Although by definition less frequently seen than centrally placed (and, by design, continually encountered) memorials, battlefield monuments require more intense and focused observance and grant a more intense and focused experience. The strength of memory they provoke is thus, potentially, more incendiary in nature, making them particularly sensitive indicators of commemorative trends.

The sites of Thermopylae, Marathon, Plataea, and Salamis have all been extensively explored by ancient historians and archaeologists, if chiefly in the interest of refighting battles. To sum up the results of this work in a nutshell, to date they have yielded relatively little evidence for specifically early Roman on-site activity. At Thermopylae this is not surprising; substantial geomorphological change has significantly transformed the location of Leonidas' last stand. This leaves arguments about its topography and subsequent memorialization inconclusive, although at least one text – as shall be seen – attests to the early imperial visibility of battle markers.[71] Marathon has been repeatedly revisited, and the location of major elements – the Grave of the Athenians (the Soros), the deme sites, the Great Marsh, and so on – either definitely or tentatively postulated (Fig. 2.12).[72] Pausanias' account of his visit to the battlefield, more than 600 years after the event, sketches out a remarkable landscape of remembrance:

> There is a deme of Marathon equally distant from Athens and from Carystus in Euboea. It was at this point of Attica that the barbarians landed, and were beaten in battle, and lost some of their ships as they were putting off to sea. In the plain is the grave of the Athenians, and over it are tombstones with the names of the fallen arranged according to tribes. There is another grave for the Boeotians of Plataea and the slaves; for slaves fought then for the first time. There is a separate tomb of Miltiades, son of Cimon ... Here every night you may hear horses neighing and men fighting. To go on purpose to see the sight never brought good to any man; but with him who unwittingly lights upon it by accident the spirits are not

70. Azaryahu 1993: 85; see also the references on p. 20, n. 25.
71. Dascalakis 1962; Pritchett 1958; 1965a; 1985a. On the geomorphological change: Kraft *et al.* 1987.
72. General topographical studies include Hammond 1968; Koumanoudis 1978; Pritchett 1960; 1965b; Themelis 1974; Vanderpool 1966a.

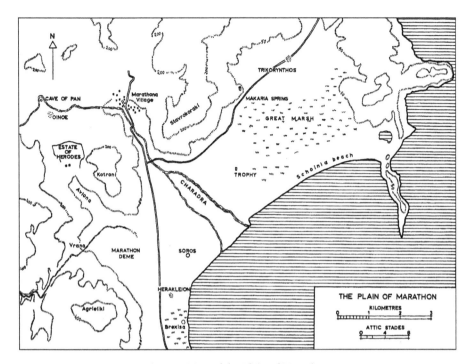

Fig. 2.12 Map of the Plain of Marathon.

angry. The people of Marathon worship the men who fell in the battle, naming them heroes; and they worship Marathon, from whom the deme got its name; and Hercules . . . There is also a trophy of white marble. The Athenians assert they buried the Medes, because it is a sacred and imperative duty to cover with earth a human corpse, but I could find no grave; for there was neither a barrow nor any other mark to be seen: they just carried them to a trench and flung them in pell-mell. In Marathon there is a spring called Macaria . . . At Marathon there is a mere, most of which is marshy. Into this mere the barbarians, ignorant of the roads, rushed in their flight, and it is said that this was the cause of most of the carnage. Above the mere are the stone mangers of the horses of Artaphernes, and there are marks of a tent on the rock.   (Pausanias 1.32.3–7)

Neither the detailed description of Pausanias nor any on-site exploration points to signs of new memorial building in the early imperial period. One possible exception is a marble trophy which may have served as support for a lost statue, although its publisher was doubtful about the piece's actual provenance.[73] The tombs of the war dead themselves, such as the Soros

73. Now in the British Museum; the style and technique of the piece point to a "late Hellenistic or possibly early imperial" date: Vanderpool 1967, esp. 109. A Marathonian trophy may also

Fig. 2.13 View of the Marathon tumulus, believed to be the tomb of the Athenian war dead.

(Fig. 2.13) – believed to be the resting place of the 192 Athenians who fell at Marathon – reveal no material signs of subsequent commemorative activity: at least as far as can be told given their eroded condition and the quality of their archaeological exploration. It has even recently been proposed that the so-called "Grave of the Athenians" is a misidentification, although that suggestion does little to diminish the evocative power the Soros possessed in the past or, indeed, in the present.[74]

As for Salamis, the Athenians had been forced to part with the island in the difficult days following Sulla's attack; they enthusiastically hailed C. Julius Nikanor (from Hierapolis in Syria) as the "New Themistocles" in thanks for its recovery, probably in Augustan times. Legislation most likely dating shortly thereafter reports the restoration of some ten shrines on the island; landmarks

appear on early imperial bronze coinage of Athens: Picard 1957: 50, 424; Shear 1936: 298–99; Vanderpool 1966b: 103. On the archaism of Athenian coin types, see Kroll 1997. The "trophy of white marble" mentioned by Pausanias has been identified by Vanderpool (1966b) with fragments rebuilt into a medieval tower; see also van der Veer 1982: 307–8; West 1969.

74. Mersch (1995) bases this argument on the date and type of grave goods discovered and the lack of evidence for hero cult. On the Soros: Hammond 1968: 14–18; Hauvette 1892; Photiou 1982: 84–93; Pritchett 1960: 140–43; Stais 1893; Whitley 1994. Tomb of the Plataeans: Welwei 1979. Gehrke, in an extremely interesting parallel study of the "meaning of Marathon" to Athenian collective identity, also discusses the battle's post-classical heritage – including appropriation and veneration of the Soros by the Greek military dictatorship: Gehrke 2001, esp. 311–12; see also Flashar 1996; Gehrke forthcoming.

mentioned include the Themistocles trophy and polyandreion, and a shrine possibly founded by Solon. Culley's reading of this legislation suggests not only an acknowledgment of extant monuments on the island, but a renewal of the cult of Zeus Tropaios and "if a cult of the Salamis dead existed, it would also be revived."[75] The emphasis, it would seem, was on restoration and renewal, rather than on the erection of further monuments.

Finally, at Plataea, Pausanias reports the following:

> Just at the entrance into Plataea are the graves of the men who fought against the Medes. There are separate graves for the Lakedaimonians and the Athenians who fell, and elegies of Simonides are carved upon them. The rest of the Greeks are buried in a common tomb. Not far from this common tomb is an altar of Zeus of Freedom ... They still celebrate games called the Eleutheria ("games of freedom") every fourth year, at which the chief prizes offered are for running. They run in armour in front of the altar. The trophy which the Greeks set up for the battle of Plataea stands about fifteen furlongs from the city.   (Pausanias 9.2.4)

The tombs mentioned by Pausanias, Plutarch (*De Malignitate Herodoti* 872E–873D), and other authors have not been found, although their locations have been posited; the altar of Zeus Eleutherios has been associated with the remains of a monumental structure (15m × 4m) discovered east of the city. Again, no particular traces of monumentalization specifically dating to the early Roman epoch emerge.[76]

To sum up this negative archaeological evidence, the Persian War battle-fields – for all the early imperial "mania" – do not appear to become a subject for monumental embellishment. Existing memorials, not fresh elaborations, were taken to be the acceptable foci of attention. It should be emphasized that this is not for want of looking, suggesting the pattern be allowed to stand as

75. For trophies of Salamis: Wallace 1969, esp. 302; West 1969: 15–17. Topographical investigations: Pritchett 1959; 1965d. Themistocles appears on early imperial issues from Athens, standing on a galley holding a wreath and a trophy, together with the owl of Athena and the serpent Cychreus: Picard 1957: 424; Shear 1936: 299. On the "New Themistocles": Habicht 1996; Jones 1978b: 222–38, though Kapetanopoulos (1981) questions the loss of Salamis and downdates Julius Nikanor to the end of the first century AD. For the restoration of shrines and the topography of Salamis: Culley 1977 on *IG* II (2) 1035. Salamis was part of an Athenian "usable past" prior to Roman times, see Higbie 1997.
76. Pritchett (1965c: 103) remarked: "in the case of Plataia the spade of the archaeologist has contributed almost nothing; to the contrary, it has destroyed much." For topographical investigations of the city and battlefield, see Grundy 1894; Konecny 1998; Pritchett 1957; 1979; 1980; 1985b; Wallace 1982. For an overview of the cult of Zeus Eleutherios, see Schachter 1994: 125–43; on the altar, Schachter 1994: 134; on the tombs, Schachter 1994: 141–42. On grave tendance in early Roman times: Plutarch, *Aristeides* 21.2–6; *De Malignitate Herodoti* 872F; 873D; 874A–B; cf. Bowen 1992.

valid. Such restraint was not necessarily a predictable development, as a comparison to the architectural revolutions of the Athenian Agora makes clear.

A lack of monumentalization should not, however, be confused with a lack of regard. As the summaries above suggest, literary and epigraphic evidence does not speak of *new* monuments, but certainly attests to commemorative rituals at old or renewed ones. Although Pausanias did not travel as far north as Thermopylae, at Marathon he found they "worship the men who fell in the battle, naming them heroes" (1.32.4). Apart from the evidence for cult on Salamis already mentioned, inscriptions of the last two centuries BC honor Athenian ephebes who (if on an apparently irregular basis) sailed back and forth between the island and Athens, and who performed sacrifices to deities involved in the sea battle, for example at the trophy of Themistocles to Zeus Tropaeus or at the festival of Aianteia.[77]

Plataea offers the richest evidence, including the contemporary testimony of Plutarch, himself a Boeotian resident. An incredibly dense network of ritual activity reverberated around the battlefield, its monuments and its meanings. The relative insignificance of the community appears to have rendered it neutral ground for communal observances, both of Boeotian cult (in the Great Daidala) and of the struggle of 479 BC. This is not the place to retail the complexities of Persian War rituals – celebrating the war dead, celebrating Eleutheria, celebrating Homonoia – which took place at Plataea annually, quadrennially, and on offsetting calendars. Plainly involved and in charge, however, was a wide spectrum of elite participants from that city and beyond; this included the attendance of such bodies as the koinon of the Hellenes (with its chief official, the priest of Zeus Eleutherios and the Homonoia of the Hellenes).

Two features of this ritual nexus can be briefly touched upon: the celebration of the Eleutheria and the *dialogos*. The penteteric festival of the Eleutheria, held every four years on the anniversary of the battle, offered all the usual major competitions – wrestling, boxing, pankration, horse-racing, oratory, and so on – with competitors coming from all parts of the Greek world, if chiefly from the mainland. Particularly noteworthy was the only element mentioned by Pausanias: the race in armor from the altar of Zeus Eleutherios. The winner of this 15 stade race (in full armor) was granted the title "Best of the Hellenes" – a title he defended at risk of his life. Prominent men in Achaian society successfully competed in this race, including individuals such as Tiberius Claudius Novius and Mnesiboulos of Elateia. The

77. Culley 1977: 294–95; Kapetanopoulos 1981: 218; 224; West 1969: 15–17.

former is everywhere visible in the Athens of the first century AD as office-holder, builder and dedicator, and priest of the imperial cult; the latter died heroically opposing the Costobocan invasion of AD 169/70.[78]

The second feature is the *dialogos*, held (probably) on a four-year cycle parallel to the Eleutheria. This ceremony, most recently reconstructed by Noel Robertson, apparently took the form of an oratorical dispute (or arbi-tration) to determine whether Athens or Sparta would lead the procession at (and possibly be financially responsible for) the next Eleutheria. The *dialogos* appears a much later innovation than the Eleutheria itself, being instituted probably only after the Achaean War of 146 BC. The attendance of ephebes (definitely Athenian, and probably Spartan) to cheer on their city's speaker may be one sign of its increased prestige under the early empire. The speeches made on this occasion, of course, rehearsed the great things done against the Medes. The rituals of Plataea, in and of themselves, neatly sum up many of the contradictory impulses at work in the memorial practices of the age: a celebration of Homonoia, yet with speeches revisiting (and revivifying) old rivalries and discords; a celebration of Greek freedom, with the "Best of the Hellenes" a priest of the imperial cult.[79]

The Persian War battlefields present a quite different commemorative pattern from the carefully constructed memorial spaces of downtown Athens or Sparta, replete though the latter were with trophies and images of the same conflict. Memorialization "on the spot" took a more controlled form, not dependent on new striking monuments or spatial configurations visible to all, but enacted chiefly through organized visitations and prescribed rit-uals, all conducted under the eyes of prominent men, ephebic cohorts, and priestly groups. This did not necessarily preclude tours by random travelers, as Pausanias demonstrates, though even he warns about those who visit out of turn: "to go on purpose to see the sight never brought good to any man." The transmission of Persian War memories in their most charged settings – on the battlefields themselves – emerges on the whole as a highly governed affair.

78. On the Eleutheria and the "best of the Hellenes": Etienne and Piérart 1975: 63–75; Robert 1929; 1949; 1968; Schachter 1994: 138–41. For Tiberius Claudius Novius: Geagan 1979b; for Mnesiboulos: Pausanias 10.34.5.
79. For the *dialogos*: Robertson 1986, especially 96, 101; also Spawforth 1994b: 235–36. A badly dam-aged inscription, from the late second century, records one Athenian speech, praising Athenian deeds and complaining about the Spartans: *IG* 2 (2) 2788. Jones (1996a: 42) notes a "tendency towards discord (stasis) and the countervailing attempt to create concord (homonoia)" as two characteristic political activities of Greek cities. I thank Renaud Gagne (who opines "Plataea was ever a battlefield," pers. comm.) and Christopher Jones for additional references and thoughts on the Plataea ceremonials.

Channels of communication and chastisement

A tight elite grip on Persian Wars memories made eminent sense, playing as it did to two of their dominant needs: to celebrate and promote particular civic histories, and to build relationships with other prominent families across the eastern empire. Positive participation in the glorious Persian Wars made the former easier for some cities than others, as the continued preeminence of Athens and Sparta in part attests. Civic rivalries – competing for resources, attention, and honors such as the right to lead at the Eleutheria – are acknowledged characteristics of the period which grew out of pressures threatening civic survival (pp. 49–50). Just who "stepped up" in the crisis of the Persian invasion (and who did not!) became one form of litmus test for civic esteem or disgrace.

Equally – if somewhat paradoxically – Persian War memories bound cities and elite families together, providing common ground for panhellenic pride. Civic connections were forged, for example, through decrees of *syngeneia* in which cities established fictive, genealogically woven kinships with desirable partners. If a city had not itself had the chance to battle the Medes, the next best thing was a relationship with one that had.[80] Distinguished families throughout the Greek provinces similarly sought such supra-local ties, as has been observed in varied kinds of behavior, including marriages, dispersed land holdings, widespread sanctuary dedications, and travel. Civic and elite bonding of this sort acted as one means of coping with a wider and more competitive imperial world – ironically enough, much like the converse practice of civic rivalry.

A further strand can be added to this investment in Persian War memories. If their remembrance created a web of shared identity across the Greek east, Rome too participated in this discourse, now replaying the conflict to recast their own enemies – the Parthians – as reincarnations of Persia. This appropriation took various material forms, not least the literal refighting of famous battles: most sensationally *naumachiae* reenacting the combat at Salamis. The Persian Wars as "shared symbol," or as channel of communication, plainly helped to compose a successful political consensus between rulers and ruled. Spawforth, in the best study of this phenomenon, suggests that Greek assiduousness in singing the Persian War blues can be traced to

---

80. Curty (1995) provides a catalogue and analysis of inscriptions dealing with relationships of *syngeneia*; on the Hellenistic and Roman periods, see esp. pp. 259–63. See also Jones 1999b, esp. 9–10 and 94–121. Related developments include the extensive use of myth in inter-state diplomacy and the rise of "academic" research into civic and ethnic origins: see Bikerman 1952; Chaniotis 1988b; Robert 1977a: 119–32; 1997b; 1981; Sheppard 1984–86: 230–40; Spawforth and Walker 1985; 1986; Weiss 1984.

this centrally based recognition and official admiration. Genuine concern for the fate of an empire threatened by an eastern menace would also revitalize internal traditions of opposition to the barbarian. Civic leaders, Spawforth concludes, would have no trouble finding "pride in the Persian wars entirely compatible with loyalty to Rome."[81]

Yet Persian War memories could be jarring as well as pleasurable; if they exalted and united the Greeks, they also chastised and disturbed. From that unassailable fifth-century vantage point, negative moral verdicts were passed on the imperial present. Apollonius of Tyana, the first-century AD sage and teacher, criticized Athenian performances of the Dionysia:

> Stop dancing away the honor of the victors at Salamis, as well as of other noble men who lie dead. For if this indeed were a Lakedaimonian dance, I would say good for you soldiers! It is training for war and I will join the dance. But if it is as delicate and leaning to the effeminate as it looks, what shall I say of the trophies raised to the defeat of your enemies? Not against the Medians or the Persians, but to your own shame have they been erected, should you lower yourself so far from those who set them up. And where do your saffron robes and your purple and scarlet garb come from? (Philostratus, *Vita Apollonii* 4.21)

Literary references to the *dialogos* at Plataea employ it, in passing, to deride the insignificance of present-day concerns: Pseudo-Lucian described men meditating speeches on love as lost in thought "as if they were about to battle for precedence at Plataea" (*Amores* 18); Dio Chrysostom disparagingly contrasts the genuine contests of earlier days with an Athens and Sparta now "valiantly struggling to lead the parade" (*Oration* 38.38). The Wars offered a severe yardstick of self-criticism, revealing an insecurity that was the flip side of the more positive nostalgia of the age. Anxiety about failure to live up to the past periodically surfaces, for example when Dio Chrysostom turns to monuments as the measure of past greatness; to look at the men of the present age is no help, "it is rather the stones which make manifest the dignity and greatness of Hellas, and the ruins of her buildings" (*Oration* 31.159–60).[82] The

81. Spawforth 1994b, quote at 246. On *naumachiae*: e.g., Ovid, *Ars Amatoria* 1.171–72; Coleman 1993: 69–70. Shayegan (1999) has recently argued that any Roman decision to celebrate the Persian Wars speaks to a desire to delineate separate spheres of influence from eastern neighbors; this is to be contrasted with more aggressive epochs, when Alexander the Great became the commemorative hero of choice.
82. Jones 1978a: 26–35, esp. 28–29. As Woolf (1994: 125) put it: "The same past that provided Greeks with the resources to jockey for position and favour in the Roman world, is now revealed as source of disquiet, promoting dissatisfaction with the present order of things and thereby inhibiting the assimilation of Greeks into it."

Persian Wars played into this strain of misgiving, and proved one especially tender and disquieting zone of memory.

Their remembrance, however, could also work against the grain of such anxieties, leading – at the extreme end of the spectrum – into the realm of outright resistance. Spawforth notes the "subversive resonance" of these particular war stories. After all, Thermopylae and the other contests had been about Greek autonomy and about keeping barbarians beyond the boundaries of Hellas. Pausanias' selective account of "what was worth seeing" among "all things Greek" endlessly emphasizes and reemphasizes the appearance of Persian War monuments; he uses that invasion and its topography of conflict to structure his discussion of other eastern wars (such as Troy) and other invasions successfully repelled (most notably the Gauls in the third century BC). In other words, the Persian Wars served as paradigm, providing Greeks of the early imperial period with a "charter of identity . . . rooted deep in tales of resistance to outsiders"; "The Persian Wars, and especially the battle of Marathon . . . had prescriptive force for future conduct."[83]

This was inherently hazardous territory, as Plutarch for one realized. In an essay on political precepts, he recommended certain historical or mythological examples for use in civic oratory, while frowning on others. The limits he sets are illuminating:

> we laugh when we see little children trying to fasten their fathers' shoes on their own feet or playfully fitting their crowns upon their own heads. But the magistrates in the cities, when they foolishly exhort the people to imitate the deeds, purposes, and actions of their ancestors which are not suitable to present times and conditions, stir up the multitudes; and although what they do is ridiculous, what is done to them is no laughing matter, unless they are simply met with utter contempt. There are indeed many acts of the ancient Greeks, a recital of which could form and correct the characters of our contemporaries: at Athens, for example, by calling to mind not warlike things, but the decree of amnesty after the fall of the Thirty Tyrants, or the fining of Phrynichus who represented in tragedy the capture of Miletus, or how they decked their heads with garlands when Cassander refounded Thebes . . . By the emulation of acts such as these, it is even now possible to resemble the ancestors, but Marathon, the Eurymedon, Plataea, and whatever other examples make the many swell with vain pride and prance about, those should be left to the schools of the sophists.   (Plutarch, *Praecepta Gerendae Reipublicae* 814a–c)

---

83. Alcock 1996: 258; Gehrke 2001: 302. Compare the effect of the Camisard rebellion, p. 6.

Voiced here is likely not a genuine worry that the "multitudes" could be whipped into a violent frenzy against Rome. Rather Plutarch (at this point in the essay and elsewhere) fears provocation of civic unrest, either within or between cities, which might invite the very real danger and embarrassment of Roman intervention onto the local scene.[84] Even in the realm of rhetorical display, as in battlefield commemorations, Persian War themes were felt best restrained within an appropriate context.

It might be more accurate to say that such themes had to be restrained, and their celebration monitored, if a quiet life was wanted. While Old Greece apparently accepted Roman rule quiescently (at least compared to regions such as Judaea or Gaul), some randomly documented reports of more violent resistance do exist; these may well be trace indicators of other, unrecorded episodes of trouble. Cassius Dio, in the third century, reported that in Augustan times a statue of Athena on the Acropolis turned and spat blood westward toward Rome (54.7), incurring for the city the active disapproval of Augustus. In a tale of Lucian, the Cynic philosopher Peregrinus used the soap-box provided by the Olympic Games to urge armed revolt against the Romans – this some years before advertising (and carrying out) his self-immolation at that same festival.[85] One final incident, from Philostratus' account of the life of Apollonius of Tyana, explicitly revolves around a Persian War memorial. Apollonius, honoring a promise made to the spirit of Achilles, visited the Thessalians to warn of the hero's anger over their neglect of his cult. He went to Thermopylae:

> As for the monument of Leonidas the Spartan, he all but embraced it, so much did he admire the man. And as he proceeded to the tumulus where the Lakedaimonians are said to have had enemy projectiles poured down upon them, he heard his company differing among themselves about which was the highest point in Hellas, the issue being provoked by the sight of Mount Oita before them. So mounting the crest of the tumulus, he said "I hold this to be the highest place of all, for those who fell here for freedom brought it up to the same height as Oita, and raised it above and beyond many like Olympus…"[86]   (Philostratus, *Vita Apollonii* 4.23)

84. *Praecepta Gerendae Reipublicae*, e.g. 814F–815B; 824A for related comments. Spawforth 1994b: 245–46; Swain 1996: 67–68, 167–68; see also Sheppard 1984–86: 241–48.
85. In AD 165. Lucian, *Peregrinus*; Jones 1986: 117–32. Jones (1986: 125) connects this call to arms with a poorly understood rebellion under Antoninus Pius: *Scriptores Historiae Augustae, Pius* 5.5; Bowersock 1965: 147, n. 5. For the incident described by Cassius Dio and the reaction of Augustus: Bowersock 1964; 1965: 106; Hoff 1989a; Oliver 1980: 44–45. Other hints of unrest in Athens date to the later years of Augustus: Bowersock 1965: 107–8; Graindor 1927: 41–45; Syme 1979: 199. In general, Bowersock 1965: 101–11.
86. Apollonius also uses the battle of Salamis as a way of turning the tables on an unphilosophical king of India (Philostratus, *Vita Apollonii* 3.31).

As the next section will argue, it can fairly be said that the memorial strategies of the Greek east tended, on the whole, toward accommodation; they sought to preserve Hellenic identity, while avoiding outright conflict. The Persian Wars, however, could pack a more dissident charge. The "mania" for them and the sheer ubiquity of their monuments, embedded as they were across the commemorative landscape of Achaian cities and sanctuaries, thus remain a provocative wrinkle in the story.

THE MOBILITY OF MEMORIES

The memorial space of the Athenian Agora and the ceremonials of the Persian Wars served often conflicting impulses: elite concerns versus those of the demos, panhellenic urges versus individual civic pride, accommodating versus hostile gestures, imperial versus local ambitions. Yet these attitudes toward, and uses of, the past were simultaneously in operation, constantly overlapping with each other. That observation raises interesting questions about just how *mobile* various memory communities might be in their commemorative allegiances.

At the level of prominent individuals, we can observe certain men shift from one form of identity (and its associated package of "right memory") to another, moving in this fashion repeatedly – polyphonically – throughout their lives. Plutarch, for example, could bemoan the fact of Roman control, yet have Roman magnates as friends; he could express undying loyalty to his small home town of Boeotian Chaeronea, yet he could travel to Rome and teach there; he could become a Roman citizen. Similar ambivalencies or, to put it better, similar permutations, can be witnessed in other documented figures of the age: Pausanias himself, for example, or C. Julius Antiochus Epiphanes Philopappus (prince of Syria, consul of Rome, and archon of Athens, whose prominent tomb marks the Athenian skyline), not to mention that self-avowed Roman citizen, St. Paul.[87] Categories of "Greek" and "Roman" – always uncomfortably blunt given the vast range of people and attitudes encompassed – grew ever more permeable over time. R. R. R. Smith, on the basis of Greek honorific portraiture, has made a closely related argument for the existence of "cultural choice" in the second century AD. To explain his portraits, Smith dismisses previous explanatory theories revolving around linear stylistic development or the "trickle-down" of imperial fashions:

---

87. Plutarch was also elected to a priesthood at Delphi and given citizenship at Athens: Jones 1971; Mossman 1997; on other aspects of his religious and political attitudes: Brenk 1987; Pelling 1986. On Philopappus: Kleiner 1983. For "two roles" played by Arrian: Oliver 1982.

It is better to look at them more positively for the roles and identities they seek to portray... Distinct concurrent strands of self-representation can be isolated in documented examples... these images are to be explained in terms not of chronology or biography but of cultural choices. The portraits cannot be fitted on any single line of formal development, nor were they concerned with a one-to-one representation of the statue's role in life. Rather they deploy a received and recognizable statue and portrait language to make and project plausible-looking statements about selected social, cultural and political aspirations.[88]

Such statements – set here in stone – would be made visible to all, but did not preclude individuals from other choices, and the selection of other images, in distinct spheres of behavior.

But does this mobility of memory apply beyond the level of the individual? The memories and identities of larger groups may have been less immediately volatile, but their flexibility too cannot be denied. Cities presented themselves in different lights, through the dedication of certain monuments or the performances of certain rituals. Depending on context and need, they could turn from local "petty" rivalries to mutual celebration of a shared past, from emphasizing a purely Hellenic heritage to displaying links to Rome. Even a Roman colony such as Corinth had no single fixed identity. In its first two centuries of existence, Corinth played the part of "centre of *Romanitas*" (and probable capital) for the province as a whole, as well as that of an antique community, competing with other Hellenic cities for prestige and status. Different strategies of self-presentation evolved to respond to the colony's changing circumstances, notably in the city's famed "re-Hellenization," but neither role ever totally eclipsed the other.[89]

To some extent, such behavior merely reflects long-lived dualities in which peoples could be fervent citizens of one polis, and yet also Hellenes united against the barbarian. With imperial annexation, however, such choices of appropriate identity, and thus of appropriate memory, became much more complex and fissured. Identification with, or rejection of, the interests of Rome added one additional texture; for the elite, a desire to develop more extensive, even empire-wide relationships contended with pre-existing, more purely local loyalties. Possible social roles, allegiances and obligations multiplied,

88. Smith 1998: 92.
89. Alcock forthcoming. The Augustan-era poet, Krinagoras of Mytilene, sneers at Corinth's "shop-soiled slaves," see Spawforth 1994. On the colony as a "centre of *Romanitas*": Cartledge and Spawforth 1989: 104; see also Engels 1990; Spawforth 1994a; 1996; Williams 1987. Welch (1999) observes this dynamic in an interesting examination of the shifting contexts for Roman spectacle in the city.

especially for those with status and authority. The conditions of "being Greek" were profoundly transformed, with inevitable consequences for their usage of memory.

The recognition that Greeks in the imperial east engaged with local, regional, and imperial concerns has sometimes led to the application of the formula "Greco-Roman" to what had once been termed "Greek." Yet "Greco-Roman" implies a kind of hyphenated assimilation, a conflation of identities into a single mass. Instead of replacing one essentializing term with another, it seems best to accept the existence of co-existing options, from which individuals and groups would continually be reconstituting and redefining themselves. Aiding in this process – indeed making it possible – was the flexibility and capaciousness of early imperial memorial spaces and commemorative practices. Complexes such as the Athenian Agora or the rituals of Persian War battlefields proved sufficiently multivalent to prompt and contain varied impulses, while on the whole channeling them in certain overriding directions: toward a continued sense of cultural separation, yet away from outright conflict.

Hybrid memories

Rejection of "Greco-Roman" should not mask the fact that new categories of identity and novel zones of memory were indeed being created at this time. This phenomenon has already been seen in action, in the abundance of places where Hellenic past and imperial present were co-mingled. Greek cities, even the archetypal Athens, took on a new architectural look, marked by Roman-derived or imperially fostered elements such as aqueducts and nymphaea, new forms of statuary, or imported building types – a transformation culminating in the eastern architectural *koine* of the Antonine age.[90] Moreover, the emperor was everywhere an unassailably commanding presence. Millar lays this out in uncompromising fashion:

> The presence of the name and the image of the Emperor has to be taken as one of the dominating features of the collective life of the Greek city in the imperial period. This applies, as noted above, very widely to the names of the cities themselves, and not merely to those transformed into Roman *coloniae*, to the personal names of individual citizens . . . to the cults and temples of the Emperors, reigning or deceased, and individual or collective . . . to the identities of public buildings . . . to the names of months in city calendars; to the names of tribes or other subunits of

90. Macready and Thompson 1987; Woolf 1994: 127; Yegül 2000.

communities; to the names of festivals; to the actual clothing of *agonothetai* or *archiereis*; to the presence of honorific statues of the Emperor and members of their families; and to the prominence of inscribed letters from Emperors, written in Greek, and of other inscriptions recording privileges granted to individuals by Emperors. It is not too much to say that the public self-expression of the "Greek-city" in the empire embodied at every level an explicit recognition of the distant presence of the Emperor.[91]

The Athenian Agora has already demonstrated Millar's point, with imperial figures at home near Theseus and the Tyrannicides. Other Achaian examples spring to mind. Members of the imperial family joined deities in traditional sanctuaries and shrines such as the Athenian acropolis or the Metroön at Olympia; imperial ritual was practiced within a Bronze Age tholos tomb at Orchomenos in Boeotia; Pausanias supplies innumerable instances where he reports old and new, heroic and imperial, without skipping a beat. Single images could encapsulate these combinations as well; for example, the breastplate of an Athenian torso of Hadrian depicted the imbricated figures of Athena, her owl, her snake, Romulus, Remus, and the wolf.[92] Only through the filter of later scholarly preference were monuments and mementoes of the "good old days" segregated from monuments and mementoes of the imperial presence. One result, as Bradley warned (p. 54), is that we cannot follow how "monuments feed off the associations . . . of other monuments" and thus how novel memories might be made. Although examples of such "mixed" spaces and contexts are ubiquitous, only two additional, in some ways complementary examples will be reviewed here, both drawn from the province of Asia, beyond the boundaries of Achaia. The first explores a sanctuary complex at Aphrodisias, the second the civic landscape of Ephesus.

91. Millar 1993: 245–46. Or see Price 1984: 235: "The emperor was honored at ancestral religious festivals; he was placed within the gods' sanctuaries and temples; sacrifices to the gods invoked their protection for the emperor. There were also festivals, temples and sacrifices in honor of the emperor alone which were calqued on the traditional honours of the gods. In other words, the Greek subjects of the Roman empire attempted to relate their ruler to their own dominant symbolic system." Rose (1997b) warns, however, that distinguishing private and imperial portraits, at least in the first century AD, may not have been all that easy; see also Payne 1984; Rose 1997a.

92. On the Acropolis Temple of Roma: Baldassari 1995; Binder 1969; Hoff 1996: 194; Schmalz 1994. On changes to the Parthenon: Pausanias 1.24.7; Carroll 1982: Hoff 1996: 185–94; Spawforth 1994b: 234–37. On the Metroön: Pausanias 5.20.9; Price 1984: 160–61. On the tholos at Orchomenos, Pausanias 9.38.2; Alcock 1993: 138, 186. On the image of Hadrian: Camp 1986: 191–93; Thompson and Wycherley 1972: 101; cf. Juvenal, *Satires* 11.100–7 (with thanks to Kathleen Coleman for this reference). For related thoughts about the "collapse or elision of past and present" in Pausanias, see Bowie (1996: 213) who notes a "peculiarity of Pausanias' presentation of the past is his frequent juxtaposition of events or monuments of quite different periods, giving the impression that they nevertheless belong closely together"; cf. Arafat 1996: 78.

Fig. 2.14 Artist's reproduction of a view, looking toward the propylon, of the Sebasteion at Aphrodisias.

Aphrodisias, on the strength of its eponymous association with Aphrodite, developed a special relationship with the Julio-Claudian family and won the status of free and allied city. Recent intensive archaeological work at the site has uncovered a major sanctuary dedicated not only to Aphrodite Prometor and the Demos of Aphrodisias, but also to the Julio-Claudian emperors (worshipped as the *Theoi Sebastoi*). This Sebasteion, constructed during the course of the first century AD, followed a symmetrical plan clearly designed to echo Roman models and experiences. A worshipper would enter through a monumental, two-story propylon and proceed to a high podium temple (about 90 meters away) at the east end, on the way passing between flanking three-storied porticoes, approximately 12 meters high (Fig. 2.14). These porticoes were decorated on the second and third levels with large sculpted relief panels, of which fewer than half of the original 190 or so survive. From what remains of this large-scale sculptural program, however, a vision of a new cosmology emerges, one embracing "the Roman empire, the Greek world within it, and the imperial family."[93]

The south portico is better preserved than the north. Its second story accommodated an extraordinarily wide selection of Greek mythological scenes,

93. Smith 1987: 95. In general on the Sebasteion, see Smith 1987; 1988. On the wider city setting and its recent archaeological exploration: Erim 1986; Genière and Erim 1987; Reynolds 1982; Roueché and Erim 1990; Smith and Erim 1991; Smith and Ratté 1995; 1996; 1997; 1998.

including such episodes as Leda and the Swan, Meleager and the Boar, Achilles and Penthesilea, and the rescue of Prometheus by Heracles. The myths selected appear by and large to have been mainstream tales, the common property of an informed Greek audience. Thanks to the uncertain original order of many panels, it is difficult to discern any tight programmatic coherence. At least one pattern, however, seems clear. As a worshipper moved closer to the temple dedicated to Aphrodite and the *Theoi Sebastoi*, some panels (the birth of Eros, Aeneas fleeing Troy, Romulus and Remus) reflected this proximity by playing upon the relationship of the city's patron goddess with Rome, as well as the origins of Rome itself.

These second-story myths architecturally supported a third tier of images: "of imperial victory, the divine emperors, and the gods."[94] Olympian gods and personifications of Nike (Victory) appear, but (to our eyes) the most striking panels exhibit the emperor and his family. One well-known scene shows Augustus by Land and Sea, with the emperor receiving the bounty of earth and the command of seas, symbolized by a cornucopia and an oar. Other scenes speak more directly to themes of imperial victory. The emperor Claudius dominates a personification of Britannia, pulling back her head to deliver the *coup de grâce*; Nero threatens a collapsing Armenia, with her oriental cap and "barbarian" hair (Fig. 2.15). Both representations, unlike the myths below, bore labels identifying the protagonists; this suggests a concern for audience familiarity. The clemency more usual in the art of Rome itself gives way here to an unusual violence of triumphant males and broken women – a violence paralleled, however, in representations of the mythic struggles of Greeks and Amazons.

Opposite this complex of images, on the second story of the north portico, was found a series of individual statue-like depictions, personifications of the numerous peoples (*ethne*) caught up in the Roman world. Preserved inscriptions name thirteen foreign peoples and three islands (Sicily, Crete, and Cyprus) scattered across the expanse of empire, from the Callaeci in Spain to the Judaeans in the Levant.[95] On the third level, above the *ethne*, stood allegorical representations and (probably) further images of emperors. The two panels remaining are personifications of cosmic significance – "Day" and "Ocean" – figures intended to place the far-flung imperial peoples shown below within the timeless sphere fitting for eternal dominion.

The Sebasteion at Aphrodisias – recently described as a "saturation bombing of the visual field" – at first glance appears a stunning monument to Roman

94. Smith 1987: 97. On the ordering of panels close to the temple: Smith 1987: 132–33.
95. Smith (1987: 50, 70–77) avers such a sculptural program must be closely modeled on attested Augustan monuments in Rome.

Fig. 2.15 Nero conquering Armenia, from the Sebasteion at Aphrodisias.

imperial might.[96] Yet inscriptions discovered at the site make very clear that this complex was paid for and dedicated by two wealthy Aphrodisian families, with each taking responsibility for half the complex. Moreover, despite its emulation of imperial fora design and certain Roman sculptural motifs, Smith (one of the site's principal investigators and analysts) convincingly argues that the Sebasteion's overall conception and sculptural program were of local origin: not least in the heroic nudity of the emperors and in the artistic quotation of Amazonomachies. How then to interpret a monumental complex that appears to celebrate a triumphant and serene world order, one that seamlessly includes the conquest and submission of provincial peoples – when that presentation was ordered and financed by a provincial people themselves?

Rather than perceiving this as a willed blindness to their actual position, or as indicating just how "free" the free city of Aphrodisias felt itself to be, a closer scrutiny of the Sebasteion – as a total package – reveals another possibility. In the series of *ethne*, people of Achaia or Asia Minor are not themselves explicitly identified. While most *ethne* bases are admittedly missing, the apparent decision to name islands with Greek populations, but not specific Greek peoples, is provocative; as Smith notes, "it was desirable that the older, Greek subjects of Rome be included not in person, as it were, but obliquely in terms of physical geography."[97] In other words, the Greeks were comprehended within the Sebasteion's imperial sweep, yet also quietly distinguished from the more vulnerable, such as Britannia or Armenia. On the parallel portico, Greek myths literally and figuratively supported the emperors above, emperors (identified for local viewers) portrayed in Hellenic manner. Imperial power was carefully located within a home-town frame of reference – associated with Aphrodite, upheld by Greek memories. It may be discomforting for eyes trained to seek out artistic origins and to dissociate "Greek" from "Roman" elements, but to pick apart the Sebasteion misses much of the point: that elements here meshed to create something new.[98]

---

96. Beard and Henderson 2001: 191.
97. Smith 1988: 57. Very few of the actual personifications survive, but it is clear that different styles were employed to convey something of the characteristics of the *ethnos* or island involved – for example, by the use of "warlike" or "barbarian" attributes. One image has been tentatively identified as an island, possibly Sicily. "Hairstyle, pose and dress seem designed to characterize the figure as unambiguously Greek and 'free,' as opposed to barbarian and captive" (Smith 1988: 65).
98. Alcock 2000; 2001b; Yegül 2000. Classical archaeology is hardly alone in this tendency: "Historically ... comparatively little attention has been given to the mechanics of the intricate processes of cultural contact, intrusion, fusion and disjunction. In archaeology, for example, the models have been ones of diffusion, assimilation or isolation, not of interaction and counteraction.

At Ephesus we are dealing not with a monumental complex, but with a ritual performance within a particular cityscape. Collective activities, such as processions or sacrifices, were key in memorial reinforcement, as the Athenian Agora and Persian War battlefields testify. More rarely, however, can their calendar and composition be traced in great detail. One remarkable exception is the foundation (recorded in an extant 568-line inscription) established in AD 104 by C. Vibius Salutaris in the Asian city of Ephesus, home to the famed temple sacred to Ephesian Artemis. Salutaris – Ephesian citizen, Roman equestrian official, possibly of Italian origin (another fine instance of multiple identities) – instituted and financially supported various practices, most notably a procession through the streets of Ephesus. Beginning at the temple of Artemis and winding along a prescribed route to pass major monuments (major gates, shrines, the theater), the procession was performed (at least for some period of time) something on the order of every two weeks, according to a thorough study of the foundation by Guy Rogers (Fig. 2.16). Ephebes and other free male citizens of Ephesus participated by marching and by carrying statues through the streets. Prominent among these was Artemis herself, together with other mythic and historic founders of the community and its tribes (e.g., Androklos and Lysimachos). Also present were the emperor Trajan, his wife Plotina, and personifications of various Roman institutions (e.g., the Senate, the Roman People, the Equestrian Order).

The organization of this "walk down memory lane," Rogers argued, worked to outline and reinforce proper civic order, while also maintaining the city's sacred identity against the "deep penetration" of Roman influence in the social fabric of Ephesus. Such a view completely accords with certain uses of social memory outlined in this chapter, where commemoration created a separate, inviolable past. Yet on another reading, far from being an alien presence, Rome stands recognized as part of the series of civic founders, as firmly integrated within the ritual.[99] Memories of the past, again, were here recontextualized and redisplayed, with Artemis of the Ephesians carried in

Significant historical work has been done on the exchange of commodities, of disease, of healing systems and of religions. Otherwise, the most productive paradigms have been taken from language": Young (1995): 5.

99. On "deep penetration": Rogers 1991, see esp. 140–49. For a more moderate reading: Spawforth 1992a. On the role of the Artemision in this city: Elsner 1997: 180–84; Oster 1990. A rich epigraphic dossier also exists for the foundation of a penteteric festival (the Demostheneia) by Iulius Demosthenes at Oinoanda in Lycia. Local and imperial cult imperatives are here woven together in dynamic fashion, with intriguing visual correlates: for example, Demosthenes promised a golden crown, adorned with images of Apollo and of Hadrian, for the *agonothete* to wear in ritual settings. See Wörrle 1988, with text at 4–17; also Coulton 1983; Jones 1990; Mitchell 1990.

Fig. 2.16 Modern tourist foot traffic through the streets of ancient Ephesus.

company with Trajan and the Roman Senate. This juxtaposition need not be accepted as a brutal intrusion, or as an act of gross sycophancy, or as a sign of "[e]quivocation and hesitancy about the meaning of the past."[100] A more complex, "in-between" explanation is also possible.

What emerges from these monumental and ritual complexes are hybrid forms of memory. Turning to the concept of hybridity allows for the possibility that more was going on here than a zero-sum competition between different, preexisting versions of the past. From processes of annexation,

100. Swain 1996: 67–68, quote at 67. It might also allow us to escape uncomfortable scholarly balancing-acts, such as "Rome did not intrude heavily upon Athenian traditions and clearly paid considerable homage to the glory that was classical Athens. Nevertheless, Rome's own presence in the city was not a minor one, and that is a point scholars continue to neglect" (Hoff 1996: 200).

synthesis, and negotiation, something novel was created that lay between the domains of "Greek" and "Roman." Hybridity is, to put it mildly, a complex phenomenon, with myriad (and evolving) definitions and a plenitude of scholarly advocates. In essence, however, it revolves around the joining of two unlike things to create a new form: it "makes difference into sameness, and sameness into difference, but in a way that makes the same no longer the same, the different no longer different." Homi Bhabha argues that hybridity challenges accepted superiorities by creating ambivalence: this "interstitial passage between fixed identifications opens up the possibility of a cultural hybridity that entertains difference without an assumed or imposed hierarchy." In hybrid spaces, "'denied' knowledges enter upon the dominant discourse and estrange the basis of its authority."[101]

What has such post-colonial argumentation to do with Athens or Ephesus? Hybrid memories, conceived and entertained in places such as the Athenian Agora, the Aphrodisian Sebasteion, or the streets of Ephesus, evaded normative schemas of domination through the creation of alternative discourses of hierarchy and authority, grounded in newly presented versions of the past. Cultural boundaries – a subject for concern on both sides, as has been seen – were elided by these combinations, though the results could remain (as Bhabha and others have noted) subject to frictions and perplexities. Whether or not to adopt such readings of these spaces and rituals would, as always, have been a matter of choice, of audience, of circumstance. One can imagine they might prove especially attractive to elite groups which – seeking to affirm themselves without open antagonism – would find such "in-between" positions persuasive and serviceable. But even for that particular memory community, they would form just one additional commemorative position, out of the broad arsenal available to the Greeks under Roman rule.

*

What is achieved by viewing Old Greece within the empire through the lens of social memory? The epoch's nostalgia no longer appears predictable or pathetic, but rather as an intriguing phenomenon and an empowering force. Upheaval in many basic aspects of life, witnessed in the framework of the landscape, meant that commemorative patterns became a matter for decision and for effort, a conclusion that sharply challenges past accusations of

101. Quotations from Young 1995: 26; Bhabha 1994: 4; 1985: 156; see also Said 1993: esp. 406. For related observations in the Greek context, see Lamberton 1997; Woolf 1994. For an application of the concept of "creolization" in the Roman empire, see Webster 2001.

Greek passivity or Roman indifference. For the Roman authorities, certain allegiances had to be erased as part of a regional reordering, while at the same time general respect for the "glory that was Greece" possessed political currency back home. For the Greek elite, an emphasis on the classical past reflected many needs: to preserve what made Hellenes unique, to augment and protect the status of the educated and wealthy, to promote a symbolic capital of use with philhellenic rulers. Perhaps above all, the ability of select memories to serve as a broad-band channel of communication – across social distinctions, among Greek communities, and reaching out to Rome – helps to explain their pervasive presence in the early imperial east.

Monuments and landscapes, however, signally failed to foster any simple or straightforward trends in remembrance. They built networks of accommodation and consensus; they served as conduits for disinclinations and dissensions that spilled over – if only rarely – into outright resistance. Moreover, new zones of memory were created, as Greek and Roman elements and images became intermingled and juxtaposed in space and time. Across this broad range of memorial stances, a growing mobility of memory can be identified, as individuals or communities moved from one political or social context to another – a flexibility especially engendered by the diverse pressures of imperial rule. Commemorative monuments and rituals allowed for variant readings of the past, and thus for the mutability of strategic positions in the present.

Commemorative choices are most visible in the realm of the elite, but we can occasionally glimpse other echelons of provincial society. Imperial disruptions struck especially hard at the traditions of rural dwellers and other hoi polloi, not least peoples who were physically transplanted or who lost local cults and gods. Increasing status distinctions in Achaian society were underlined by certain elitist uses of the past; to live poor and undistinguished in a "museum" could not always have been easy. Yet aspects of Greek memory were still monumentalized and made public, allowing the persistence of widespread pride in a common Hellenic heritage. For all that, a dominant, no doubt largely elite-driven trend in memorial manipulation can be seen at work – one encouraging a sense of ongoing cultural distinction, while chilling actively hostile anti-Roman sentiments. Hybrid memories harmonized local interests with those of the ruling power; the more volatile remembrances of the Persian Wars came in for a degree of surveillance.

Remembering the past as perfect in a tense present is a common human phenomenon, something too often perceived as comfortable, but somehow not admirable – pleasant, but also passive. I would argue that such patronizing attitudes, together with other reigning misconceptions about the nature of early imperial Achaia, have badly hindered understanding of this province's development. As Thelen has argued: "Instead of dismissing the construction of imagined pasts as romantic, escapist, inaccurate or neurotic, we should try to understand why it is so common."[102] In the particular case of these "neurotic" Greeks, the motivations and consequences of turning to the past – in all their multiple confusions – begin, with the aid of material evidence, to take shape before us.

102. Thelen 1989: 1125–26.

3

CRETAN INVENTIONS

With its absorption into the Roman Empire, brutally as it was conquered
and at first repressed, Crete entered a period of prosperity such as it had not
known since the palmy days of Late Minoan I.
(Pendlebury 1939: 365)

Comparing Roman Crete to its Late Minoan predecessor (periods separated, after all, by more than a millennium) might strike some as an odd thing to do. Yet John Pendlebury's comment reflects what was long quite standard thinking in Cretan studies. Attracting attention and gaining the island renown was its prehistoric, Minoan heritage – typically leaving the later centuries of insular history either neglected or interpreted through the lens of that Bronze Age past. The obvious inadequacies of such a perspective are today provoking various forms of reassessment; here I extend that reconsideration to historic patterns in Cretan commemoration. What can the evidence of landscape and of monuments disclose about the island's uses of its past?

Picking up on Pendlebury's comparative approach, this chapter will contrast two contiguous periods – the Hellenistic age (c. 323–c. 69 BC) and the Roman "period of prosperity" (c. 69 BC–c. AD 250). As will be seen, the two epochs are differentiated in all manner of ways: political configurations, distributions of cities, settlement patterns, economic priorities, external connections. Corresponding distinctions can, on the arguments made so far in this book, be predicted for each epoch's treatment and employment of the past. To that end, the chapter briefly surveys Cretan history in both periods, before reviewing and comparing their memorial priorities and strategies – the contingent ways in which they imagined and "invented" memories.

A SENTIMENTAL HOLD

The turn-of-the-century discoveries of Sir Arthur Evans at the Knossian Palace of Minos, and the subsequent revelation of other palace centers such as Phaistos and Malia, early set Cretan archaeology on a prehistoric path. The lure of Minoan art and culture, romantically and practically fostered, for

decades possessed a "sentimental hold" (in Sarah Morris's phrase) on archaeological research; as Didier Viviers put it: "Crete is before all else the island
of Minos."[1] In 1976, Ian Sanders (an early proponent of post-prehistoric
research on the island) wryly remarked of Pendlebury's standard volume,
The Archaeology of Crete (1939):

> It is symptomatic of the study of the archaeology of Crete that Pendlebury
> took 255 pages to cover the Minoan period of about 2000 years but only
> 74 pages for the remaining 1750 years, with a mere 22 pages devoted to
> the Hellenistic and Roman periods, from c. 300 BC to the Arab conquest
> in the early ninth century AD.

Pendlebury's untroubled comparison of "palmy days" in Late Minoan I and
Roman times makes sense as part of such a world-view. Rather like patronizing
attitudes toward the nostalgia of the Second Sophistic, this prehistoric bias is
on its way out of the door, as more and more Cretan field projects are oriented
to historic periods and as an increasing number of detailed epigraphic and
numismatic analyses appear.[2]

Yet it must also be recognized that the "sentimental hold" continues to
be influential, if now in more subtle ways. There remains a readiness to recognize continuities in Cretan life, to expect conservatism in Cretan behavior.
One sphere where such traditionalism has been identified is that of religious
practice, with the same deities and cults assumed to have stayed in place
and to have commanded enduring respect across the ages. Examples cited by
Sanders include the ongoing veneration (running well into the Roman era)
of apparently prehellenic deities such as Diktynna or Britomartis; or the care
taken to preserve ancient sanctuaries such as the famed temple of Apollo
Pythios (the Python) at Gortyn, first erected in the seventh century BC
but still in use in the Roman period. The Cretans of historic times are

---

1. Morris 1992: 173; Viviers 1994: 229. See MacGillivray (2000) on *Sir Arthur Evans and the Archaeology of the Minoan Myth*. Starr (1983: 9) once remarked: "Minoan civilization is the only great
civilization created in the twentieth century."
2. Sanders 1976: 131, although even he felt constrained to acknowledge Minoan Crete as of
"infinitely greater" importance than later periods; cf. Harrison 1993: 1, 39–176. Another index of
this prejudice is provided in Pendlebury's illustrative material: of his thirty-five plates illustrating
Cretan material culture, only three depict anything of post-Bronze Age date and only one anything
post-fifth century BC (1939: pls. ix–xliii). Willetts (1977) gives the Roman period a single para-
graph. For a collection of essays from a conference on post-Minoan Crete (admittedly a still-biased
nomenclature): Cavanagh and Curtis 1998; see also Chaniotis 1999a. Major projects focusing on
the historic epochs include recently instituted British research at historic Knossos (Bingham
1995) and ongoing work at Gortyn (with major publications on the Hellenistic and Roman
periods) by the Scuola Archeologica Italiana di Atene. See also Frost and Hadjidaki 1990; Whitley
et al. 1995.

imagined – explicitly or implicitly – as ensnared within what has been called "the abiding influence of tradition."[3]

In her book *Daidalos*, Morris warns about the modern genealogy of such attitudes:

> A romantic attachment to the unanticipated culture of Bronze Age Crete has exaggerated "Minoan" elements in the material and literary culture of Crete in archaeological scholarship for the sake of continuity, to demonstrate Greece's (and Europe's) link to a glamorous past. Modern affection for prehistoric Crete, whose discovery (just after the liberation of Crete from Turkish rule) took place during a strong drive for Greek roots, has overestimated this past and signs of its "revival" or "renaissance." Moreover, European eagerness to identify roots as old as possible for Greek civilization, as if in competition with the discovery of Mesopotamian prehistory, precipitated notions of cultural continuity.[4]

The implausibility, or at least the untested nature, of these beliefs may seem fairly obvious, but so far it has proved easier to doubt than to replace them. Not in question here is the likelihood that the past was on display, as an active force, in historic Crete; what I do dispute is the notion that uses of that past remained innocently unchanged. To assume cultural continuity is to ignore the altered circumstances of the island over time, as well as its possible variety of memory communities, each with their own commemorative obligations and desires. A more detailed examination of relevant Cretan landscapes and monuments is required, to allow a more rigorous comparison of what was remembered, and where, and how.

HELLENISTIC CONFLICT, ROMAN CONQUEST

If Pendlebury alluded to "palmy days" for Roman Crete, the Hellenistic period, by contrast, has been called an era of "warring city states," a time when Crete "must have been a very uncomfortable place."[5] Explaining this contrast can begin with the nature of the island's external relations. While

3. Willetts 1962: 42. On traditionalism and the "persistence of religious traditions": Sanders 1982: 40, 132–33; see also Bosanquet 1939–40: 75–76; Chaniotis 1995a; Willetts 1962: 191. Recent study of the Pythion has shown that it was reconstructed in Roman times – in part, significantly, with inscribed Archaic blocks: Di Vita 1992: 96, 100; cf. Di Vita and La Regina 1984: 84–89; see also Ricciardi 1991. On the sculptures of the Apollo Pythios temple: Romeo and Portale 1998: 24–33, 47–90 (the work of Ilaria Romeo).
4. Morris 1992: 183; more generally, see Herzfeld 1982. For similar problems in the study of Roman Greece, see pp. 36–38.
5. Rackham and Moody 1996: xvii; Bosanquet 1939–40: 72. Pendlebury (1939: 354) even compares the period to the Wars of the Roses.

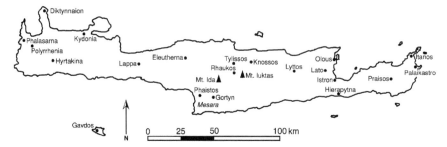

Fig. 3.1 Map of Crete, showing the location of principal places mentioned in the text.

Rome would conquer and annex Crete, converting it into a province (yoked with Cyrenaica in North Africa), no single Hellenistic power dominated the island as a whole, although numerous treaties were agreed with particular groups of cities. Hellenistic royal policy instead encouraged internal divisions among the independent Cretan polities; as John Davies dryly put it: "no one king had an interest in damping down such squabbles."[6]

Their strategy was successful, for a principal defining characteristic of Hellenistic Crete is the island's well-attested, endemic, and often violent inter-city conflict and competition. Squabbling emerges as particularly active in the third and second century BC, marked by the successful expansion of certain cities at the expense of other, usually smaller communities. Notable "winners" of the time were Gortyn, Hierapytna, Kydonia, Lyttos, and Knossos; "losers" included Tylissos (to Knossos), Phaistos (to Gortyn), Rhaukos (to Gortyn and Knossos), and Praisos and Istron (to Hierapytna) (Fig. 3.1). This is only a very partial list of clearly grim proceedings. Polybius (a roughly contemporary, but personally and politically biased observer) presented one unfortunately influential assessment of these internecine traumas, which he found predictable for the base, craven, greedy, and treacherous Cretans. As just one taste of Polybian invective, for the year 181 BC he reported: "the beginning of great troubles in Crete, if one can indeed speak of a 'beginning of troubles' in Crete. For owing to the persistent nature of their civil wars and the savagery of their treatment of one another, 'beginning' and 'end' are much the same thing" (Polybius 24.2.3). Today, less essentialist, more sophisticated explanations are gaining ground. Apart from externally provoked antagonisms, causal factors proposed by scholars such as Angelos Chaniotis include a rising population (suggested by Cretan mercenary numbers) and increasingly asymmetrical land divisions. It should be noted that civic violence was not

6. Davies 1984: 309; see also Bosanquet 1939–40: 72–73. On treaties with Hellenistic monarchs: e.g., the Eumenes treaty: *ICr* IV.179; Ducrey 1970. The Ptolemies implanted a garrison at Itanos: Spyridakis 1970; for recent work in the site's hinterland: Kalpaxis *et al.* 1995.

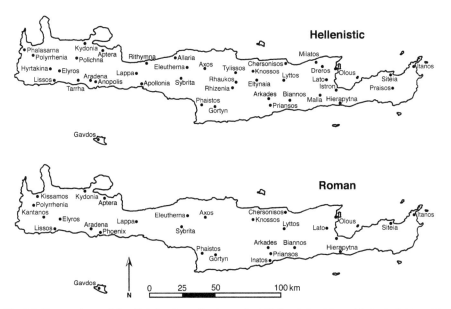

Fig. 3.2 Comparison of the distribution of independent Hellenistic cities with that of sites with evidence for city status in Roman times.

the only response to these pressures; cities and citizens also fostered more co-operative connections and cultivated survival strategies ranging from piracy to pastoralism.[7]

These struggles had one pronounced effect on the political map of Crete. In Archaic and Classical times the island was divided into numerous, often very small-scale polis units, although Homer's "Crete of the hundred cities" (*Iliad* 2.649; or "the ninety cities," *Odyssey* 19.174) was always something of an exaggeration. In the quarrelsome Hellenistic age, however, the number of independent civic units markedly declines. Detailed chronological understanding of this process is not currently possible, but two distribution maps compiled by Sanders illustrate a major shift between the Hellenistic and Roman situations (Fig. 3.2). In his reckonings, "Crete of the hundred cities" in early Hellenistic times contained about thirty-five or forty functioning civic units; by the time of the Roman conquest in the 60s BC, "further warfare seems to have reduced the number of states to something over twenty."[8] Some

7. Chaniotis 1995b. On political and territorial changes in the Hellenistic period: Callaghan 1992: 134–36; Chaniotis 1996; 1999b; Rigsby 1986; Sanders 1976; Souza 1998; Spyridakis 1970; van Effenterre 1948: 109–273; Watrous *et al.* 1993: 232. For a collection of other Polybian remarks on the Cretans, see Ager 1994: 1; also van Effenterre 1948: 283–312.
8. Sanders 1982: 11–12. No one appears substantially to disagree with the orders of magnitude suggested by these figures, which are based chiefly on complex epigraphic and numismatic data: Baldwin Bowsky 1994: 38, n. 95; Perlman 1996: 282–83. Viviers (1994; 1999) argues for dynamism in the Cretan landscape of Archaic and Classical times as well.

of these communities survived their loss of political independence, but others were clearly eradicated. All of these intertwined developments form the background against which the construction of social memory in Hellenistic Crete must be assessed.

As in other parts of the Greek east, Roman intervention in Cretan affairs began well before the island's formal incorporation. Unlike other Greek provinces (including Achaia), however, Roman forces violently subdued Crete, taking the island in three campaigns (69–67 BC) led by Q. Metellus (later titled Creticus). With Augustan provincial reorganization (c. 27 BC), the island was paired with Cyrenaica to form a single senatorial province, an arrangement that endured until the Diocletianic reforms. Compared to preceding periods, fewer and more substantial political units were now distributed across the island's landscape in a relatively stable pattern, although certain cities did alter in status. Gortyn in the central Mesara plain, for example, was selected as provincial capital: no doubt in part because of its position's accessibility to Cyrenaica, in part because of its rich agricultural hinterland, in part because of long-standing ties to Rome (Figs. 3.1, 3.3). By contrast, the antique city of Knossos, one of Gortyn's chief Hellenistic rivals, became

Fig. 3.3 View of excavations in the "basilica" of the Praetorium, the official seat of the proconsul, at Gortyn.

a Roman colony, *Colonia Julia Nobilis Cnossus.*[9] Such transformations led to the creation of a new, now pan-Cretan political hierarchy.

Roman annexation of the island brought significant, and quite visible, change in its wake. New patterns of trade, commerce, and agricultural activity responded to wider imperial markets; new building materials and styles of personal display reflect a broader Mediterranean awareness; new inhabitants of the island and new alliances across the empire can be traced in the study of Cretan onomastics.[10] Martha Baldwin Bowsky has also argued for a redefinition of relationships among the island's dominant elite families, a redefinition familiar elsewhere in the Roman east:

> To the ancient eye ... Crete may not have been so divided into separate cities and districts from west to east. Prominent Hierapytnans, Gortynians, and Lyttians, if not Knossians, belonged to a pan-Cretan aristocracy, to a network of notables active between and among towns, a supra-civic elite, even a supra-provincial network of Greeks prominent in the Roman world and also in Hellenic cultural life.[11]

Another indicator of this increasing social and cultural integration is the recorded participation of three cities – Lyttos, Gortyn, and Hierapytna – in the Hadrianic Panhellenion, whose members were drawn from all parts of the Greek world.[12]

What emerges from this combination of evidence is an early Roman Crete with a more deliberately "outward"-looking orientation, at least at the level of elite behavior and decision-making. This posed a challenge to antique institutions and practices. Strabo, writing in the late first century BC/early first century AD, ended his lengthy review of Cretan mores and myths on this note:

---

9. Knossos was also forced to yield revenues from a portion of its territory to the Italian town of Capua: Rigsby 1976. For archaeological work at Gortyn, see the ongoing series of publications from the Scuola Archeologica di Atene e delle Missioni Italiane in Oriente, beginning with Di Vita 1988; see also Di Vita 1992; Di Vita and La Regina 1984: 69–116.
10. On all these developments and on Roman Crete more generally, see Baldwin Bowsky 1994; 1999; Beschi 1974; Chaniotis 1988c; 1999b; Haggis 1996b; Harrison 1988; 1991; 1993; Marangou-Lerat 1996; Piatkowski 1981; Sanders 1982: 3–15; Spyridakis 1992a. On long-term trends in the adminstrative organization of Crete: Bennet 1990.
11. Baldwin Bowsky 1994: 38, arguing especially for Hierapytna as "one of the most progressive cities of Roman Crete, open to Roman ways and practices as much as to Greek tradition." See also Baldwin Bowsky 1999 for a detailed prosopographical study of Roman-period changes.
12. All three were represented through the Cretan *koinon*; individuals from Gortyn and Hierapytna are attested as officeholders in the Panhellenion. See Romeo forthcoming; Spawforth and Walker 1985: 78, 80–82, 85; Spawforth 1999: 348–49. For other references on the Panhellenion, see p. 68, n. 55.

I have assumed that the constitution of the Cretans is worth describing because of its peculiar character and because of its fame. Few of these institutions endure, however, for the administration of affairs is carried on chiefly by means of the decrees of the Romans, as is also the case in the other provinces.   (Strabo 10.4.22)

All of these intertwined developments form the background against which the construction of social memory in Roman Crete must be assessed, and compared to its predecessor.

MEMORIES OF A DIVIDED ISLAND

Changes in the land

We can begin with the landscape of the Hellenistic island. One question, of course, is how far the turmoils reported actually affected the material frameworks of life, given the possible consequences for social memory such change might entail. Regional surveys carried out in various parts of the Cretan countryside can begin to address this issue. Several such projects have been conducted on the island and, while many remain at a relatively early stage of publication, a fairly good picture can be built up of developments in at least two zones: east Crete and the Mesara plain – the areas especially affected by the activities of Hierapytna and Gortyn respectively (Fig. 3.1).[13]

In the eastern part of the island, much work has targeted the so-called "Isthmus" (the island's narrowest transshipment point). Even within this geographically limited zone, a variety of localized trajectories have been re-covered. The Vrokastro survey, for example, noted the disappearance of Istron and Oleros as independent centers: a "decapitation" of local settlement hierar-chies which generated a diversity of rural responses across the area explored. Elsewhere on the Isthmus, the expansion of Hierapytna stimulated settle-ment, as in the territory of the Kavousi–Thriphti survey which passed under the specific control of Hierapytna in the second century BC. Haggis ties the resulting rise in habitation directly to that city's strong maritime interests and desire to utilize the Isthmus route.[14]

Further east lies the site of Praisos, the ancestral home of the Eteocretans (or "true" Cretans, reputedly the autochthonous inhabitants of the island)

---

13. For a list of recent surveys, see Moody *et al.* 1998. Great strides are now being made in the study of historic Cretan pottery chronologies, notably by work at Gortyn; see also Erickson 2000. Such data were not available for the results discussed here, leaving chronological refinement of these developments cruder than would probably now be the case. Cretan ceramic traditions do appear, however, to be highly regionalized in both prehistoric and historic times: Haggis 1996a: 387.
14. The Vrokastro survey: Hayden *et al.* 1992; the Kavousi-Thriphti survey: Haggis 1996a. For Late Hellenistic and Roman Hierapytna, see Baldwin Bowsky 1994; Haggis 1996b.

until its destruction by Hierapytna around 145 BC. Recent archaeological prospection on the urban site and in its immediate hinterland testifies to a flourishing city in Classical and earlier Hellenistic times and to its harsh mid-second-century BC termination.[15] The Ziros project, working in the high tablelands to the southwest of Praisos, may offer one glimpse of what happened to that displaced population. The two small upland basins it examined demonstrate no signs of permanent occupation until the Hellenistic period; the principal investigator, Keith Branigan, posits a link to the destruction of Praisos: "It is indeed tempting to speculate that the initial Hellenistic re-settlement . . . was stimulated . . . by the dispersal of the former inhabitants of Praisos in the mid-second century B.C."[16]

This handful of surveys attests to substantial and multi-faceted change in the Hellenistic landscape of east Crete; we witness both civic expansion and civic destruction, the abandonment of certain areas and the encouragement of others. The expansionist activities of one dominant city influenced, or dictated, much of what happened. A similar story can be told of the fertile Mesara plain and the rise of Gortyn. Several cities (of which Phaistos, situated on the site of a Minoan palace, is most famous) were subsumed under Gortynian control in the later Hellenistic period. Since the early work of Sanders, regional surveys have underlined this epoch as a time of marked rural change; one recent reexamination of the western Mesara, for example, deemed the effect of Gortynian hegemony "radical." Gortyn's "flexing" of its muscles has also been related to developments – "a drift towards Gortyn and the Mesara" – observed in the Ayiofarango Valley, to the south of the plain proper. Finally, survey in the hinterland of the Minoan town and historic sanctuary at Kommos reports a "radical shift in and growth of population" in Hellenistic times; the third century BC saw an especial concentration (with site numbers tripling in one area) around the increasingly important port site of Matala. In all these cases, it can sometimes be difficult to disentangle the influence of Gortyn in its early imperial incarnation from its previous Hellenistic activities, but the shockwaves of the city's growing ascendancy seem quite clear.[17]

15. Whitley 1998; Whitley et al. 1995; AR 39 (1992–93): 77–79; AR 40 (1993–94): 82; AR 41 (1994–95): 70; AR 43 (1996–97): 117. To the north of Praisos, along the coast of the Gulf of Siteia, the Agia Photia survey pointed to some settlement increase in Hellenistic times, a pattern even more pronounced in the Roman period although total site numbers for this survey remain small: Tsipopoulou 1989.
16. Branigan et al. 1998: 90.
17. Alcock 1994a: 180 for another review of this evidence. On the Mesara: Sanders 1976, esp. 136–37; Watrous et al. 1993: 232–33. For the Kommos Survey, see Hope Simpson et al. 1995: 397–99, quote at 398. The Ayiofarango pattern echoes a previous, prehistoric development: "It may be that there was a repetition of the events of the beginning of the Middle Bronze Age, with Gortyn now taking the role previously played by Phaistos . . . It does seem possible that there was

These two clusters of survey evidence, briefly reviewed, make a very simple point: the transformation of Hellenistic political topographies, at least in these regions, involved more than just a redistribution of urban centers. Instead, the redrafting of political boundaries led to often dramatic reorganization of rural settlement and to movement of peoples. But what ramifications did this landscape instability possess for the placement and transmission of memories?

Returning to old ground

This vulnerability of the Cretan landscape, I would argue, was reflected and contested in contemporary ritual and commemorative practices. Cults marking civic boundaries, for example, promoted claims to particular territories; in some documented quarrels they were even cited as a formal *casus belli*. Such border shrines include the sanctuary of Ares and Aphrodite at Sta Lenika (disputed between Lato and Olous), the sanctuary of Zeus Diktaios (aptly described as an "Apple of Discord" between rival east Cretan cities), and the western Diktynnaion (a focus for competition between Kydonia and Polyrrhenia). Following the vicissitudes of conflict, such sanctuaries could change hands frequently. Others were permanently lost; for example, an annual procession from the expansionist Hierapytna to the sanctuary of Athena Oleria signaled the annexation of a once independent Oleros.[18]

The use of border cults both to assert and to defend civic prerogatives was not new to the island in Hellenistic times, but it became more visible and emphatic.[19] Side-by-side with that development, moreover, stands another

a drift towards Gortyn and the Mesara in the second/third centuries, just as we have suggested there was in Middle Minoan I–II towards Phaistos and other growing centres further north" (Blackman and Branigan 1977: 75; see also Blackman and Branigan 1975). Other areas of Crete have been surveyed, some of which show little or no trace of Hellenistic activity: e.g., the area of the Minoan palace of Malia (most recently, Müller 1996), the island of Pseira (Hope Simpson and Betancourt 1990), and, most surprisingly, the Lasithi plain (Watrous 1982: 22–24). Limited reconnaissance has recently been carried out in the *chora* of Gortyn itself: LaTorre 1993.

18. Ares and Aphrodite: Baldwin Bowsky 1989; Bousquet 1938; Chaniotis 1988a: 23–25; van Effenterre 1942; van Effenterre and Bougrat 1969. On the architectural restorations at the site by Lato after its final, arbitrated victory: Baldwin Bowsky 1989: 340–42. The fragmentary remains of the "Hellenic" temenos, temple, and altar of Zeus Diktaios, dating back probably to Archaic times and running into the Roman period, were discovered in early excavations at Palaikastro: Bosanquet 1939–40; Chaniotis 1988a: 26–28; Crowther 1988: 43–44; Dawkins *et al.* 1904–5: 298–308; MacGillivray and Sackett 1984; Perlman 1995: 163–65; Spyridakis 1970: 53–58; Watrous 1996: 104–105; Willetts 1977: 201. On the "Apple of Discord": Spyridakis 1970: 49. For the Diktynnaion: Sanders 1982: 173–74 (20/29); Spyridakis 1970: 53–54; Willetts 1962: 192; Philostratus, *Vita Apollonii* 8.30. On the Athena Oleria procession (second/first centuries BC): Hayden 1995: 96, 123–24, 141.

19. On extra-urban cults more generally, Polignac 1984; also Alcock and Osborne 1994; Daverio Rocchi 1988; Sartre 1979. For a wide-ranging study of this phenomenon on Crete, Chaniotis 1988a; see also Cucuzza 1997.

detectable pattern, a florescence of small shrines in the countryside. Sanders observed these were "all of Hellenistic date, a period when there seems to have been a revival in religious activity which did not in all cases last into the Roman period."[20] More remarkable in this context is the location of many of these Hellenistic shrines, for they mapped onto what would have been recognizably "old" places – good examples of what Halbwachs termed *cadre matériel*, his material traces of the past in the present. These sites usually (if not always) date to the epoch termed Minoan in modern scholarship.

The Mesara plain, in particular the hinterland of Phaistos, is a good place to begin examining this phenomenon. Only 2 kilometers from Phaistos lay the Minoan villa site of Ayia Triada, intermittently excavated since the early twentieth century and the source of famous Bronze Age finds, including its eponymous Late Minoan IIIA sarcophagus. Also unearthed, however, were signs of Early Iron Age ritual activity (dating specifically to the Protogeometric B/Orientalizing epoch, or the ninth to seventh centuries BC). A subsequent long hiatus in occupation was broken by the foundation, in early Hellenistic times, of a small village no doubt dependent on Phaistos. Cult was then renewed in at least two loci, both nestled firmly within the Late Minoan ruins: an altar in the northwest corner of the "Piazzale dei Sacelli" and a shrine dedicated to Velchanos, an indigenous Cretan deity (Fig. 3.4). Additional votives found in the vicinity may point to still other shrines on site, and suggest that one of the deities worshipped was a fertility goddess. To explain the Iron Age florescence of cult, Anna Lucia D'Agata points to the political interests of Phaistos, who "re-occupied the site of Ayia Triada in order to use it as a sanctuary site, so asserting clearly its rights over an area to which neighboring centers were making claims."[21] A similar scenario can be envisioned for the Hellenistic age – a hypothesis much strengthened by the fact that settlement and cult at Ayia Triada end around the same time (the mid-second century BC) that Phaistos was subdued by Gortyn.

Other examples of a "return to old ground" are visible in the Hellenistic Mesara. A small Demeter shrine of late Classical/Hellenistic date was found close to Kamilari Tomb I, the largest of the three Minoan tholoi excavated at that locale (Fig. 3.5). To the north of the circular tomb lay an enclosure containing an "altar" together with Middle and early Late Minoan pottery. In association with this complex (believed to have been visible in later times) lay the historic cult building and an associated votive deposit; excavated and surface

20. Sanders 1982: 39. In addition to the examples to be discussed, he mentions a shrine of Pan at Pateraki and one at Afrati in east central Crete.
21. D'Agata 1998, quote at 24; Banti 1941–43; D'Agata 1997; La Rosa 1992a: 74–77; 1993; Sanders 1976: 137.

1. Shrine of Velchanos
2. Small stone building with Hellenistic material
3. Altar

Fig. 3.4 Plan of the multi-phase Bronze Age site of Ayia Triada, showing the location of subsequent Hellenistic finds (areas shaded in gray).

finds included terracotta plaques, female figurines, and miniature horns of consecration.[22] The western Mesara survey contributed further instances of related activity. A fourth-century BC skyphos found at the Late Minoan IIIC

22. Cucuzza 1997: 72–74; Levi 1961–62b; see also Alcock 1991: 459, n. 53 for other references.

Fig. 3.5 Balloon photograph of Kamilari Tholos I.

cemetery at Liliana was identified as a possible votive, as was a perforated cup base found in Late Minoan chamber tombs at Kalivia. The investigators summed up the situation bluntly: "Minoan sites in the Mesara became the focus of cult during the Hellenistic period."[23]

Additional cases can be found beyond the borders of the Mesara plain. To the east, along the island's southern coast, stood the Late Minoan IB country house and shrine at Pyrgos. Following its fiery Bronze Age destruction, the site was "barely visited" until the Hellenistic period (Pyrgos V). At that time a circular late Hellenistic shrine was superimposed atop the Minoan house's lightwell and staircase (Fig. 3.6). Gerald Cadogan (the site's excavator), for one, believed this intrusion was not fortuitous: "I feel sure that something of the Minoan house stood when the Hellenistic shrine was founded ca. 200 BC."[24]

Inscribed votives name the Pyrgos deities as Hermes and Aphrodite, the same pair honored at the upland shrine at Syme, located high on the remote slopes of Mount Dikte. Syme – remarkably – demonstrates genuine continuity in cult from Minoan through Roman times; fertility and vegetation

23. Watrous *et al.* 1993: 231–32, quote at 231.
24. Cadogan 1981: 169–71, quote at 171; 1977–78; 1992: 202–9. The shrine covered roughly the area indicated by the numbers 1–4 on Fig. 3.6.

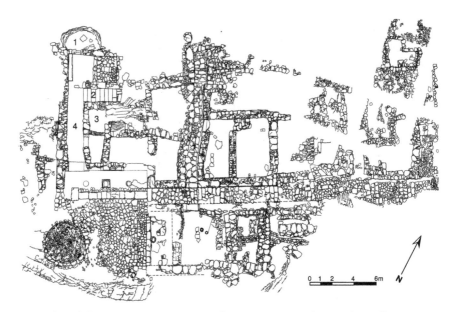

Fig. 3.6 Plan of the Late Minoan IB country house at Pyrgos. The circular Hellenistic shrine was built over the structure's lightwell and staircase (roughly the area indicated by nos. 1–4).

deities were worshipped at least from the Archaic period and possibly before. Syme, obviously, is not a "new" Hellenistic shrine returning to an "old" place, yet it offers other support for an intensified Hellenistic investment in the past.[25] The excavators, Angeliki Lebessi and Polymnia Muhly, describe the site's major late Hellenistic structure (Building D, extended in Roman times as Building C–D) in provocative terms:

> Built with a high bench against its back wall, it has the plan of a "house-shrine," a type of building well known in Crete in the Late Minoan III and later periods. On the bench of Building D, several Minoan stone vases that were being reused were found together with HL [Hellenistic] terracotta figurines and lamps.[26]

Such mixing and reuse of finds may have been a frequent occurrence at Syme; the sacrificial area was regularly raked, leveled, and reorganized, continually bringing up the detritus of past offerings and keeping "the Minoan past very much alive for the pilgrims of later periods." We can be sure, however, that the Hellenistic period witnessed such practices; apart from the design of the

25. Lebessi 1983; 1992: 268–71; Lebessi and Muhly 1987: 112; 1990: 336; Lebessi and Reese 1990;
    Praktika 1989: 296–303; see also Chaniotis 1988a: 33–34; Watrous 1996: 68.
26. Lebessi and Muhly 1987: 106; Watrous 1996: 65–68.

Hellenistic "house-shrine" and its mixture of offerings, small votives drawn from earlier periods were also built into its walls.[27]

The western portion of the island, at least on present evidence, has less to add to this discussion than either the center or the east.[28] One place that can be mentioned, however, is the well-preserved Late Minoan IIIB tholos tomb at Stylos Sternaki. A dozen vases, described as of "advanced" Hellenistic date, were found perched on the lintel of the tomb's relieving triangle; fragments of similar vessels were discovered inside the tomb and in the filling of the dromos.[29]

Settlements, caves, tombs, and symbols

Patterns of return and repossession occur in other Hellenistic material settings as well. Settlements overlay settlements, in some cases with Hellenistic buildings resting directly upon Minoan wall foundations. No systematic catalogue has been attempted, but examples would include the Protopalatial complex at Monastiraki or the Late Minoan settlement at Ayia Pelagia. In the Chalara quarter of Phaistos, a Hellenistic structure stood atop a late palatial house, even using "bits of the ancient ruins for its foundations and for the lower part of its own walls."[30] While accidental superimposition is always a possibility, as with the reuse of itinerant elements in the Athenian Agora, we must resist the temptation to write this off as merely efficient building practice.

Literally hundreds of caves dot the island of Crete, dozens of which – from earliest prehistory onwards – were entered and utilized in some fashion. Cave cult is a constant feature in discussions of Cretan religion; the sites involved range from extensive and famous caverns (such as the Idaian and Psychro Caves) to numerous, less distinguished grottoes. Positive identification of

27. Lebessi and Muhly 1987, quote at 111. *Praktika* 1993: 209–30; *Ergon* 1997: 67–70; *AR* 43 (1996–97): 105; *AR* 44 (1997–98): 116.
28. To an extent this may reflect an archaeological bias, with western Crete (blessed with fewer major Minoan sites) receiving less attention than other parts of the island. But the west appears to diverge from the center and east in certain distinct ways, including the manner of celebration of cave cult: Guest-Papamanoli and Lambraki 1980; Tyree 1974: 147–50. For a collection of historical sources on the western half of the island, Gondicas 1988.
29. Davaras 1971; Mavrigiannaki 1972; see also Alcock 1991: 463, no. 12. Another possible Cretan example of post-classical tomb cult has been noted at Episkopi (Pedias): Alcock 1991: 467.
30. Monastiraki: *Kretike Estia* 2 (1988): 313; 5 (1994–96): 313–14. Ayia Pelagia: Alexiou 1972; *ArchDelt* 29 (1973–74 [1980]) Chr. 883–85; 33 (1978 [1985]) Chr. 355–57. Phaistos: Levi 1964: 11–12. Also preserved there was a ramp built in Protogeometric times, with Hellenistic houses respecting its alignment. Along this ramp, one very fine building preserved a portion of an ancient staircase. Levi reported the discovery of half an Orientalizing pithos: "probably a valuable family relic preserved and repaired during the habitation of the Hellenistic house."

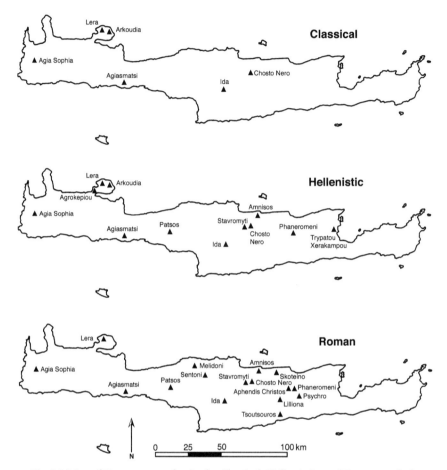

Fig. 3.7 Map of Cretan cave cults, in the Classical, Hellenistic, and Roman periods.

a cave's function in a particular epoch can be difficult, a problem exacerbated when early investigations provide our only source of information. At the Psychro Cave above the Lasithi plain, for example, dynamite was employed to access the innermost reaches and villagers were offered rewards for finds of "better objects."[31] Discovery of certain categories of material (votives, figurines, or pyres) can stand, however, as fairly definite indicators of ritual practice. Mapping the places where such finds date specifically to the Hellenistic age reveals a definite expansion in cave cult, compared to the preceding Classical distribution (Fig. 3.7). Each instance of Hellenistic activity took

31. "[T]he villagers, both men and women, worked with frantic energy, clinging singly to the pillars high above the subterranean lake, or grouping half a dozen flaring lights over a productive patch of mud at the water's edge. It was a grotesque sight, without precedent in an archaeologist's experience": Hogarth 1899–1900: 100–1.

place in caves previously utilized, usually in prehistoric times. Traces of that earlier usage would quite likely have been visible to later visitors in many, if not all, cases. Again, emerging here is an apparent "desire to visit 'old' cult places."[32]

The final places to which people "returned" were tombs, with the association of Hellenistic burials and older graves. Returning to the Mesara, at Ayios Ioannis near Phaistos, a rectangular funerary enclosure with cist graves of Hellenistic date rested above a Geometric tholos tomb; at Petrokephali, Hellenistic ceramics (of fine Hadra type) came to light in association with a Protogeometric deposit, arguably from a tomb context.[33] The most unequivocal display, however, comes from the North Cemetery at Knossos. A massive campaign of rescue excavation revealed Hellenistic graves honeycombing this Iron Age cemetery, and indeed other necropoleis in the vicinity. Inhumations were inserted – quite consciously it appears – among the older graves (Fig. 3.8):

> Many of these late graves were neatly arranged in groups suggesting funeral enclosures. They very rarely encroached one upon another; markers for individual graves seem likely. *This reuse of an old necropolis must have been deliberate. The cemetery plan even suggests that the precise areas of the old graves may have been well known and sought after for burial.* The same behavior was observed at Fortetsa, and seems to have extended as far N as Khaniale Teke. How strange the contrast for the burial parties between the clean kouskouras upcast from such graves as 128, 130, 131, 133 dug in a virgin patch, and the heap of dark soil littered with broken pottery and laced with cremated bone at the graves they had dug into the old Ts. 75 or 104.[34]

Coldstream employs the phrase "Minos redivivus" in attributing a nostalgia for the Minoan past to the Early Iron Age users of this same cemetery. A similar

32. Tyree 1974: 150. Fig. 3.7 is based on Tyree 1974, with modifications following my consultation of recent publications, especially Rutkowski and Nowicki 1996 and Watrous 1996. Paul Faure worked extensively on Cretan caves (e.g., Faure 1964), but his presentation and interpretation of data are not helpful in this regard. Complete publications of cave cults are all too rare, but see Guest-Papamanoli and Lambraki 1980; Kourou and Karetsou 1994. Peak sanctuaries, it should be noted, are another Cretan "peculiarity," but, with the exception of Iuktas (pp. 124–25), such sites do not seem to play a part in this pattern of reuse and later veneration.

33. Agios Ioannis: *Kretike Estia* 5 (1994–96): 334; *AR* 44 (1997–98): 112; Petrokephali: Cucuzza 1997: 74; La Rosa 1984: 810, 814; Levi 1961–62a: 467–68; Rocchetti 1969–70: 54–58.

34. Coldstream and Catling 1996, quote at 722 (my emphasis). *Kouskouras* is the limestone soil matrix of the cemetery. See also Catling *et al.* 1982. Study of the Hellenistic and Roman graves, in their own right, will be published separately, although finds of later periods "infiltrating especially from HL or R burials" are to be found in the 1996 North Cemetery publication. This direct parallel between Iron Age and Hellenistic behavior is also seen, of course, at Ayia Triada and elsewhere.

Fig. 3.8 Hellenistic graves carefully inserted between larger, flanking Iron Age tombs, Knossos North Cemetery.

desire to attach themselves back in time is manifest with these Hellenistic tombs.[35]

One last category of evidence to cite is the reappearance of ancient symbols. Excavations at the border sanctuary of Ares and Aphrodite at Sta Lenika discovered a dedication to Aphrodite of *c.* 120 BC, in the middle of which was an inscribed sign. The best parallels for this "curieux signe" – despite the inscription's date – come from the Linear B script of the Late Bronze Age. Two further signs ("aussi mystérieux") were discovered on the walls of the temple chamber assigned to Aphrodite. Links between the Minoan mother goddess and that later deity are assumed in Bousquet's original analysis; less specific associations back in time are undoubtedly a safer conclusion. Finally, a dedication from the Psychro Cave yields another instance of apparent symbolic survival (if not survival of the signs' original meanings). Below the text (itself inscribed in a script reminiscent of Eteocretan) are three slightly larger and deeper incisions which either belong to, or closely resemble, Linear A

35. Coldstream 1998; Coldstream and Catling 1996: 719. For Ayia Triada, see D'Agata 1998. Evans reported the discovery of a "Mycenaean" ring (decorated with images straight from the Shaft Graves) in a Hellenistic tomb from Chania; there are, however, "rightful doubts" about the authenticity of the piece: Cohen 1995: 503, n. 57 for references.

Fig. 3.9 Probable Hellenistic dedication from the Psychro Cave, with three deep-cut "Linear A" symbols.

(Fig. 3.9). The inscription has been somewhat variably placed in time, but is most often agreed to be of Hellenistic date.[36]

Any one, or even several, of the individual examples so far adduced could be dismissed as accidental, meaningless, or not proven. It might be claimed that a certain circularity is at work here: later finds turn up in "old places" because "old places" (chiefly Minoan places) are where we have principally looked. There may be some element of truth to that argument, but it is not sufficient to upset the entire applecart. Taking the assembled evidence *in toto*, a pattern of reappropriation and return takes shape for Hellenistic Crete. Moreover, such acts are often unprecedented, or only follow after a long hiatus – in other words, there is nothing *continuous* about Cretan inventiveness with their past.

36. On the Sta Lenika inscription: Bousquet 1938: 405–8 (no. 4), who reproduces a photograph taken in the Great Court at Knossos to underline his point about the Linear B resemblance. He also comments on how others, including Sir Arthur Evans, noted similar survivals into historic times. Marinatos (1958: 227) places the Psychro inscription in the third or late fourth century BC; see also Watrous 1982: 62, no. 66; Stieglitz 1976. In a later study, Watrous (1996: 55) suggests a Roman date, given the lack of Hellenistic finds from the cave.

Local memories

These processes of return and reuse argue for widespread memorial invest-ment in the island's past during the Hellenistic period. That leaves two ob-vious and central questions: which past, and whose memories? Once upon a time, it would have been natural to assume a Minoan flavor to what was here recalled. Given textual evidence for Hellenistic interest in the heroic age, a link to the figure of King Minos and his associated cast of characters and venues (Theseus, Ariadne, the Minotaur, the labyrinth) is far from implausi-ble. To insist upon anachronistic preconceptions about the centrality of that particular epoch, however, would be a backward step. Unfortunately, other substantive suggestions are difficult to muster, given the nature of much of the archaeological evidence – shrines set in ruins, votives in caves – and lack-ing strong epigraphic or literary contexts for such anonymous dedications. The themes behind this commemorative behavior – what exactly was being remembered and called upon – remain obscure, and likely always will.

If the precise *content* of those memories is hidden, their *context* may still be informative. The case can be made that many of these Hellenistic acts were intended to celebrate local memories of a local past. They were fre-quently anchored to the kind of places – tholos tombs, ruined foundations, neighborhood cemeteries – known and valued by people living close by, but of limited interest and attraction for those at any great distance. The subse-quent history of these commemorative practices, often failing to survive their host community, likewise speaks to their essentially local character. Cults at Ayia Triada, for example, were not adopted by Gortyn following that city's reduction of Phaistos. Presumably the site was not sufficiently connected to Gortyn's own history or needs, lying at a parochial level below the interests of this expanding polity. Similarly, Hierapytna's annexation of Praisos saw not only the destruction of the city, but the end of any evidence for a specif-ically "Eteocretan" identity. Admittedly, precisely what constituted such an identity – apart from the non-Greek Eteocretan language – is ambiguous, and once easy assertions about the continuity of Eteocretan independence (as a kind of "Cretan Wales") seem deeply dated.[37] None the less, Hellenistic epigraphic evidence for the use of Eteocretan bespeaks at least some degree of regional self-awareness. No such inscriptions postdate the mid-second cen-tury, however, and it is assumed that "being Eteocretan" (in whatever sense

37. On the "Cretan Wales": Bosanquet 1939–40: 64. Ancient sources on the Eteocretans include Diodorus 5.64.1; 5.80.1; Strabo 10.4.6; 10.4.12. For more recent discussions, see Whitley 1998; 1992: 256–61; Whitley *et al.* 1995. On Praisian politics in Hellenistic times: Spyridakis 1970: 22–32.

that possessed) did not long survive Hierapytna's overwriting of the land-scape of Praisos.[38] Out of all the cases reviewed, one clear exception to this emphasis on locality is the remote pilgrimage site of Syme, but that seems a somewhat solitary counter-example. On the whole, Hellenistic investment in the past worked on the small scale, was geared to more bounded inter-ests.[39] When those local concerns became irrelevant, so too did their points of commemoration.

As for why a local Cretan past might have possessed particular appeal in the Hellenistic present, at least one central factor can be safely identified. As Chaniotis has observed in relation to sanctuary affairs more generally, the period's antagonisms are no doubt key, leading as they did to increasingly challenged civic boundaries and to conflicts that might end in gain or loss. In a politically dissected landscape marked by unstable divisions, the promotion of border sanctuaries was one obvious, but not isolated, response. Highlighting and controlling venerable points in the landscape similarly expressed a sense of belonging and possession.

Turning to the question "whose memories?," one group looms large in the picture. Inscriptions attest that the polities of Hellenistic Crete were largely dominated by cadres of elite families. Such groups were clearly be-hind the formal use of border shrines in civic struggles, as indicated by the epigraphic dossiers from the sanctuary of Zeus Diktaios or from that of Ares and Aphrodite at Sta Lenika.[40] Certainly control of the *cadre matériel* – including the reuse of ruined buildings and of ancient inscriptions – was a constant concern to dominant actors in any society, as illustrated in chapter 1 by the actions of Nabonidus and other Mesopotamian dynasts. Yet not all the manifestations reviewed here readily conform to a model of elite intervention and formal civic ritual. Pots left within old tombs or unpretentious cave cult

38. Official inscriptions in Eteocretan continue as late as the second century BC: Hall 1995b: 89–90; Whitley 1998, esp. 37–38. It is unclear whether at its end Eteocretan was a spoken tongue or an archaic ritual language.
39. Local patriotism and a concern for civic memory are, of course, a wider Hellenistic trend, and one could ask to what extent these developments are particularly Cretan. Confronting this issue in an analysis of Hellenistic sanctuaries, Chaniotis (1995a) prefers to consider the Cretan evidence in its own light, owing to the island's intensification of territorial conflict. This does not rule out the likelihood, however, that comparable pressures led to comparable responses elsewhere in the Hellenistic world. For epigraphic attestation of civic patriotism: Boffo 1988; Chaniotis 1988b; Isager 1998.
40. For one well-documented elite network: Baldwin Bowsky 1989. For epigraphic evidence from the sanctuaries of Zeus Diktaios and Ares and Aphrodite, see n. 18. As noted earlier, elite interests supported cooperation between cities as well; this could be mediated at shared sanctuaries such as Syme. There, inscriptions attest to votives or building contributions from men of Lyttos, Priansos, Hierapytna, perhaps Knossos, and more: see Chaniotis (1988a: 33) for references.

speak to a more pervasive memorialization of the past, one also practiced by smaller rural communities or by individual families. As the evidence of regional survey suggests, such people faced a very real threat of disruption and displacement; if inequities in land holdings were indeed becoming more pronounced, that too would add a measure of anxiety. For these, and doubtless other, unrecoverable reasons, a broad spectrum of people appears to have turned to old monuments and sites in their own backyard.

One set of "memory communities" does, however, deserve special mention, and those are the communities made up by the island's dependent populations.[41] Hellenistic inscriptions testify to the existence of various forms of dependency; for example, the island of Gavdos, most famous as a shipwreck site of St. Paul, owed Gortyn military support and tithes of produce, including goods for the temple of Pythian Apollo. Another inscription speaks of the Artemitai, a group bonded in some fashion to Eleutherna; the officials of that city could require military service of these people, could fine them, and could restrict their movements and their participation in public cult.[42] Whatever the precise political status of any of these peoples, their relationship to the past would not have been identical to that of the full-fledged citizens of Eleutherna or of Gortyn.

The rich agricultural land of the Mesara plain also housed several dependent communities, many of them newly brought to that status through the Hellenistic expansion of Gortyn. Even Phaistos (and its outlier of Ayia Triada) may have been under some form of Gortynian control prior to its second-century reduction. The relatively recent loss of independence by these Mesara communities, their continued use of *ethnika* in personal and collective contexts (e.g., *hoi Amyklaioi; hoi Rittenioi*), together with the fact that Gortyn ultimately had to attack Phaistos: all suggest a degree of resistance to this subordinate status. In this scenario, what took place at Ayia Triada would express not only Phaistian claims to that territory, but also an ongoing sense of separate communal identity, rooted in remembrance of the past. The other

41. Another intriguing – if quite difficult – line of investigation would be to trace the gendering of memory, given the emphasis on male age-grade rituals in Cretan society and their developments over time: Strabo 10.4.20–21; Leitao 1995. On changes in the structure of Syme which may reflect alteration in such rites of passage: Lebessi 1992: 268–71; Lebessi and Muhly 1987: 112; 1990: 336; Lebessi and Reese 1990; see also Chaniotis 1988a: 33–34; *Praktika* 1989: 296–303; Watrous 1996: 68.

42. Gavdos: *ICr* IV.184A.18–19. Artemitai: *ICr* II.xii.22. Chaniotis (1995a) also suggests that the Artemitai may have been bonded specifically to live near a sanctuary of Artemis; see also Perlman 1996: 252–54. Perlman (1996) offers a general review of the evidence for dependency (with earlier references). Dependent communities are another feature of Cretan life too often taken as unchanging and "natural": Willetts 1965: 149; cf. van Effenterre 1982: 44.

Mesara cases discussed (pp. 109–11) may have served a similar purpose.[43] The relative abundance of evidence from the Mesara is intriguing in this context. At present, however, it is impossible to determine whether dependent communities accentuated that region's reliance on the past, or whether the rich data are instead a function of the area's impressive history of archaeological prospection.

MEMORIES OF AN IMPERIAL ISLAND

Roman dispositions

Gortyn's indifference to the shrines of Ayia Triada did not alter with its promotion to provincial capital, and a Roman-period wine-press ultimately adorned the shrine of Velchanos. In fact, Hellenistic reactivations of ancient places generally – if not universally – met with rejection in early Roman times. In some cases, of course, this abandonment predated Roman conquest and resulted from internal Hellenistic conflicts (as at Ayia Triada and Phaistos), but that explanation fails to fit all, or even most, of the assembled examples. Significant changes in patterns of commemoration, including a diminution in the power of the local past, would seem to follow Roman conquest and annexation.

This hypothesis is reinforced by the nature of those sanctuaries that *do* endure under Roman rule. Prime examples are the pan-Cretan sanctuary at Syme (where pagan cult runs at least into the third century AD and with evidence for early Christian churches), or the Idaian Cave (see below, pp. 126–28). Both were pilgrimage sites of wide appeal; both were distant from any single controlling community. Also pertinent in this context is an Asklepieion which in Hellenistic times provided a focus for settlement in the relatively isolated Ayiofarango Valley. This cult was abandoned around the time of the Roman take-over, with devotions apparently transferred to another Asklepios sanctuary at Lebena – a sanctuary administered by Gortyn in a dependent coastal town.[44] Sanctuaries that survived, it would appear, were

43. On dependencies in the Mesara: Perlman 1996: 258–70. The status of Hellenistic Phaistos is somewhat ambiguous. Although still formally independent in 182 BC, it appears to have been *de facto* subject to Gortyn in the later third century BC. Gortyn would subdue the city in the mid-second century, but there is some evidence that it, like the settlement at Rhytion, survived as a Gortynian *kome*, or village: Strabo 10.4.14; Cucuzza 1997: 87–92; La Rosa 1992b: 238; Sanders 1976: 134–35; Watrous *et al.* 1993: 232–33.
44. Blackman and Branigan 1977: 65, 72–76; see also Blackman and Branigan 1982. On Lebena and its Asklepieion: Philostratus, *Vita Apollonii* 4.34; Perlman 1996: 248, 251, 255; Tarditi 1992. The abandonment of cult at Kommos (possibly the dependent Gortynian community of Amyklai),

those that could serve a larger, non-local audience, and that were capable of accommodating a more widely shared, non-local sense of the past.

One site where direct imperial intervention in the memorial sphere might be predicted is Colonia Julia Nobilis Cnossus; this is also, of course, a site for which we have detailed archaeological evidence. From the Hellenistic city, the Knossos Survey reported at least three likely heroa, none of which remained active in the Roman era. The best understood example is KRS 76, a shrine lying some 300 meters west of the ancient palace; Peter Callaghan postulated this was the heroön of Glaukos, son of Minos and Pasiphaë. Within the shrine, finds of whole pots, ranging over some four centuries in date, led the investigators to posit the existence of interior storage shelves where antique pottery and dedications were deliberately preserved. The Glaukos heroön has been convincingly linked by its votives (equestrian figures, snakes, and many drinking cups) to male age-grade rites of passage.[45]

The end of the "manly" rituals of the Glaukos cult is very proximate to the time of conquest, a correlation seized upon by Callaghan:

> The importance of the shrine lasted only so long as Knossos remained an independent city...Whatever did happen at Knossos on its capture by Metellus, the new rulers can hardly have been sympathetic to a cult so intimately connected with military training, and in a city which had been their most formidable adversary on the island...[The colonists] obviously had no time for the local and, to them, foreign hero.[46]

Callaghan's general point is well taken, yet there is more to this than colonial caution about the possibilities of smouldering opposition. The disappearance of Glaukos, together with the other unidentified heroes, forfeited ties to an indigenous Knossian past. That disjunction may not be so surprising at the site

---

which had housed a sanctuary since the tenth/ninth centuries BC, can also be cited. In the last two phases of "Temple C" (AD 50–150), the building appears to have been used as a residence rather than as a shrine: Shaw 1992: 148, 152, with references.

45. Callaghan 1978. The Glaukos shrine is somewhat like Syme in its persistent presentation of ancient votives, as well as in its devotion to male rites of passage. Of the other two heroa, one lay to the east of the Little Palace (Knossos Survey no. 185) and was assigned to the Hellenistic period on the basis of votives in terracotta and a limestone relief; the other, on the summit of Lower Gypsadhes (Knossos Survey no. 312), was redated to that era by Callaghan. Hood and Smyth 1981: 22–23, 48. On Hellenistic and Roman Knossos: Callaghan 1981; 1992; 1994; Callaghan *et al.* 1981; Catling *et al.* 1982; Paton 1994; 1998; Sackett 1992.

46. Callaghan 1978: 28. See also Harrison 1993: 44–48; Huxley 1994: 132; Paton 1994: 147; Willetts 1962: 63–67. Callaghan comments on how the colonists maintained worship of the goddess Demeter, but cult practice at the famous Knossian Demeter sanctuary also altered around the time of Roman conquest: Coldstream 1973: 186–87 and *passim*; Hood and Smyth 1981: 20, 56 (no. 286); Huxley 1994: 132–33; Paton 1994: 147.

of a Roman *colonia*; what is provocative is how well it agrees with developments observed elsewhere on the island.

Dominant traditions

Both positive and negative evidence, therefore, suggests that Hellenistic re-inforcement and celebration of more local forms of memory diminished radically on Crete in early Roman times. This is not the same as saying that the past became unimportant. Distinct new inventions of what was vital to remember do emerge in Roman times, with these diverging in two significant ways from their predecessors. First, they stress prominent myths and legends, memories promulgated and accessible to all. Second, they are best attested in literary sources; archaeological evidence for Roman memorial practices, to date, remains rare on the ground. Three traditions appear especially high-lighted: Minos and his nexus of associations; the participation of Cretan heroes in the Trojan War; and the island's claim to both the birthplace and the tomb of Cretan-born Zeus (Zeus Cretagenes).

The web of stories around Minos, son of Zeus, embraced several mem-orable figures, events, and locales – Theseus, the labyrinth, Pasiphaë, the Minotaur, Rhadamanthus, Ariadne, and Daedalus – while extending to lesser players as well, such as Androgeos, son of Minos, who possessed an altar at Phaleron in Attica. Pausanias did not visit Crete and speaks of the island sparingly in his *Periegesis*, but these are the stories he tells and the names he mentions.[47] Apollonius of Tyana, by contrast, did visit the island (giving up the ghost, according to one version of his demise, at the western sanctuary of the Diktynnaion). Philostratus reports:

> And he sailed toward Cydonia and passing along to Knossus, where a labyrinth is pointed out which once, I believe, contained the Minotaur. As his companions wished to see this sight, he let them do so, but refused to himself be a witness to the injustice of Minos. He thus advanced to Gortyn because he longed to see Ida.   (Philostratus, *Vita Apollonii* 4.34)

The "injustice" here referred to was the Athenian tribute, demanded by Minos, that brought Theseus to Crete. Apollonius would not escape Minos on Mount Ida, however, for the Idaian Cave was frequently associated with the king in his more positive role as a wise law-giver – with the laws received from colloquy

---

47. Pausanias 1.1.4; 1.17.3; 1.21.4; 1.24.1; 1.27.9; 2.31.1; 2.15.1; 7.4.5–6; 9.40.3. Also mentioned is Britomartis/Diktynna (2.30.3). Pausanias comments upon disagreements between Cretan and other accounts, for example about the origin place of Eileithyia (1.18.5) and about the identity of Cretan city founders (8.53.4). On the mythic figure of Minos in earlier times: e.g. Huxley 1968; Morris 1992: esp. 172–94; Perlman 1992.

with Zeus within a cave.[48] The Roman-period celebrity of the Idaian Cave, and the association of Cretan caves with wisdom, will be further discussed below.

The second tradition of note is the Trojan War, and the part played in it by Cretan figures such as Idomeneus and Meriones. If veneration of certain Knossian heroes ended with Roman conquest, by contrast the residents of Knossos (according to Diodorus, writing in the late first century BC) held the tomb of these particular warriors "in special honor as eminent heroes" (5.79.4). A fascinating text purports to be the Trojan War diary (*Ephemeris Belli Troiani*) of Dictys Cretensis, a Knossian companion of Idomeneus. This journal, which promoted the Hellenic side in the conflict and minimized the role of gods and heroes, was said to have accompanied the author to his grave. Circumstances of its rediscovery appear in two prefaces added to the account, one of which retails:

> After many centuries the tomb of Dictys at Cnossus (formerly the seat of the Cretan king) collapsed with age. Then shepherds, wandering near the ruins, stumbled upon a little box skilfully enclosed in tin. Thinking it was treasure, they soon broke it open, but brought to light, instead of gold or some other kind of wealth, books written on linden tablets. Their hopes thus frustrated, they took their find to Praxis, the owner of that place. Praxis had the books transliterated into the Attic alphabet (the language was Greek) and presented them to the Roman emperor Nero. Nero rewarded him richly.

While the *Ephemeris* is best known in its Latin form (notably influencing medieval interpretations of the saga), that text was actually a somewhat altered and occasionally distorted version of a Greek original (with both versions first surfacing in Severan times). The ductility of this tale has indicated to some that "we are dealing with a two-layered forgery"; a two-layered invention, reinforcing the linkage of Crete and Knossos to Trojan heroics, may be a better way to put it.[49]

Finally, there is Zeus. The tomb of Zeus, a highly controversial notion in antiquity, is traditionally identified with Mount Iuktas to the south of Knossos. To modern-day archaeologists, Iuktas is well known for its Bronze

48. Diodorus 5.78.3; Plato, *Laws* I.624b; Strabo 10.4.8; Morris 1992: 177–78.
49. Champlin 1981: 195. Champlin, who undertakes a detailed examination of the *Ephemeris* and its relation to other texts of the time (such as Philostratus' *Heroikos*), has tied the Latin version of the text to Serenus Sammonicus, a courtier and author slain as a partisan of Geta in AD 211. Translation of the preface is from Frazer 1966: 19. The alternative preface modifies this version in various ways, for example reporting the tomb exposed by an earthquake and the shepherd's master giving the linden tablets to the island's governor: Frazer 1966: 7–11, 20–21.

Fig. 3.10 Summit of Mount Iuktas, with the chapel of Afendis Christos at no. 1. The other numbers indicate elements of the Bronze Age peak sanctuary: altar (2); chasm (3); terraces (4, 5); rooms (6).

Age peak sanctuary, marked by a deep chasm. Few finds of historic date come from the mountain top itself, but a Roman-period altar inscribed to "Zeus the Savior" was reported from its east side; Sanders also believed a Roman-period shrine lies under the present-day church of Afendi Christos, which stands on the summit near the peak sanctuary (Fig. 3.10). At Archanes on the slopes of Iuktas, third- or fourth-century AD tombs contained, in a secondary context, a dedicatory inscription to the Kouretes, the beings who assisted in the birth of Zeus.[50]

Various places associated with that birth were tirelessly promoted in Roman times. Diodorus, for example, mentions a site sacred to Zeus' mother at Knossos: "where even now men point to the foundations of a house of Rhea and to a grove of cypresses given over to her from antique times" (5.66.1). Evans linked this sanctuary of Rhea to a "Hellenic" temple discovered within the southwestern quarter of the Palace of Minos; its foundations bordered on the central court and followed the principal outlines of the palatial complex

50. Karetsou 1981: esp. 137; Sanders 1982: 154 (no. 8/9); see also Chaniotis 1988a: 33; Evans 1921: 153–59; Rutkowski and Nowicki 1996: 41; Watrous 1996: 70–72. Cook (1914: 157–63; 1940: 939–45) reviews the ancient literary references, probably the most famous of which is Callimachus' *Hymn to Zeus* (1.8–9). On the controversy, see Spyridakis 1992b; Verbruggen 1981: 63–70, 222. Late Roman tombs: *Kretike Estia* 2 (1988): 321; *ArchDelt* 42 (1987 [1992]) Chr. 530.

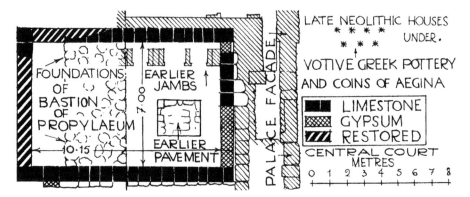

Fig. 3.11 Plan of an early Greek temple within the Palace of Minos, identified by Evans as the "Temple of Rhea."

(Fig. 3.11). Even in ruins, the site was remembered, at least as a place of touristic interest.[51]

Zeus Cretagenes himself was born in a cave. Of the championed rival claimants, a chief contender was the Idaian Cave, located on the central massif

Fig. 3.12 Excavations in the 1980s at the Idaian Cave.

51. Evans 1928: 6–7, 334; Hood and Smyth 1981: 20, 50 (no. 209). The temple immediately overlay the "wall stumps of a palace chamber," although Evans thought this "doubtless for convenience sake." Evans saw the Rhea cult as embodying the continuous worship of the great Minoan Goddess. Interestingly, these were the only "Greek" remains Evans recognized within the confines of the Palace.

ARCHAEOLOGICAL REPORTS FOR 1985–86

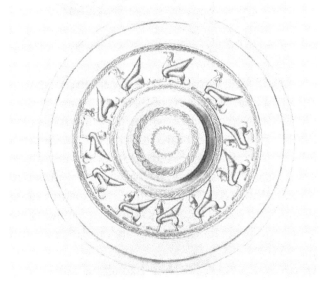

Fig. 3.13 Sixth-century BC shield cover, rededicated in early imperial times at the Idaian Cave. This find was selected for the cover of *Archaeological Reports*, an annual newsletter of archaeological discoveries in Greece.

of Mount Ida at an altitude of some 1500 meters. While a focus for almost continuous human activity since prehistoric times, in certain epochs this cavern patently experienced a pronounced intensification in use and probable significance. Archaeological investigation, most recently in the 1980s by Yannis Sakellarakis, revealed the later Geometric and Orientalizing periods (roughly the eighth to sixth centuries) as one such time (Fig. 3.12). The early Roman era (beginning in the first century BC) was clearly another. At this time the cave emerges as one of the premier cult sites on the island, with a remarkable density of offerings. An altar and statue-bases stood outside the entrance, while inside were literally hundreds of finds – jewellery, plaques, coins and, most notably, lamps. Older votives, ranging from a sixth-century bronze shield-cover to a Neolithic pot, also appear to have been rededicated in early imperial times (Fig. 3.13).

With its remote, often snow-bound location, the cave was *de facto* a site of pilgrimage, clearly attracting visitors (in addition to Apollonius of Tyana)

Fig. 3.14 Provincial coins of Crete depicting Zeus Cretagenes; to left, from the reign of Titus, to right, from the reign of Trajan.

from all over Crete and from various parts of the empire.[52] Apart from interest in his possible birthplace, the appeal of the Cretan-born god is also echoed on coinage of the imperial province, where Zeus Cretagenes (together with other Zeus motifs) frequently appeared (Fig. 3.14). One particular symbol associated with the god – seven stars and a ball – was eventually appropriated to the emperor's image, transformed into a symbol of imperial dignity. An issue by the Cretan Provincial Council under Caligula, for example, depicts the stars surrounding a seated Augustus – thus, in Sanders's words, linking "Zeus Cretagenes, the father figure of the island, with Augustus, father of the empire" (Fig. 3.15).[53]

Minos, Trojan War heroes, and Zeus had all, of course, attracted attention and commemoration prior to the Roman conquest. The point here is that they became more *emphasized*, evidently at the expense of other, less widely compelling memories, in the early Roman era. Additional material confirmation of this pattern would obviously be welcome, but these Cretan developments already accord with those observed (in chapter 2) for other parts of the Greek east. Election of prominent and recognizable themes – be it the Persian or the Trojan Wars – played a part in fostering communication across the new expanse of empire. At one level, this would work among Greek communities themselves, and among those individuals who now belonged, as Baldwin Bowsky observed, "to a pan-Cretan aristocracy, to a network of notables active between and among towns, a supra-civic elite,

52. For overviews and further references on the excavations at the Idaian Cave: Sakellarakis 1985a; 1985b; 1988; Sines and Sakellarakis 1987; see also Rutkowski and Nowicki 1996: 26–29; Watrous 1996: 59. On material evidence for imperial-era tourism, Sapouna 1998: 172–73. On Mount Ida: Verbruggen 1981: 71–99. On alternative birthplaces of Zeus: Cook 1914: 148–54; 1940: 932–39; Verbruggen 1981: 27–49.
53. Sanders 1982: 38; Svoronos 1890: 334 and pl. 32.2. On imperial assumption of the Cretan symbols of Zeus, see Verbruggen 1981: 180–81. For the coins illustrated in Fig. 3.14, see Svoronos 1890: pls. 33.10, 35.1. For other provincial coins with Idaian Zeus on the reverse: Svoronos 1890: 334–56; Willetts 1977: 203.

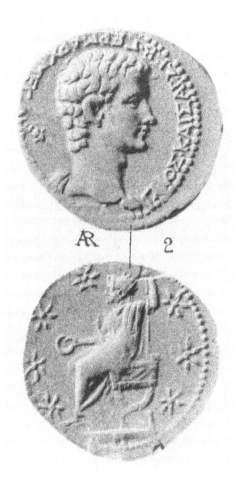

Fig. 3.15 Provincial coin of Crete with Caligula on the obverse. The reverse depicts a seated, radiate Augustus associated with the symbols of Zeus Cretagenes.

even a supra-provincial network of Greeks prominent in the Roman world and also in Hellenic cultural life."[54]

These accented traditions also linked the island to the center of Rome itself, where aspects of Cretan heritage were met with appreciation and redeployed in turn. Acceptance of the symbols of Zeus Cretagenes is one sign of this development, as may be the fiction that Nero acquired (at some expense) the story of Dictys Cretensis. The emperor Galba publicly displayed a family tree traced back, on his maternal side, to Pasiphaë, wife of Minos. Legends of the Minotaur, and Cretan mendacity in claiming a tomb for Zeus,

54. See p. 105. Morris has argued that the popularity and strategic uses of Cretan myths, especially of Daedalus, in Athenian mythography help to explain their spread and popularity in the Second Sophistic (Morris 1992: 184, 386, and *passim*).

appear as themes in Latin poetry – often with a contemporary political twist. Word plays on forms of *daedala* conveyed a sense of archaism in Latin poetry; Daedalus appears in the *Aeneid* and his flight with Icarus became a popular theme in poetry and art.[55] The Elder Pliny described the Knossian labyrinth and related it to the *Lusus Troiae* ("Troy Games"), an equestrian militaristic spectacle supposedly instituted by Ascanius. Held in the Circus Maximus, the Games involved high-born boys who had not yet taken the toga virilis; "the performance was showy and popular." Virgil too connects the labyrinth and the games, knitting ancestral connections between Troy, Crete, and the Julian family.[56] In these and other ways, themes of the Cretan past were woven into a broader commemorative tapestry and served – like the Persian Wars – as a shared point of understanding for central and provincial audiences within the empire.

*

This narrative seemingly proposes a fairly neat picture. With the annexation and provincialization of Crete, and with all consequent developments, changes in memorial patterns not unexpectedly followed. Different aspects and uses of the past now claimed priority, with less overt focus on reinforcing local or regional structures and more intense emphasis on stressing a pan-Cretan, widely recognizable myth-history. Local identities and backyard legends gave way to memories suited to a unified island – surely a perspective more comfortable to the new insular imperial elite.

One category of evidence, however, already refuses to fit comfortably into this scenario, and that is the fact that cave cult reaches an all-time high under the empire (Fig. 3.7).[57] Some of these grottoes, of course, do correlate well with popular themes in Roman times; apart from the Idaian Cave, for example, the Psychro Cave also competed for recognition as the birthplace of Zeus. Moreover, these better-known caverns possessed further associations

---

55. Suetonius, *Galba* 2. For poetic uses of Cretan themes: e.g. Martial 9.34; Lucan 8.871–72. On Daedalus: Morris 1992: 67–68. For Roman-period representations of the birth of Zeus, see Verbruggen 1981: 163–73. A good example is the so-called Ara Capitolina in the Capitoline Museum, which portrays scenes from the life of Zeus. A seated female figure, wearing a mural crown, is present in the birth scene; she probably personifies the island of Crete: Helbig 1895: 379–80, no. 515.

56. Favro 1999: 213–14, quotation at 213; she also discusses the "power of place" of the Vallis Murcia, which contained the Circus Maximus; see also Paton 1994: 144. For ancient references to the spectacle: Pliny, *Naturalis Historia* 36.19.85; Suetonius, *Divus Iulius* 39.2; *Divus Augustus* 43.2; Virgil, *Aeneid* 5.588–91, and Favro 1999: 218–19. Ancestral links: Virgil, *Aeneid* 3.108.

57. Sanders 1982: 40; Tyree 1974: 162–65. The range of types of Roman finds in most of these caves, however, tends to be rather limited, being predominantly pottery and lamps.

with wisdom, law, and learning; Pythagoras and Apollonius of Tyana, as well as Minos, were all believed to have spent time in Cretan caves in quiet contemplation, philosophical discourse, or interaction with the divine. In the cultural atmosphere of the Second Sophistic, visiting and venerating such grottoes made eminent sense.[58]

The problem is that not all caves with traces of Roman material could boast such notable pedigrees. More limited, humble observances at sites such as Tsoutsouros or Melidoni argue for the continuation of alternative rituals – neither civic-sanctioned nor elite-dominated – under the empire.[59] It can only be guessed what memories were entertained in these settings. One intriguing, if unprovable, hypothesis might be that these practices again revolved around the promotion of local allegiances, now working against the grain of much-changed political circumstances and offering an arena for symbolic resistance to local authorities, or to Rome itself. Whether that suggestion is at all on target or not, the need to explain the imperial-period florescence of cave cult militates against accepting too overly tidy a reconstruction of events.

The patterns of commemorative change here proposed make a simple, but significant, point. Hellenistic Crete was quite unlike Roman Crete (and *vice versa*), in terms not only of political and social organization, but also of memorial priorities and preferences. That conclusion should not surprise us, although the precise forms these differences take are revealing and instructive. It does undoubtedly cause problems, however, for any lingering sentiments about the Cretans dwelling under "the abiding influence of tradition." As the material framework of their lives altered, through their own actions or those of others, so too did inventions of the Cretan past.

---

58. Chaniotis 1988a: 34–35. Psychro Cave: Boardman 1961; Hogarth 1899–1900; Rutkowski and Nowicki 1996: 9–11, 18; Watrous 1982: 20–24, 61–62, no. 66; 1996. On caves as sources of wisdom, for the case of Pythagoras, see Porphyry, *Pythagoras* 17; for Appollonius, see Philostratus, *Vita Apollonii* 4.34; for Minos, see n. 47. Marinatos (1940–41) pushed this point too far, arguing for the existence of theological academies in Cretan caves; cf. Spyridakis 1970: 52–53.
59. Tsoutsouros: Rutkowski and Nowicki 1996: 40, 82; Tyree 1974: 31, 218. Melidoni: *Kretike Estia* 2 (1988): 305–7; 3 (1989–90): 273–75; 5 (1994–96): 291–93; Rutkowski and Nowicki 1996: 65.

4

BEING MESSENIAN

> But though the Messenian exiles have been restored to their homes, their calamities
> and long exile from Peloponnese have effaced from their memory much of the
> ancient history of their country, so that it is now open to any one to lay claim to
> traditions to which the true heirs have forgotten their right.
>
> (Pausanias 3.13.2)

In the minds of ancient historians, the most memorable thing about the Messenians is the fact that they lost. In the traditional narratives of what became known as the First and Second Messenian Wars (traditionally dated to the late eighth and seventh centuries BC), Spartan forces crossed the barrier of the Taygetos mountain range and captured, after vicious and hard-fought struggles, the land of Messenia: "rich for plowing, rich for planting" (Tyrtaios, *Fragment* 3). Later accounts, of which Pausanias' Book IV (*Messeniaka*) is the most comprehensive, purport to record the major events, locales, and players of these conflicts – Eira, Mount Ithome, the Battle of the "Great Trench," Aristocrates and, above all, the intrepid Messenian freedom fighter Aristomenes.[1]

What actually happened in these wars, and indeed their very historicity, remains murky territory for us. With the take-over, Messenia enters a kind of black hole, with little reported of the region's inhabitants (not least the famed helots of antiquity) and with little surviving indigenous testimony. This state of affairs endured for some 300 or so years, more or less the entire span of the Archaic and Classical periods. With the liberation of 370/369 BC by Epaminondas, that imposed silence drops away: helots were freed, exiles recalled, the city Messene founded on Mount Ithome, the centuries of dispossession ended (Fig. 4.1).[2] In the post-liberation period (defined here as

1. There is a vast literature on the Messenian Wars, e.g. Cartledge 1979: 102–30; Fuqua 1981; Huxley 1962; Kiechle 1959; Lazenby and Hope Simpson 1972: 84–86; Meier 1998; Oliva 1971: 102–14; Richer 1999. For Book IV of Pausanias, see the commentaries of Frazer 1898b; Musti and Torelli 1991. In this chapter I follow the present *communis opinio* about helot origins and conditions; for revisionist treatments of this subject: Luraghi 2002; in press.
2. At first Messene was called Ithome, before being renamed for the region's eponymous heroine; the city and its remarkable fortifications offered a well-populated, well-protected physical deterrent to Spartan aggression, somewhat akin to the contemporary foundation at Megalopolis. On this foundation and the history of Hellenistic Messenia: Roebuck 1941; 1945; Shipley 1997: 231–32. On Epaminondas, see Hanson 1999: 17–120.

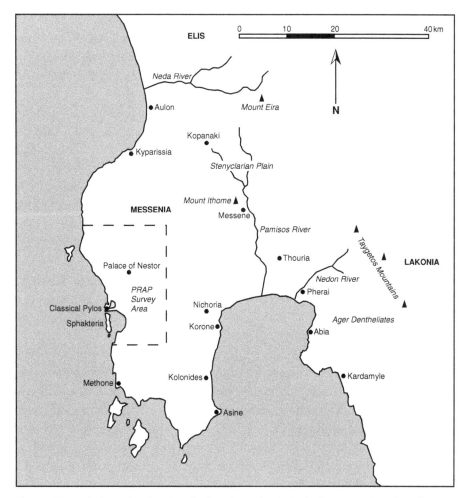

Fig. 4.1 Map of Messenia, showing the location of principal places mentioned in the text. Almost all the territory represented (except for the upper northwestern sector) was explored by the University of Minnesota Messenia Expedition (UMME); the boundaries of the study area of the Pylos Regional Archaeological Project (PRAP) are indicated.

the late Classical and Hellenistic periods, or the mid-fourth to first centuries BC), Messenia reassumed its place within the wider orbit of Greek political developments and alliances, retaining its independence until the Peloponnese passed under the supervision of Rome.

I raised in the previous chapter the question of social memory among dependent communities, although little definite could there be said. Messenia provides another opportunity to broach this subject with a broader, if still far from ideal, range of evidence in hand. As with the Cretan study, the

Messenians also offer the chance to compare commemorative behavior in two very different settings – in the years under Spartan rule and in the years following liberation by the forces of Epaminondas. What was chosen for remembrance, and how was it remembered, in these two connected, but so dissimilar, epochs?

First, however, an even more basic point needs to be established: just what group is here being labeled "the Messenians"? No one answer will please everyone, nor is there any reason why a unitary definition should hold across the entire span of time to be considered here. For the first part of the chapter, I assign this name to the principal population of the area, the helots. The origins and workings of helotage are notoriously opaque, and terming this population "Messenian" implies neither that all helots were necessarily descended from early "free" Messenians, nor that this is necessarily what they always called themselves, nor that they alone lived in Messenia. Other classes of inhabitants, such as perioikoi, also dwelt in the region, but in far fewer numbers and in scattered communities (pp. 152–53). As for the period following liberation, with all its consequent changes, a more diverse body would be entitled to, and would claim, that designation.[3]

We can begin, then, with an emphasis on helot behavior and memorial traditions. Given the marked silence of our textual sources (which has led to quite variant interpretations of the same few scraps of material) the evidence of landscape and of monuments becomes more essential than ever. Even following emancipation and the resulting growth in literary and epigraphic testimonia, we will need this evidence to contextualize an apparent Messenian "commemorative splurge," and to weigh their consumption of a strictly controlled diet of memories.

SPARTAN MESSENIA

As the region passed under Spartan control (usually imagined as a gradual, westward-moving process), the landscape was divided into *kleroi* (allotments) for convenient control of resources and of manpower. Messenian

---

3. "The majority of the Helots were descended from the Messenians who were enslaved of old. Hence all were called Messenians" (Thucydides 1.101.2, trans. Cartledge 1979). Helotage was known in Lakonia too, but Lakonian and Messenian helots should not be conflated into a single unit (although they acted as such on occasion). Despite similarities in many aspects of their lives, differences in the histories of these two groups, in their links to Spartiate society, and in their behavior at certain critical junctures, are equally apparent. On the composition of the Messenian population following liberation, see pp. 164–67.

residents who did not flee into exile were assigned to these allotments, in some cases possibly being attached to their own former holdings. If the precise status of these individuals – somewhere "between free men and slaves" (Pollux 3.83) – remains blurry, their fundamental role does not. The helots of Messenia and Lakonia underpinned the structured militaristic organization of Spartiate life, with their primary function to feed and service their masters in a state of collective servitude. For laborers in the more distant, fertile region of Messenia, food production must have been the principal burden. Little else is clear, but Messenian helots appear to have lived in self-reproducing family units and to have possessed some rudimentary form of property rights, possibly allowing long-term attachment to particular plots of land.[4]

Helot rights, however, seem very limited when compared to the more frequently rehearsed brutalities of their treatment. Helots were marked out by personal stigmatization; they were intimidated by arbitrary beatings or killings, and by an annual declaration of war; they were forced to mourn for Spartan kings, or forced into drunkenness as living examples of non-Spartan behavior. Other instances of normative inversions, terror tactics, and institutionalized contempt could be cited. The relevant sources, however, are not numerous and are usually quite late in date, leaving the frequency or general application of such practices in question; for instance, Lakonian helots were surely more subject to close observation and personal humiliation than the more distant Messenians. For all that, with a decidedly outnumbered ruling group attempting to keep control of a far-flung subject population, harsh tactics seem all too likely and should not be overly minimized. Their cardinal intent – to keep subordinates in their place and to draw distinct social boundaries between Spartans and others – is clear enough, and the inhabitants of Messenia would not have been exempt.[5]

Perhaps not surprisingly, when the Messenian helots do surface in our sources, often they are expressing discontent with their lot. Rebellions did

4. On the organization of helot life: Hodkinson 2000: 113–29, esp. 117–25; see also Cartledge 1979: 160–77, 347–56; 1987: 170–77; Ducat 1978; 1990; Hodkinson 1992; Powell 1988: 248–52; Ste. Croix 1981: 92–93, 149–50; Whitby 1994; cf. Luraghi in press. They may also have possessed a right to asylum, as Lakonian helots did at the sanctuary of Poseidon at Tainaron (although this right is also known to have been violated): Thucydides 1.128.1; Schumacher 1993: 72–74.
5. In addition to the references in n. 4, see Ducat 1974 for a general review: "Aux hilotes est ainsi réservée une sorte de sous-culture ou de contre-culture; d'où leur exclusion, rapportée par Plutarque, de la véritable culture spartiate. Toutes ces pratiques visent à déshumaniser les Hilotes; déshumanisation qui est à la fois la condition et le résultat de mépris." He argues (1974: 1454–55), however, for caution in assuming all these practices to be in use, all the time. On drunkenness and humiliation specifically, see David 1989; Fisher 1989.

Fig. 4.2 View of Mount Ithome, showing the line of the renowned fourth-century city wall of Messene.

occur, although their periodicity and severity remain unknown. The best-attested episode, sometimes referred to as the Third Messenian War, took place *c.* 460 BC. Triggered (in one account) by a pulverizing Lakonian earthquake, the Messenian helots revolted; the insurgents took refuge on Mount Ithome, dwelling there (in one account) for as long as ten years before sueing for truce (Fig. 4.2). Exiles from this revolt were resettled at Naupaktos by the Athenians; descendants would later be played back into their homeland during the Peloponnesian War.[6] Spartan domination would survive this episode by less than a century. When a coalition of Greek forces, led by Theban Epaminondas, marched into Messenia and on Lakonia, a final helot uprising joined the parade.

Stark and lacunose as this brief recital may seem, it represents in essence most of what we know about helots under Spartan rule. Problems with sources will be further discussed below, but their fragmentary and biased nature has led to one ironic consequence: when the Messenians *do* attract attention, they are chiefly considered as part of the story of Sparta and "Of the making

6. For ancient references to the fifth-century rebellion: Thucydides 1.101.2–103.3; Diodorus 11.63–64, Plutarch, *Cimon* 16.4; Pausanias 1.29.8, 4.24.6, 7.25.3, Aelian 6.7. See also Bauslaugh 1990; Oliva 1971: 152–63.

of books on ancient Sparta there is, it seems, no end."[7] One result of this Lakonocentric vantage point (fed by the demographic imbalance of masters and menials and abetted by the judgment of Athenian observers) is the casting of helots as a lurking threat: "most Spartan institutions have always been designed with a view to security against the helots" (Thucydides 4.80.2); the helots "are like an enemy constantly sitting in wait for the disasters of the Spartans" (Aristotle, *Politics* 1269a37–39). Later scholars pick up on this notion of the enemy within, the "helot danger."[8] Such a perspective transmutes the Messenians into an amorphous menace, a stormcloud upon the horizon, a largely undifferentiated mass whose inner workings seem hidden and unknowable.

The tantalizing fact remains that, despite these centuries of Spartan domination, once freed from servitude the region's inhabitants were well able to enumerate and praise their ancestry, their heroes, their mythic history: they apparently possessed a strong vision of just what it was to "be Messenian." How far this was a false, "invented" past has been the usual, rather unhelpful question; instead, the focus in the latter part of the chapter will be on the pressures and opportunities at work in shaping that vision. But first we can try to analyze the storm cloud, to explore the possibility that memorial practices are indeed there to be retrieved.

A sense of regional identity has before been postulated for the Messenians in Archaic and Classical times. Evidence for this recognition of common cause (and the resulting ability to take "effective action in common") comes in bits and pieces, often from late, indirect, or external sources. Plato and Aristotle both issue warnings:

> (Man) is a troublesome piece of goods, as has often been shown by the frequent revolts of the Messenians, and the great mischiefs which happen in states having many slaves who speak the same language . . . Two remedies alone remain to us – not to have the slaves of the same country, nor, if possible, speaking the same language.   (Plato, *Laws* 777B–C)

---

7. Cartledge 1987: vii. A recent electronic library search came up with at least two dozen books written about Sparta or Lakonia in the decade or so since this statement.
8. Translations follow Cartledge (1979: 347, 355), who offers an alternative version of Thucydides 4.80.2: "As far as the Helots are concerned, most Spartan institutions have always been designed with a view to security." In a modern voice, "The Helot danger was the curse Sparta had brought upon herself, an admirable illustration of the maxim that a people which oppresses another cannot itself be free": Ste. Croix 1972: 292. On the demographic imbalance: Herodotus 9.10.1, 9.28.2, 9.29.1; Thucydides 8.40.2; Cartledge 1987: 37–40, fig. 4.2. For a more minimal view of this "danger," Roobaert 1977; Talbert 1989; Whitby 1994: esp. 107–11.

> The very best thing of all would be that the farmers should be slaves, not
> all of the same people and not spirited; for if they have no spirit, they will
> be better suited for their work and there will no danger of their making a
> revolution.   (Aristotle, *Politics* 1330a25–28)

The displeasing stubbornness of helot behavior was especially pointed up by
comparison to displaced, deracinated chattel slaves.[9] As for signals from the
people themselves, religious votives dedicated in the name of "the Messenians" were deposited in both local and panhellenic sanctuaries in the fifth
century (pp. 144–45); those in exile represented themselves as members of
an ongoing corporate body. Finally and most crucially, of course, was the
demonstrated ability to cooperate in rebellion back in Messenia itself.

This does not seem the behavior of an atomized community, and from
such hints and traces, some form of collective identity has been tacitly accepted. Quite when this emerged is unknown, and is likely to stay so, but
there is little cause to argue for any highly developed degree of political unity
and regional autonomy (the formal existence of *hoi Messenioi*) prior to conquest. Indications of these folk actually conceiving of themselves as specifically
"Messenian" dates for the most part to late in the course of their subjugation,
though this may be a function of our available sources. Conquest itself, of
course, no doubt had a great deal to do with defining social and geographic
boundaries, with severe Spartan treatment provoking sharp divisions between
ruler and ruled.[10] Yet even if domination proved an enabling factor in this
process of self-definition, it cannot explain everything about the forms taken
by local identities, the degree to which they were rooted in the past, or their
precise articulation on the ground. That is where the evidence of landscape
and monuments comes into play.

Silences and contentions

While more is known of the helots than of any other servile group in Greek
history, that is hardly saying much. Most disturbing in this context is the total
lack of indigenous narratives; for the years of Spartan control the name of not
a single Messenian helot is preserved, let alone their personal or communal

---

9. For a detailed analysis of this distinction, Cartledge 1985; translations from Cartledge 1979:
   347–48. "Effective action in common": Ste. Croix 1981: 93. Awareness and unease over the
   Messenian plight, and this large-scale subjugation of Greek to Greek, have been detected elsewhere, for example in Euripides' play *Kresphontes*, which revolves around early usurpations of
   power in Messenia: Harder 1985; Treves 1944: 103.
10. On ethnic development, see Hall 1997: esp. 26–33. For Messenia, see Ducat 1990: 181–82;
    Figueira 1999: 224.

Fig. 4.3 A rare visual representation of helots found in *The Cartoon History of the Universe*; the episode depicted is the extermination of helots discussed in Thucydides 4.80.3–4.

histories.[11] Our most detailed and connected account postdates – by no negligible margin – everything here under consideration. Much of the scholarship on Pausanias' Book IV, not unexpectedly, has revolved around issues of *Quellenforschung*, especially his use of the Hellenistic authors Myron of Priene and Rhianos of Bene.[12] The problems of back projection – from a second-century AD author to the fourth century BC, still less to the seventh century BC – are manifest, running the risk of presenting memorial traditions as some kind of static essential. We must resign ourselves to having little direct evidence of precisely what Messenians said, or felt, or thought, at particular points in time.

Nor – until recently – has the archaeology of the region done much to compensate for these difficulties. To be fair, many of the usual sources of evidence are simply lacking. Art historians, for example, are stymied by the absence of definite artistic representations of Messenian helots, executed either by themselves or by others (Fig. 4.3); helot Messenia did not erect civic monuments or create urban spaces.[13] Research on historic-period sites has been

11. Powell 1988: 248. See also Davis 1998b: xxxiv–xxxix.
12. Torelli and Musti 1991a and 1991b. For studies of the attitude of Pausanias to Messenians and their history: Auberger 1992a; 1992b; Elsner 1992: 15–16; Piolot 1999, esp. 207–13. See n. 62 for references on Messenian "pseudo-history."
13. In a search for an illustration of a helot, the first (and only) image found was in Larry Gonick's superb *The Cartoon History of the Universe* (1989).

undertaken, not least ongoing excavations at the major site of Messene, but the bulk of attention has been paid to Messenia's rich Bronze Age heritage. This fairly consistent neglect stems both from a general bias against losers and from the more specific assumption that helots would leave behind little worthwhile to find. Historic Messenia thus has suffered from a double-whammy – the stigma of conquest (like Roman Greece) and an archaeological preference for prehistory (like historic Crete) – that accounts for its relative oblivion.

These silences, in original source material and in subsequent investigations, inevitably distort what can be recovered of Messenian memories in Archaic and Classical times. Nevertheless, certain contentions can be put forward. First, their identity was anchored in memories accommodated within, and facilitated by, communal dwellings and shared cult activities. Second, one particular form of ritual – tomb cult at monuments perceived to be antique – generated and fed a sense of local belonging rooted in the past. And third, the existence of co-existing memory communities can dimly be perceived, encompassing not only different groups within Messenia itself, but also exiles from that homeland. The chapter will then turn to the upheavals that accompanied liberation, and will argue for their deep impact on Messenian social memory – not least in introducing new complexities and in fostering a need for aggressive self-assertion.

Communication in the landscape

If discerning the *content* of Messenian memories, the precise nature of their commemorative narratives, is beyond our ken, better targets become not so much questions of what or who, as questions of where and how. In other words (as in the Cretan case study), the *contexts* for Messenian memory become vital matters, locating the places where legends, jokes, songs, tall tales – whatever means they used to recount themselves – were transmitted and shared.

So where did Messenian helots live? Rural settlement is rarely a subject for ancient commentary, and Messenia, not unexpectedly, proves no exception. Debates over Messenian residential patterns, therefore, have tended to work from probabilities, imagining what would work best in terms of reconciling a limited Spartan presence with a need for consistent Spartan exploitation. The possibility of nucleated or communal settlement, in the interests of more effective surveillance, has been entertained, but the more common surmise was that paranoid Spartiates preferred to keep potential troublemakers scattered about, on their *kleroi*, in a kind of divide-and-conquer strategy.[14] Whichever scenario is chosen, the scant textual evidence leaves it largely an argument *ex silentio*.

The only way to bring something fresh to this debate is through archaeological investigation. As noted, until fairly recently (and with certain notable exceptions), archaeologists by and large allied with ancient historians in neglecting Archaic and Classical Messenia, especially in light of the discovery of the Bronze Age "Palace of Nestor" on the Englianos ridge near Classical Pylos.[15] Yet the discovery of the Palace led to regional survey work (the University of Minnesota Messenia Expedition, or UMME) in the area, conducted from the 1950s through the 1970s. While chiefly focused on "reconstructing a Bronze Age regional environment," the project noted the location and characteristics of historic-period sites as well.[16]

The settlement patterns generated by UMME for the period of Spartan control remain, however, somewhat ambiguous. Uncertainties about ceramic identifications meant that, to a certain extent, Classical and Hellenistic sites could not be distinguished, thus eliding a presumably major historical disjuncture. Considering the pattern discerned just for the Archaic period (700–500 BC), however, points to settlement across the region, with an emphasis on more fertile zones (e.g., the fertile Pamisos valley, the Stenyklarian plain) and with some evidence for the abandonment of old sites and the establishment of new ones – one very crude measure of disruption in the landscape. Few other specific data are available about these settlements. While in some cases site size estimates are provided, these often prove unreliable, lumping together as they do all phases of surface occupation on what were frequently multi-period sites. What can be discerned, however, is a pattern of more extensive Archaic settlements (such as hamlets or villages), rather than of isolated dwellings inhabited by one or two families. In the Classical/Hellenistic period (500–146 BC), when site numbers markedly increase, the same suggestive evidence for larger groupings continues. Similar patterns have been sketched out by

14. E.g. Cartledge 2001: 150; Lukermann and Moody 1978: 95; Powell 1988: 248; for a review of the arguments, see Harrison and Spencer 1998; 159–61. Ancient references, none very explicit, include Thucydides 5.34; Strabo 8.5.4 and Livy 34.27.9. For a parallel, seemingly innocuous but very compelling question, see Garnsey (1998): "Where did Italian peasants live?"

15. Historic exceptions to this pattern include aspects of Valmin's regional investigations (1930; 1938) and the excavations at Messene (Orlandos 1976; Themelis 1993; 1994a; 1994b; 1998). See Spencer 1998 for a general review of the region's archaeological history.

16. On the degree of attention paid to post-prehistoric material, see McDonald and Rapp 1972: 123, 143. For the data and their interpretation, McDonald and Hope Simpson 1972: 130–46 and McDonald and Rapp 1972, 310–21 ("Register B"). See also McDonald 1984.

a more localized investigation (the Five Rivers Survey) in the hinterland of Nichoria.[17]

This pattern renders Messenia somewhat anomalous when compared to other surveyed areas of Greece. Almost all other projects, for this equivalent span of time, reported more of a hierarchy of site sizes, ranging from villages to small rural sites (and normally with more of the latter than the former).[18] Yet it is difficult to know how much faith to place in the UMME findings, given the project's self-admitted prehistoric focus and non-intensive survey methodology. A desire to test these results was one motivating factor for the Pylos Regional Archaeological Project (PRAP), which in the 1990s worked in the southwestern sector of Messenia, in the vicinity of the Palace of Nestor (Fig. 4.1). Given that PRAP's investigation was both more intensive and more overtly diachronic than that of UMME, it was predicted that if smaller Archaic and Classical sites – the putative dispersed homesteads of helots – had indeed dotted the Messenian landscape, this project would be in a stronger position to detect them. This enterprise, however, only confirmed Messenia in its unusual settlement history. Almost no small isolated sites can be assigned to the period in question; instead, what population there was in the PRAP study area appears to have gathered in larger, village-like groupings.[19]

That study area lay at the far western reaches of Spartan-controlled territory; regions closer to the Lakonian border (or with more fertile land, such as the Pamisos valley) may have been differentially controlled and inhabited. One other indication of more "concentrated" settlement does now exist, however, from the village of Kopanaki in the northern Soulima valley. There a domestic structure was found, so large (some 30m × 17m) and sturdy that it was originally thought to be a Late Roman villa. Pottery finds, however, proceeded to date the building from the sixth to the second quarter of the fifth century BC, when it was violently destroyed. The excavator, Nikolaos Kaltsas, came to propose the site as the substantial center of a large Spartan landholding, with helots living in attendance and under a landlord's eye; the destruction is aligned with the helot rebellion of the 460s.[20] Obviously these two forms of consolidated settlement are hardly identical: the sites found in

---

17. On all these patterns, McDonald and Hope Simpson 1972: 144–46; Lukermann and Moody 1978: 95–97, 104.
18. See, for example, Alcock *et al.* 1994: 157–65; Jameson *et al.* 1994: 248–57, 383–94; Snodgrass 1990.
19. Alcock *et al.*, in prep.; Davis *et al.* 1997: 456–57; Harrison and Spencer 1998. Especially notable is PRAP I04 Romanou *Romanou.*
20. Kaltsas 1985; see also Harrison and Spencer 1998: 161–62. Luraghi (in press) has suggested a correlation between this site and the *phrourion* at Filaki, excavated by Valmin (1941), which would affect its interpretation.

the Pylos area appear to represent agglomerated settlement, unlike Kopanaki's plantation-like structure. Yet what has still to emerge – from either excavation or survey – is any evidence for dispersed helot farmsteads. Our few archaeological indicators instead combine to point, if in different ways, toward a preference for concentration in settlement.

This may seem a long way to travel to make a simple point, but the ramifications for social memory are significant. Community dwelling not only helps to explain pragmatic things (such as how helots could plan rebellion), but provides the day-to-day context for other forms of communication as well. In his study of displaced African slave populations in Brazil, Roger Bastide noted a more successful survival rate for "home memories" in the cities than in the countryside:

> It is the structure of the group rather than the group itself that provides the frameworks of collective memory; otherwise it would be impossible to understand why individual memory needs the support of the community as a whole. If we need someone else in order to remember, it is because memories are articulated together with the memories of others in the well-ordered interplay of reciprocal images.[21]

For the masters, dictating, or at least permitting, such communal dwelling would prove a double-edged sword. Nucleation abetted external watchfulness; it also, as shall be seen (pp. 153–54), allowed the creation of local Messenian support networks – a not unimportant consideration for Spartans requiring a more-or-less constant flow of labor and produce. On the other hand, such dwelling together also affirmed emotional ties of kinship and of common concern which could, potentially, ignite into violent resistance.

At what other points in the landscape might Messenians meet? Sanctuaries apparently offered, as for contemporary free Greeks, an outlet for sociability, display, and communication, although little is known of helot religion.[22] Certain cults in the region hint at continuing activity – through textual references, excavated dedications, or surface remains – during the period of Spartan domination, including Zeus at Ithome, Apollo Korynthos on the Messenian Gulf, the mysteries at Andania in the Stenyklarian plain, and the recently discovered Sanctuary Ω-Ω at Messene, where Petros Themelis proposes a small heroic cult to the legendary pre-Dorian king, Leucippus and his family.[23] Worship of the river god Pamisos in the Kalamata plain is also

---

21. Bastide 1978: 247.   22. Parker 1989: esp. 145.
23. Ithome: Thucydides 1.103.2; McDonald and Rapp 1972: 314–15, no. 529; *Praktika* 1987: 87–90. See Cartledge 1979: 193; Lazenby and Hope Simpson 1972: 89; and Roebuck 1941: 34 for other references. Apollo Korynthos: Versakis 1916 for the original excavation; also Bauslaugh

Fig. 4.4 Inscription of "the Methanioi" ("the Messenians") on a bronze spear butt from the sanctuary of Apollo Korynthos.

attested, but the sanctuary's position suggests it may have belonged in perioi-kic territory, as more surely did the sanctuary of Poseidon at Akovitika, with its Pohoidaia festival managed by the perioikoi of Thouria.[24]

Of these shrines, two in particular – Zeus Ithomatas on Mount Ithome and Apollo Korynthos at Longà on the Messenian Gulf – have been suggested as appealing to a pan-Messenian clientele, at least in classical times. Ithome, of course, served as the Messenian refuge site in the major rebellion of the 460s BC (exiles departed under the protection of Zeus Ithomatas), and was chosen as the site for the post-liberation center of Messene, with Zeus continuing as patron deity (Fig. 4.2). Pausanias recounts how (in his own day) the dis-covery of a statue of Zeus Ithomatas in the nearby town of Lakonian Leuctra immediately emboldened claims that "Leuctra belonged to Messenia of old" (3.26.6) – a late testimonial to the deity as unifying figure. The evidence from Apollo Korynthos takes the form of a dedication (an inscribed spear butt) from "the Messenians" commemorating a victory over the Athenians (Fig. 4.4). This probably is again to be connected with the mid-fifth-century

1990; Jeffery 1990: 203–4, 206, nos. 3, 7, 10, 11; McDonald and Rapp 1972: 312–13, no. 504; Valmin 1930: 173–75. Andania: Breuillot 1985: 799–802; Jeffery 1990: 206, no. 6; McDonald and Rapp 1972: 316–17, no. 607; Piolot 1999; Roebuck 1941: 7–10, 35–36; Valmin 1930: 92–98. On excavations at Sanctuary Ω-Ω: see Luraghi 2002; Themelis 1998; together with recent reports in *Archaeological Reports* and by Themelis in *Praktika*.
24. For the Pamisos excavations: Valmin 1938: 419–65, esp. 424–25; see also Baladié 1980: 47; Breuillot 1985: 795–99; Jeffery 1990: 206, no. 1, 448; McDonald and Rapp 1972: 314–15, no. 530; Roebuck 1941:17, 36–37. Akovitika: Jeffery 1990: 448; Themelis 1969; 1970. For recent discussion, see Luraghi 2002.

revolt; the Archaic and Classical shrine in general is thought to display a certain "warlike" aspect. Such places of shared veneration are reminiscent of the "gathering" role played for scattered groups by Hambledon Hill, although for some helots it may have been more a matter of knowing of, than actually traveling to, these places. Like dwelling together, however, the existence of such communally conceived and occasionally visited places combats the disbelief of some: "that many helots, of all people, could be inspired by loyalty to a region as amorphous as Messenia, rather than just to their own local centre or neighborhood."[25]

Other, smaller and less distinguished cult places have been identified through explorations at Nichoria, with one possible shrine at the site itself and two others (one Archaic, one Classical) noted through survey work in the region. The Pylos Regional Archaeological Project offers, provisionally, one additional shrine, with Geometric-Archaic and Classical fine wares discovered around a deep natural sinkhole.[26] Only very detailed surface reconnaissance can discover such sites, suggesting that still others may dot the remainder of the Messenian landscape. While these all appear to have been more small-scale rural shrines with a more localized clientele, they too offered places at which people could assemble.

We know little, archaeologically or epigraphically, from any of these sanctuaries, and the debate about their nature is ongoing. If the helots of Messenia, despite external domination, continued to participate in traditional religious practices, it is less certain whether they were in control of these shrines, or acted alone at them. Robert Parker has noted that Spartans used, and may even have supervised, sanctuaries in perioikic territory, and that may be a possibility here as well; certainly some finds (for example, votives and figurines from Apollo Korynthos or Sanctuary Ω-Ω) have strong Lakonian parallels. Perioikoi too may have been involved in these cults.[27] Clarity is impossible with our available evidence, but two observations can safely be made. First, the

25. Talbert 1989: 28. In general, Talbert characterizes helots as "relatively ignorant, simple people, almost without education or awareness of the outside world" and as knowing the place of "the lower orders in many societies throughout human history" (1989: 30). On dedications from "the Messenians," see Bauslaugh 1990; Ducat 1990: 142–43.

26. Nichoria and environs: Coulson and Wilkie 1983: 332, 337; Lukermann and Moody 1978: 110–12, no. 100 (Nichoria), no. 517 (Panayitsa, Archaic), no. 50 (Ayios Nikolaos, Classical/Hellenistic). PRAP shrine (?): PRAP M02 Gargaliani *Kalantina* (2); Davis 1998a: 277–78; http://classics.lsa.umich.edu/PRAP.html. On the difficulties of identifying shrines through survey evidence: Alcock 1994b.

27. Parker 1989: 165, n. 15. Luraghi (2002) certainly declares Apollo Korynthos to have "as strong a Spartan flavor as that of any sanctuary in Laconia itself," based on the Lakonian style of votives, inscriptions, and a column capital (much like one from Amyklai). In general, he would place control of these cult places in perioikic hands.

size and position of some of the shrines, notably the survey-derived examples, make such outside interest unlikely. And second, participation by non-helots does not render the cults solely "Spartan" or "perioikic" in nature, nor does it necessarily erase their meaning and influence for the subject population. Sanctuaries, whether solely operated by and for helots or not, thus provided another arena in which Messenians congregated, an alternative place for the communication and transmission of tradition.[28]

Tombs and tomb cult

Messenia, as a quick glance at any basic Aegean prehistory text would affirm, is rich in Bronze Age graves, especially tholos and chamber tombs dating to the Late Helladic period. Their archaeological exploration dates back as far as Heinrich Schliemann himself but, not surprisingly, such investigations tend to focus on tomb construction and initial Mycenaean use. Also periodically noted however, if only in passing, was the presence of later material such as fine and coarse-ware ceramics, tiles, coins, or specifically votive objects – in some cases found with traces of pyres and ash or with animal bones. This has been taken to demonstrate Messenian participation in tomb cult, loosely defined here as ritual activity based at a monument perceived to be ancient and intended to link contemporary society with a form of power located in the past.[29] Tomb cult, I would argue, offered an additional means for creating and cementing a sense of belonging through acts of commemoration.

   Measuring the distribution of such activity in time and space is nowhere easy. Interpretation of the later material found – unless it is demonstrably votive or in clear association with animal sacrifices – is beset with difficulties, as the "archaeology of cult" (in Cretan caves, for example) so often is. In some cases such finds have been dismissed as accidental intrusions, and the tomb sites written off as garbage dumps, shelters, or animal pens. Ambiguous as much of the evidence may be, it seems unwarranted to dismiss all cases in this fashion. Tomb cult, after all, is by no means a Messenian preserve, but has been reported in numerous parts of the Greek world. But Messenia stands out as a particularly popular venue, matched in the Geometric period only by the Argolid and Attica, and it is downright preeminent in late Classical

---

28. Solidarity through religion in American slave societies has been the subject for much study. "The rise of a religious community among the slaves, with that looseness of organization inevitable in a slaveholding society . . . ordered the life of the collective": Genovese 1974: 659; see also Bastide 1978.
29. For recent general studies of tomb cult: Antonaccio 1995; Coldstream 1976; Korres 1981/82; Morris 1988; Whitley 1988. For this particular, deliberately flexible and open-ended definition of tomb cult, see Alcock 1991: 448, n. 3.

and Hellenistic times (with some 40 percent of presently catalogued examples). Moreover, tomb cult elsewhere appears largely confined to those
two main bursts of activity, rendering the Messenian pattern again somewhat anomalous. While that bi-modal (Geometric/Hellenistic) distribution
is strongly marked, there are also signs that such practices endured – if neither
continuously nor in the same places – throughout the intervening era.[30]

Geometric activity in the region, for example within the chamber tomb
cemetery at Volimidia, would have dated either before or around the pre-
sumed time of Spartan annexation; following liberation, tomb cult would
flourish as never before. As for what happens in between, adopting a generous
attitude toward the evidence identifies some fifteen tombs displaying activity
during Archaic or Classical times. Of these, nine contained finds specifically
termed Archaic by the excavator or later examiners; eight held objects similarly determined as Classical (Fig. 4.5).[31] These classifications, unfortunately,
are rarely well supported by illustration or detailed publication.

Nor can their deposition through specifically ritual acts always be confirmed, though some cases are clearly stronger than others. At Koukounara,
for example, Korres (a notable skeptic about cult activity) accepts it for the
late eighth century on the basis of an Orientalizing pyxis in Tomb 4; this tomb
also contained later pottery, quantities of animal bones, and the remains of a
pyre. An Archaic olpe and kyathiskos was found in Volimidia, Angelopoulos
10 – a tomb that also held burned animal bones, some deliberately placed on
tiles. Cult at Tourliditsa has been argued on the basis of large animal bones

30. Activity at certain tombs continues into the Roman period, in Messenia and elsewhere. For more
    detail on chronological patterns, see the citations in the previous note and Alcock 1991: 452,
    figs. 2–3. See also Spencer 1995.
31. Two tombs demonstrate signs of both Archaic and Classical activity. *Archaic:* (1) Kaminion
    Kremmidia; (2) Karpophora (Akones); (3) Koukounara Tomb 4; (4) Koukounara Tomb 1; (5)
    Papoulia: Ay. Ioannis; (6) Tourliditsa; (7) "The Tholos at Vasiliko"; (8) Volimidia, Angelopoulos
    10; (9) Volimidia, Angelopoulos 11. Included here are tombs with material that would date to
    the very end of the eighth century (e.g., the Orientalizing pyxis from Koukounara Tomb 4) and
    thus possibly belong to the years immediately following the Spartan annexation. *Classical:* (1)
    Kaminion Kremmidia; (2) "The Tholos at Kopanaki"; (3) Nichoria, Tholos F; (4) Tourliditsa;
    (5) Vathirema; (6) Psari; (7) Peristeria; (8) Osmanaga. Historic material from the tombs at
    Peristeria and Osmanaga has been placed in the "Hellenic" or Classical range, although a later,
    post-classical date has also been suggested and on balance may be more likely. For bibliography
    on all these tombs, see Alcock 1991: 456, 460–62, 465–66, modified and augmented by recent
    reports in *ArchDelt, AR* and Antonaccio 1995: 70–102, whose site nomenclature is adopted. Not in
    this list is Ellenika (at the site of ancient Thouria) where pottery of Mycenaean, Protogeometric,
    and Hellenistic date, Lakonian-type tiles, and animal bones were discovered in a tholos context.
    The Protogeometric material (usually dated to the eleventh and tenth centuries BC) puts this
    earlier than the time-span (and other examples) discussed here. Thouria, of course, became a
    perioikic settlement, and one said to have joined the helots in fifth-century rebellion. On this
    evidence: *ArchDelt* 47 (1992 [1997]) Chr. 121–22.

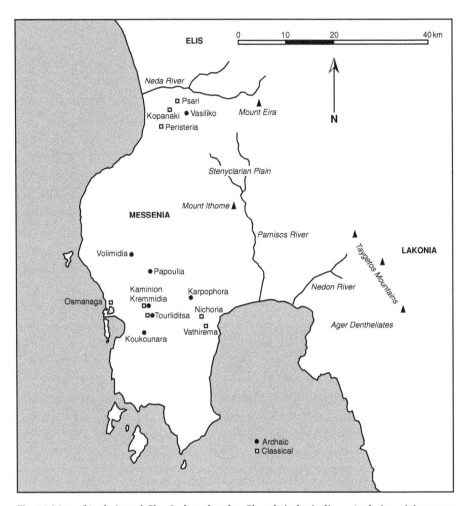

Fig. 4.5 Map of Archaic and Classical tomb cults. Closed circles indicate Archaic activity; open squares, Classical activity. Koukounara and Volimidia each possess more than one relevant tomb.

found in conjunction with ceramic material, including Archaic, Classical, and Hellenistic finds. The excavator of the "Tholos at Kopanaki," M. N. Valmin, thought the grave "a kind of temple rather than a tomb" and the site of a continuous hero cult signaled by "Hellenic and Hellenistic sherds."[32]

32. Koukounara 4: Coulson and Wilkie 1983: 333; Korres 1981/82: 381–92; with other references in Alcock 1991: 465, no. 26 and Antonaccio 1995: 75–77. Volimidia, Angelopoulos 10: Korres 1981/82: 415; with other references in Alcock 1991: 466, no. 31 and Antonaccio 1995: 97. Tourliditsa: Hope Simpson and Dickinson 1979: 137 (D29), with other references in Alcock 1991: 461, no. 5 and Antonaccio 1995: 74. "The Tholos at Kopanaki": Valmin 1927–28: 201–9, 216–24; Alcock 1991: 465, no. 23; Antonaccio 1995: 85–87, although the definite fifth-century material mentioned is associated by Valmin with a later burial.

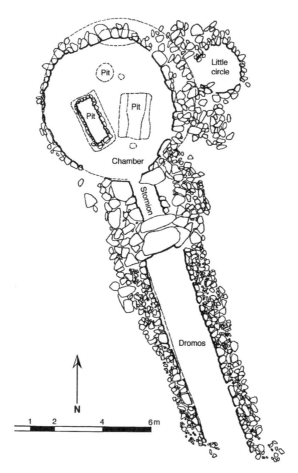

Fig. 4.6 Plan of Tholos F at Nichoria. A black ash and charcoal stratum (containing significant quantities of animal bone, especially pig) covered the north end of the stomion and most of the chamber floor, suggesting repeated fires were lit near the center of the tomb.

Two fairly well-grounded Classical cases have been recognized in the Five Rivers area of Messenia. Vathirema (though published versions of its sequence of use are confused) possessed "a good group of black-glazed Classical pottery," and cult there has been accepted by various of the site's interpreters. Most unambiguous is Tholos F at Nichoria; not coincidentally, this is the best excavated and published (under the subtitle "the hero cult in the tholos") of the tomb sites (Fig. 4.6).[33] The tholos yielded cooking and dining ceramics (including skyphoi, mugs, lekythoi, and coarse wares) dating to the

33. Vathirema: Coulson and Wilkie 1983: 333; see also Alcock 1991: 461, no. 6; Antonaccio 1995: 89–90. Nichoria: Coulson and Wilkie 1983: 332–39; see also Alcock 1991: 460–61, no. 3. Antonaccio (1995: 92–94) prefers to interpret the Nichoria tomb as a shelter.

last quarter of the fifth century and the first quarter of the fourth century BC – in other words, the generations immediately prior to liberation.

Where does this review leave us? During the years of Spartan domination, there appears interest in, and likely veneration at, ancient tombs in the landscape – if at a low and discontinuous level. Selection of perceptibly ancient monuments as a focus for ritual performance speaks at very least to cultivation of links to the past. More specifically, such acts have been taken to show reverence for ancestors or local heroes: in either case figures closely linked to a territory and its history. Beyond that, we cannot be more precise about the identity of cult recipients, as is the case in most instances of the phenomenon elsewhere. In Messenia, the only possible exception is the "tomb of Thrasymedes" (the son of King Nestor), described by Pausanias as lying "a little way" from Pylos (4.36.2). This tomb has been fairly convincingly associated with the Middle and Late Helladic tumulus and tholos tomb complex at Voidokoilia on the headland opposite Classical Pylos (Fig. 4.7). Cult activity at Voidokoilia – clearly marked through the deposition of animal sacrifices, figurines, vessels, votive plaques, and the construction of a small cult structure near the tomb – only began, however, in post-liberation times.

Even lacking specific names and genealogies, tomb cult furnished a local source of authority for communities under duress, a condition met by Messenia in these centuries. A comparative glance at other oppressed communities makes clear that what tends to be remembered – indeed exaggerated in remembrance – are the "good old days" before troubles came; similarities with aspects of the Achaian case study come readily to mind.[34] The attractions of tomb cult, with its emphasis on direct access to a better past from an uncertain present, are thus patent. One closely related, more aggressive reading is also possible. In their publication of the Nichoria tholos, W. D. E. Coulson and Nancy Wilkie suggested that perhaps "such practices became symbolic of the Messenian 'resistance movement.' The cult of Messenian heroes would be an effective way of perpetuating local traditions in the face of occupation by the hated Spartans."[35] This proposition may be reinforced by the fact that tomb cult is not a very visible practice in Lakonia, at least on present evidence.[36]

34. "Perhaps the most familiar theme of social history is that people have resisted rapid, alien and imposed change by creating memories of a past that was unchanging, incorruptible, and harmonious. They mobilize those memories to resist change": Thelen 1989: 1125; see also Scott 1985: 178–79.
35. "During this period of Spartan occupation local traditions were evidently kept alive through hero worship which took place in tombs of earlier date": Coulson and Wilkie 1983: 338.
36. Antonaccio is cautious on this matter, however, and does note that the instances known, interestingly, are placed in other "stress" zones, such as perioikic territory: 1994: 98; 1995: 142.

Fig. 4.7 View down over the acropolis of Classical Pylos, looking into the survey territory of the Pylos Regional Archaeological Project. In the bare patch on the headland opposite (in the middle ground) lay the Hellenistic tomb cult of Voidokoilia (possibly the "Tomb of Thrasymedes").

Other episodes of Greek tomb cult make the convincing case that co-existing or competing agendas inhabited these ritual spaces, with impulses toward unifying corporate worship set side-by-side with claims derived from more limited familial or class interests. In the social world of helots, such internal status distinctions may have been less apparent, but they did (as shall be seen) exist. Nichoria's evidence for feasting and food storage (possibly observed, if less clearly, in other tomb assemblages as well) suggests that cult administration included the control of commensality, thereby offering one pathway to local authority. Eating and drinking, with all the sensations and thoughts stimulated, has long been perceived as wielding great mnemonic power, as Proust's madeleine famously demonstrated.[37] Tomb cult thus emerges as a vital context both for the ongoing organization of Messenian society, and for the stimulation of its memories.

DIFFERENT POPULATIONS, DIFFERENT REMEMBRANCES

Settlements, sanctuaries, and ancient tombs combine to argue that the Messenians under Spartan rule possessed means and opportunities to com-municate and celebrate memorial traditions among themselves and to trans-mit them onwards. This necessary focus on a relatively limited set of places could easily allow us to slide into imagining these people as a homogeneous and egalitarian collective, all acting and reacting in the same fashion over time. It would be a sad mistake, however, to move from one monolithic view of the Messenians (that shadowy threat on the horizon) to another (that of a united party in opposition). Assuming an uncomplicated "one for all, and all for one" mentality is at best fanciful; at worst, it creates an insidious Messenian equivalent to the Spartan mirage.[38] Instead, we should search for the possible presence of multiple, alternative memory communities, both within Messenia and among the Messenians.

A distinction here is drawn between "in Messenia" and "among the Messe-nians." Other peoples were resident in Messenia under Spartan control, most importantly the perioikic communities. Perioikoi appear to have formed a discrete entity within the body of *Lakedaimonioi*, being separate from and not equal to (but not necessarily oppressed by) the Spartiates proper. The major-ity lived in Lakonia; one recent review identified at most only five securely attested perioikic poleis in Messenia: Aithaia, Asine, Aulon, Thouria, and Kardamyle (Fig. 4.1). Only Thouria definitely lay inland, in the rich Makaria plain; the other known sites are coastal in orientation, thus effectively forming

37. Hamilakis 1998: esp. 117, 126; see also Eves 1996. Such feasting would be an example of a more "incorporated" memorial practice. On rival claims expressed through tomb cult, see especially Morris 1988; Bérard 1982. Pottery finds with parallels from Olympia or Lakonia indicate that individuals involved had contacts with the world beyond Messenia: Antonaccio 1994: 98; Coulson and Wilkie 1983: 338. This need not necessarily mean, however, that parties other than helots were involved in these ritual practices. Stephen Hodkinson is currently preparing a systematic study of tomb cult in Archaic and Classical Messenia and its socio-political implications.
38. Spartan mirage: Ollier 1973; cf. Whitby 1994 on "the choice between shadows." There are whiffs of this glorification in Treves (1944: 104), an Italian Jew in exile in England at the time, who speaks of "an unshakeable national solidarity, and the determined fidelity to a glorious and revered tradition that, in favorable political circumstances, caused the refounding of Messenia," and in Shero (1938: 500), "generations of serfdom had not robbed them of their national consciousness and martial spirit."

"a barrier between the helot population and the sea." Perioikoi from Thouria and Aithaia are said to have joined in the mid-fifth-century revolt based at Ithome, but for the most part these groups are assumed hostile to the helot population and – until late days – aligned with Spartan interests.[39]

To complicate the picture further, at least two communities, Asine (modern Korone) and Methone, were the result of supposed Spartan resettlement of refugees from the Argolid. Asine, at least in the fourth century, also held a Spartan garrison. These towns maintained, or subsequently cultivated, memories of their alien origins; Pausanias makes clear, for example, that the Asinaeans made much of their Dryopian identity: "it gives the Asinaeans the greatest pleasure to be called Dryopians, and it is plain that they have founded their holiest sanctuaries in memory of their old sanctuaries on Parnassos" (4.34.11). Finally, we are told of a Spartan colony at Pherai. Little is known about any of these communities, perioikic or other; and while we can accept that they were the possessors of communal experiences and histories (on occasion overlapping with, on occasion diverging from, those of the helots), these will not here be pursued.[40]

Variability can be sought, however, across the body of those we are terming "Messenians." Diversity both of status and of attitudes toward the Spartans arguably does exist, diversities potentially shaped and reflected in different accounts of the past. Beginning with social status, Stephen Hodkinson has made the case for a degree of internal economic stratification emerging from a combination of factors: "differential reproduction and mortality and diverse conditions of cultivation led to the development of inequalities among the helots in their access to land." The term *monomoïtos* (glossed as "leader of the helots" by the fifth- or sixth-century AD lexicographer Hesychios) perhaps represents such individuals. Thinking through the logistics of exploitation, Hodkinson also proposed a system of sharecropping as the most "effective

39. On perioikoi: Hall 2000; Mertens 1999; Shipley 1997; see also Cartledge 1979: 178–93; Kiechle 1959: 68–71; Roebuck 1941: 28–31; Shipley 1992. Luraghi interprets this evidence quite differently, arguing that perioikic settlements occupied "a significant portion of the region," and that they "should be assigned the leading role in Messenian ethnogenesis in the fifth century"; he finds it remarkable that they are usually omitted from discussions of Messenian identity – as I fear they are here (2002). For the perioikic revolt: Thucydides 1.101.2; Shipley 1997: 194–95, quote at 195. The location of Aithaia is unsure, but it probably lay in the southeastern part of Messenia. Shipley (1997: 212) suggests these perioikic settlements would probably not have become well-developed urban entities until the late Classical or Hellenistic periods.
40. On the garrison at Asine and the colony at Pherai: Xenophon, *Hellenica* 7.1.25; Lazenby and Hope Simpson 1972: 84, 86; Roebuck 1941: 30. On "short-distance colonization" and resettlement: Hall 1995a: 581–84; 1997: 74–75, 77; Malkin 1994: 83–89. Referring to the communities of Asine and Methone, Cartledge points to Wade-Gery's marginal note on "the Ulster of the Messenian Ireland": Cartledge 1979: 119.

means of sustaining the long-term economic relationship between Spartiates and helots"; such a system balanced agricultural needs against environmental constraints, and a "political" against a "moral" economy. Sharecropping, Hodkinson argues, ensured that no one starved. Such a system would, however, require "middle men" to help facilitate the flow of goods between ruler and ruled; such bailiffs could well have been the more prosperous (if such a word can cautiously be used!) among the helots.[41]

It is not a bad idea, at this point, to recall the geographical separation of Spartiate possessors and helot workers. Sparta itself, domicile for most Spartiates, lay about 45 kilometers from Messene, about 70 kilometers from coastal Pylos – with the looming presence of Taygetos in between. Even more marked was the social gulf dividing the two. In times of trouble (such as widespread crop failure), Messenian helots could not easily or comfortably turn for Spartan assistance. Sharecropping might avert some disasters, but more was necessary: "If in times of subsistence crisis Messenian helots were thrown upon their own resources, and local self-help and intra-community patronage were their main source of protection, local community organization is likely to have been highly developed."[42] The better-off of the helots, again, would be the natural organizers and patrons of their communities.

While these "leaders of the helots" are not yet directly visible in our archaeological data, such men no doubt became closely associated with the administration of sanctuaries and tomb cult, as well as the day-to-day running of community life – all the contexts argued for the articulation of social memories. Their co-optation was surely neither fortuitous nor innocent; the helots could have been drawn into what James Scott calls the "ultimate dream of domination": "Certain combinations of atomization, terror, repression, and pressing material needs can indeed achieve the ultimate dream of domination: to have the dominated exploit each other."[43] Yet atomization does not seem to have been achieved here, and this helot "elite" must have been pulled in different directions: if they cooperated with Spartans in some circumstances, not least to protect their own positions, they also participated in

41. Hodkinson 2000: 125–31, quotations at 125, 131. Opportunties for contact with individual Spartiates might have brought additional authority or reward; this is certainly seen in the case of Lakonian helots. The Neodamodeis, for example, were manumitted ex-helots who, in return for military service, had been rewarded with higher status. This differentiation may well have become more pronounced in the later years of Spartan domination, e.g. the fifth and fourth centuries BC: Thucydides 7.19.3; 7.58.3; Cartledge 1987: 174–76; Ducat 1978: 36–37; 1990: 159–66; Oliva 1971: 163–79.
42. Hodkinson n.d.; 1992. I thank Steve Hodkinson for letting me cite his unpublished work.
43. Scott 1985: 302.

Messenian forms of ritual commemoration, and – in some cases – may have engineered rebellion as well.

This ambivalence can perhaps be scented in one other context. The bluntest expression of helot feelings toward the Spartans is that they wanted to "eat them – even raw" (Xenophon, *Hellenica* 3.3.6). Predictable though such heartfelt hatred might be, it is not always reflected in actual descriptions of helot behavior. In Thucydides' detailed account of the conflict at Sphakteria and Pylos (425 BC) – a vanishingly rare peep into local reactions to the Spartan presence – some contrarieties do surface. On the one hand, we are told that the Spartiates trapped on Sphakteria were temporarily sustained by food smuggled by helots who sailed or swam over to them. Admittedly, Thucydides says they were promised freedom and sums of money, but that is not the same as grim compulsion. At the same time, Messenian exiles numbered among the Athenian-led force at Pylos, and helots "deserted" to that base after the unexpected victory. Divergences of behavior demonstrated in this unique vignette point to different ways of calculating and offering allegiance within the body of "the Messenians."[44]

These divergences could merely be assigned to differences in social status, with the "leaders of the helots" remaining more loyal to their masters, or they could simply be taken as proof that the Spartan combination of "terror, indoctrination and incentive bonuses" worked better on some individuals than on others.[45] Yet other factors, including variant family or local histories, may lie behind such choices. These whispers of differences, as well as decrying the existence of any monolithic Messenian community, thus also hint at the existence of diverse versions of the past, imperceptible to us in any other way.

The shadow of Sparta

One profoundly alternative memory community, of course, would be that of the overlords themselves. Spartiates periodically crossed into Messenia, not least to terrorize the enemy within, but little evidence attests to their substantial or continual presence. None the less, the Spartans possessed their own memories of this same landscape, remembrances categorically unlike those held by the Messenians. After the liberation, Sparta resisted public acknowledgment of territorial losses, refusing to accept the existence of Messene and plotting various ways to retrieve "ancestral" territories. These sentiments

---

44. Thucydides 4.9.1; 4.26.5–9; 4.32.2; 4.41.2–3. See also Xenophon, *Hellenica* 1.2.18; Diodorus 13.64.5.
45. Cartledge 1987: 407. For similar sentiments, see Ducat 1978: 30, n. 86; Powell 1988: 98. For a commentary on the actions at Pylos in 425 BC: Wilson 1979.

are forcefully expressed by the speaker in Isocrates' *Archidamus* (c. 366 BC), purportedly giving the Spartan position in a debate about recognizing an independent Messene:

> Were they restoring those who are in truth Messenians, they would still be performing an unjust act, but at least they would have a more sensible reason for wronging us. As the case stands, however, it is the Helots whom they are trying to settle right beside us, so that the most bitter fate which threatens us is not that we shall be deprived of our land contrary to justice, but that we shall behold our slaves made lords of it. You will assuredly perceive from what follows both that we are now harshly dealt with and that in the past we held Messene justly.   (Isocrates, *Oration* 6.27–28)

Bitter enough to lose land rightfully and traditionally theirs, even worse to lose it to former (and illegitimately freed) slaves. Isocrates, as an Athenian, may have ultimately been more concerned with Theban power than with Spartan anger, but there seems little reason to doubt such emotions and opinions existed. Discrepancies in memory (and in the claims to which memory gave rise) between these two populations were long-lived, as shall be seen later in the chapter.

The probable part played by harsh Spartan treatment in generating a sense of Messenian identity has already been touched upon. In other senses, however, the Spartan role in shaping Messenian memorial traditions seems oddly ineffectual, at least when compared with the strategies of other expansionist states. The Spartans – who shared important gods and heroes with the Messenians – did not, for example, despoil or uproot sacred sites, one proven tactic for undercutting social cohesion and regional loyalties (pp. 46–47). Controlling Messenia for centuries, they seem to have inscribed few deliberate signs of that control upon it: no equivalent to triumphal arches, no aggressive boundary markers, no emphatic monuments upon Ithome. Such reticence conforms to the accepted image of laconic display; the expanse of territory involved and the relative scarcity of Spartiates no doubt also played their part.[46] As one result of this relative Spartan invisibility, the land "lost" by the Messenians was in some ways not radically transformed; its memory was still securely rooted in the visible world.

If the landscape and monuments of Messenia escaped direct prescriptive action by the Spartans, obviously its people did not. Out of the many

---

46. Although former assumptions of a total "lack" of Spartan art are increasingly untenable: Förtsch 1998; Stibbe 1996.

forms of Spartan intimidation and violence, one struck particularly at the transmission of Messenian memories. One of the punitive tactics reported of Spartiates was the arbitrary extermination of helots, be it through the *krypteia* (a rite of passage involving their assassination) or through the destruction of those who appeared overly "sturdy."[47] As already noted, the frequency of such acts has been debated, but there seems no reason to doubt the removal of individuals perceived to pose a threat. Thucydides recounts the best-known episode of such extermination when he describes a period of Spartan vulnerability during the Peloponnesian War – in fact after the successful Athenian action at Pylos in 425 BC:

> Athens at the time posed an immanent threat to the Peloponnesus and especially to the very land of the Lakedaimonians. The latter nevertheless had a hope: to deter the Athenians by sending an expeditionary force to one of their allies, which would trouble them [the Athenians] in turn. The allies were prepared to receive it and to defect as soon as it appeared. At the same time the Lacedemonians were looking for a pretext for expediting Helots to a foreign theatre lest they take advantage of the presence of the Athenians at Pylos to foment revolution. Fearing their youthful ardor and their number (for the Lacedemonians, the central issue in their relations with the Helots had always been to keep them under surveillance), they had, on a previous occasion, already resorted to the following measures. They had let it be known that all those [among the Helots] who felt that through their conduct in the face of the enemy they were so deserving should have their credentials for emancipation inspected. It was, from their perspective, a test: those who demonstrated sufficient pride to believe they should be first to be freed were thus the prime candidates for a future rebellion. About two thousand of them were selected; adorned with a crown, they ran the circuit of sanctuaries as free men. Shortly thereafter, they were made to disappear, and no one knew in what manner each of them had been eliminated.   (Thucydides 4.80.3–4)[48]

The impact of such losses on social memory could take many forms, not least making martyrs of these men. Killings like these also eliminated individuals who, thanks to their own strength or capability, may well have been among the more engaged actors in Messenian society. To return to Bastide's

47. *Krypteia*: see references in n. 4, together with Vidal-Naquet 1986: 112–14, 147–52. On the dangers of becoming "sturdy": Athenaeus, *Deipnosophistae* 657D, quoting Myron of Priene.
48. Translation from Vidal-Naquet 1992: 99–100. On this episode: Cartledge 1979: 246–47; 1991: 381; Powell 1989b: 173–74. Doubting its authenticity: Talbert 1989: 24–25; Whitby 1994: 97–99. This is the scene represented in Fig. 4.3. See also pp. 174–75.

study of Brazilian slave culture, he emphasized that "collective memory can indeed be regarded as a group memory provided we add that it is a memory articulated among the members of the group. It was precisely these articulations that slavery shattered."[49] His stress on the importance of memory networks as a "system of relationships between individuals," and in particular on how the loss of particular actors in rituals and performances can lead to gaps in memory, is apposite here. In Bastide's study, it was exile and slavery that forced the survival, loss, or re-creation of collective memory. In Messenia, random strikes by the Spartans, on top of general conditions of servitude and significant losses to exile, would have had similar shock effects. If imagining any single reconstruction of Messenian memories is fallacious, so is any notion of their untroubled and uncontested transmission.

The Messenian diaspora

Exile was a dominant feature of the Messenian experience. At its height, the diaspora community was distributed as far afield as Sicily and North Africa; in the calculations of Pausanias they suffered the most prolonged banishment of any Greek population: "the exile of the Plataeans is found to have lasted the longest, but even it did not extend over more than two generations. But the Messenians wandered for nearly three hundred years far from Peloponnese" (4.27.10–11). According to his account, exiles departed after the defeats of both the First and Second Messenian Wars; another wave followed the mid-fifth-century rebellion, leaving their land under the explicit protection of Apollo, who recognized them as suppliants of Zeus Ithomatas. That other helots, in smaller numbers, may also have sought to escape their lot is suggested by stray pieces of evidence, for example a treaty (datable only between the late seventh and early fifth centuries) between Sparta and Tegea. Although the text is open to varying interpretations, the Tegeans may be pledging to expel, not enfranchise, runaway helots in return for Spartan support.[50]

Little is known of the earlier exiles. Some have been traced to Italy (to Rhegium) and later to Sicily (to Zancle). The invitation to join the latter colony has generated a great deal of puzzlement, chiefly thanks to an apparent mix-up of centuries by Pausanias. In the *Periegesis*, he claimed that Anaxilas, tyrant of Rhegium and himself of Messenian descent, invited survivors of the

49. Bastide 1978: 240–59, quote at 245; 1970; Wachtel 1990: 8–9. Another parallel is offered by the "disappeared" of Argentina: Arditti 1999; Crossland 2000; Taylor 1997.
50. Aristotle, *Fragment* 592; Jacoby 1944; Kiechle 1959: 16–19; more recently Braun 1994; Osborne 1996: 287–88. On the truce from Ithome: Pausanias 4.24.7.

Fig. 4.8 Statue of Zeus Ithomatas represented on a civic coin of Messene.

Second Messenian War to aid in the seizure of Zancle, which was thus dated to the 29th Olympiad (664–661 BC). Colder fact makes clear that Anaxilas actually lived much later, expelling Samian refugees from Zancle in the early fifth century BC and replacing them with Messenians who renamed the city "Messene" (shortly replaced by the Doric form "Messana"). Untangling this mess runs to many scholarly pages; what is clear is that Pausanias' confusion on this point, whether deliberate or not, essentially elides the "unimportant" centuries when Messenia lay under Spartan control.[51] Renaming a new home after an old homeland is, of course, a frequently observed occurrence among other willingly or unwillingly displaced peoples: "the memory of the ancestral homeland is invariably an important component of ethnic consciousness."[52]

The Athenians cannily resettled the final batch of fifth-century exiles at Naupaktos on the Corinthian Gulf, a base from which they in turn attacked local peoples such as the Acarnanians (Pausanias 4.25.1–10). This group is also known to have commissioned a statue of Zeus Ithomatas by Ageladas of Argos, an image that would ultimately be brought back to Messene, appearing on their first series of civic coins (Fig. 4.8). Pausanias states that the statue was still kept, some six centuries or so after its fashioning, in the home of the

---

51. Pausanias 4.23.6–10; Diodorus 15.66.2–6; Kiechle 1959: 6–9, 109–13, 119–23; Pearson 1962: 421–25; Shero 1938: 520–21; Torelli and Musti 1991a, 237–39; 1991b, xviii. Luraghi (1994) suggests that Pausanias was well aware of what he was doing. For another discussion of chronological manipulations in Spartan and Messenian history, Den Boer 1956. A separate body of Messenians, transplanted to the city of Tyndaris in Sicily, is described as living in concord in a well-established community (Diodorus 14.78.5–6)
52. Hall 1997: 25; on other problems of nomenclature in colonial settings: Cronon 1983: 8–9. On Messene/Messana: Jeffery 1990: 205; Kiechle 1959: 112; Shero 1938: 530.

city's eponymous priest.[53] Members of this particular exilic community are most famous, of course, as key players in the Athenian campaigns at Pylos and Sphakteria. When Demosthenes first argued for establishing a base at Pylos, he made a case for utilizing their passions and skills:

> The others declared that there were many empty headlands in the Peloponnese, if he wanted to occupy one at cost to the city; but Demosthenes thought that this place had significant advantages when compared with any other. There was a harbour next to it, and the Messenians had been natives of this land in former times; they spoke the same dialect as the Lakedaimonians, and could do much damage if they made it a base of operations and, at the same time, they would make a steadfast garrison of it.
>
> (Thucydides 4.3.3)

The success of the garrison in recruiting at least partial support from local helots has already been noted. Although Thucydides' description of the attack on Sphakteria can be variously interpreted, one reading suggests that it was Messenian knowledge of a "secret passage" that led to the breaking of Spartiate resistance.[54] The chronology of all these events must be kept in mind; at least a generation would have passed between the time of exile (c. 460–450 BC) and when these men of fighting age returned to Messenia (425 BC). Personal experience was not counted upon to make the Messenians valuable, so much as their traditions of hostility and their family memories – if not necessarily of pathways on Sphakteria. The exiles publicly celebrated their stunning victory with dedications at Delphi and Olympia, including the famed Nike of Paionios (dedicated at Olympia by "the Messenians and the Naupaktians"; Fig. 4.9), and they continued to harass Spartan forces from Pylos.[55] The Spartans ultimately (c. 409 BC) regained control of that base, reexpelling the Messenians to Naupaktos and Kephallenia, from which points they would soon be further scattered to Sicily and North Africa. The Messenian diaspora thus reached its peak not long before the recall home.

We can observe, in all these fragments of testimony, the endurance of a strong Messenian identity in exile, anchored in particular to the remembrance

---

53. On the Zeus of Ageladas: Pausanias 4.33.2; Pliny, *Naturalis Historia* 34.49, 55, 57; Ducat 1990: 142; Habicht 1985: 58; Pollitt 1965: 24–25; Roebuck 1941: 34.
54. Thucydides 4.36. Wilson (1979) is a skeptic on this passage: "even today the possible paths are far from common knowledge. At best the Messenian leader might have been prompted by some dim memory on the part of one of his countrymen" (pp. 117–18, quote at 117).
55. On these monuments: Hölscher 1974; Jacquemin and Laroche 1982; Jeffery 1990: 205–6, nos. 12–13.

Fig. 4.9 Plaster cast of the Nike of Paionios in the Museum of Classical Archaeology, University of Cambridge.

of Messenian topography and cult, to a sense that Messenia was home.[56] A refusal ever truly to relocate is certainly asserted by later authorities, and Messenian loyalty and steadfastness much celebrated. Pausanias speaks of how after Leuctra:

56. Attachment to a lost homeland is a constant theme of diaspora populations, modern as well as ancient and medieval: see Clifford 1994, for one review essay. Critical writing on modern diaspora (Jewish, Islamic, African), like its cognate topic of social memory, is currently a very productive space. On the Messenian diaspora: Asheri 1983. Figueira (1999) analyzes the role of the diaspora in the "evolution of the Messenian identity," which he thinks a relatively late creation and one stimulated by Athenian attitudes and interventions. It is worth observing that at least one Messenian leader, in Pausanias' account, urged the exiles to forget Messenia and their hatred of the Spartans (4.23.5).

the Thebans sent messengers to Italy, Sicily and the Euesperitae, inviting all Messenians in any part of the world whither they had strayed to return to Peloponnese. They assembled faster than could have been expected, for they yearned towards the land of their fathers, and hatred of Sparta still rankled in their breasts.   (Pausanias 4.26.5)[57]

Distance and duration are emphasized in this no doubt elaborated account of the "many sufferings of the Messenians," who were finally brought back safe from exile "to the ends of the earth and to lands the farthest from Peloponnese" (4.29.13). While the actual return rate is unknown, such exiles undoubtedly formed a significant part of the new population at Messene.

Also heralded by Pausanias is Messenian conservatism. Despite having wandered for nearly three hundred years, "in all that time they are known to have dropped none of their native customs, nor did they unlearn their Doric tongue; indeed, they speak it to this day with greater purity than any other of the Peloponnesians" (4.27.11). Other evidence corroborates Pausanias on this linguistic archaism, which has been observed in both Lakonia and Messenia (if especially the latter). Messenian isolation and subjugation cannot be invoked to explain this "backwardness," for most of the relevant linguistic data belongs after 369 BC, and was thus the product of a reconstructed society that included not only the former helots, but the Messenians of the diaspora as well.

> One would normally, then, have expected the Messenian dialect to be rather diverse and heterogeneous. The fact that it is instead so conservative may in fact represent a deliberate and conscious policy on the part of a community that was anxious to equip itself with the history, traditions and general ancestral identity which had been denied to it for so long.[58]

Stubborn adherence to certain memories and practices as a claim to the past is again highlighted, if here as much for the age following liberation as for the exilic period itself.

The act of remembering Messenia in exile – commissioning a statue of Zeus Ithomatas, renaming a Sicilian town, joining the Athenian forces at Pylos, maintaining native customs and language – all presuppose a long-distance selection and attachment to certain memories and mores of the homeland. Inevitably, however, much would also have been forgotten or

57. On this "summoning," see also Diodorus 15.66.1; Plutarch, *Agesilaus* 34.1; Plutarch, *Pelopidas* 24.9. Among the returned exiles numbered members of old priestly families: Roebuck 1941: 34
58. Hall 1997: 180; see also Hall 1995b: 91. On the paucity of evidence for exilic script: Jeffery 1990: 204. For other references to the Messenians and their Doric: Pausanias 3.112.4, 4.30.4, 4.31.2

transformed. Disjunctions in memory – between people who remain in place, and those who depart and whose "descendants" return – were sympathetically explored by Halbwachs when discussing the Crusaders in the Holy Land. There the shock of outsiders returning to the genuine landscape of Christ led to a clash between local traditions and external expectations:

> Since Christianity took possession of the Holy Land and returned there legitimately, the Christians returned triumphantly, like descendants of noble or royal families returning to the castles and the lands of their ancestors who had been chased away and dispossessed in the past – and their memories returned with them. But how can spatial memories find their place where everything is changed, where there are no more vestiges or landmarks? If the newly arrived Christians had limited themselves to what the Christians who dwelled and lived in Jerusalem all their lives had told them, they would have learned that the buildings supposed to commemorate certain events told in the Gospels were in fact buildings from which living tradition had disappeared in the distant past. These buildings had in fact been destroyed in part, and what remained was deformed, of doubtful significance, and of uncertain authenticity.

> But the crusaders could not be stopped by discouragements and scruples of this kind. They came with the authority of an immense community. They somehow felt that behind them operated the pressures of innumerable generations. This is why they did not hesitate to resume in their own way the work of commemoration or, more exactly, the reconstruction of the holy places... They proceeded with a great deal of assurance, since they were the legitimate possessors of a tradition that the Christians of Jerusalem had forgotten or not known. The Crusaders behaved as if this land and these stones recognized them, as if they had only to stoop down in order suddenly to hear voices that had remained silent.[59]

The Crusaders proceeded to fashion a Holy Land in the image they required, adopting some existing commemorative sites and practices, ignoring others, and creating still more new ones. This comparison raises tantalizing, if unanswerable, questions about likely tensions between those who had remained resident in Messenia (the now freed helots) and the returning exiles. If the Holy Land was reworked and remapped to create localizations and landmarks to match expectations, just what happened in Messenia following the termination both of Spartan rule and the diaspora?

59. Halbwachs 1992: 231–32 (1941: 200–2); see also Bastide 1978: 247; Wachtel 1990: 7.

LIBERATION AND THE PAST

The confusions of liberation – in political, social, economic, and demographic terms – would be difficult to overestimate. The end of Spartan control finished off a by now long-established system of landholding and labor. A new and mixed population was introduced to the region with the creation of Messene, a foundation which involved not only former helots and returned exiles, but apparently perioikoi who joined the Theban forces and other landless Greeks who fought for Epaminondas.[60] All this required some profound measure of land redistribution, on a massive scale. In time, perioikic communities shook off Spartan suzerainty and became independent; other new cities were established. These varied civic units appear to have bonded, usually under the aegis of Messene, into a federal league of "the Messenians" which quickly became embroiled in the power politics of the Hellenistic age. A more complex political scene thus evolved, both within Messenia itself and in the region's external relations. All this did not happen at once; some portions of the region were not liberated, for example, until later in the fourth century BC. But that does not significantly reduce the magnitude of change at work here, and the "revolutionary novelty" of the whole situation.[61]

Before turning to what landscape and monuments reveal about this dramatic transformation, we must address one issue central to previous discussions of the epoch: just how far were Messenian notions of the past a product only of post-liberation times, a kind of "pseudo-history"? For a very long time, most ancient historians believed that "being Messenian" was an invention of the fourth-century moment, the instant myth-making of a people desperately in need of a cosmetic, quick-fix past. Two things are particularly distressing about this argument in its most extreme incarnation. First is an underlying disdain for invented traditions and an over-ready assumption of their instrumentalist nature. Second is an apparent conviction that a people without freedom or political organization can have no sense of self, no memories, no "history" – or at least none worth worrying about: "It is an axiom of Greek political life that a polis, in order to have dignity and standing, must have or acquire a history. But how can there be any history of a people that has had no existence as a nation or a city-state?"[62]

---

60. Roebuck (1941: 27–57) collects the ancient sources; see also Roebuck 1945; Luraghi 2002. On civic institutions: Fröhlich 1999. In the later Hellenistic and early imperial period, Messene became an important center for *Rhomaioi*, Italian businessmen settling in Achaia.
61. Borrowing a phrase from Treves 1944: 103. On the federal league: Lazenby and Hope Simpson 1972: 90; Roebuck 1941: 109–17.
62. Pearson 1962: 402; cf. Musti 1996. Pearson (1962: 397, n. 2) provides a lengthy list of historians who deal with the "problem of Messenian history," most of whom (going back as far as George

Lionel Pearson was here writing in the early 1960s, and obviously few today would define history in such a narrow sense. Certainly this chapter so far has argued that the Messenians, even powerless under Spartan rule, had the ability to remember and promulgate their own versions of the past. Dismissing phrases such as "pseudo-history" or "false invention," what now requires explanation is how those versions – those memories – were transformed with freedom's radical restructuring. What elements were retained, what dismissed, what newly forged? Did new contexts emerge for the expression and communication of social memory?

Freeing up the landscape

Earlier in this chapter, I presented the human landscape of Archaic and Classical Messenia as composed of small communities, with a very few possible regional cult centers augmented by more local shrines. Modifications would have taken place across that time-span, but the essential outline endured. That pattern alters drastically, beginning roughly around the mid-fourth century and continuing through the Hellenistic period – or (in terms of historical events) in the wake of Epaminondas. One obvious development, of course, is the rise of polis units, the creation of independent cities and their hinterlands. While Messene is the chief example, other poleis were founded or else developed at former perioikic sites; by Pausanias' day major settlements included Pherai, Thouria, Korone, Abia, Kolonides, Asine, Methone, Pylos, and Kyparissia (Fig. 4.1). Change did not stop there, however, but swept through the entire settlement hierarchy. Results of the Pylos Regional Archaeological Project (PRAP) indicate an efflorescence of settlement across a wide spectrum of site types: it is at this time, for example, that small isolated farmsteads are detected in the Messenian countryside.[63] A much altered physical environment would have met the eye of any Hellenistic traveler, compared to what he would have seen in preceding centuries.

The ritual landscape of Messenia likewise was transformed. As cities were founded or freed, they went on to articulate their own political trajectories and mythic histories, inevitably generating their own cultic networks and calendars; individuals now made dedications, and received honors, in their own

---

Grote) agree totally or in part with his position. Arguing against: Kiechle 1959; Shero 1938; Treves 1944; Zunino 1997. Reexamining this issue of "pseudo-history": Alcock 1999; Luraghi 2002.

63. Alcock *et al.*, in prep.; Davis *et al.* 1997: 456–57. Other small, possible farmstead sites were discovered in the hinterland of Nichoria by the Five Rivers survey: Coulson and Wilkie 1983: 337; Lukermann and Moody 1978: 108–12. For general reviews of post-liberation change: Harrison and Spencer 1998; Alcock 1998a.

name.[64] Regional survey again has discovered rural shrines, with one on-going and one new example from the Nichoria hinterland, and with two likely late Classical/Hellenistic sanctuaries documented by PRAP and others.[65] In these latter two cases, associated finds of cut blocks speak to some form of monumental building; both were also found in elevated hilltop locations – possibly indicating a new willingness (indeed ability) to locate places of worship in prominent and visible locations. In other words, the decades following liberation saw the rise of a more densely packed, more complexly articulated ritual landscape than the foregoing period had allowed.

Tomb cult proved no exception to this pattern of development and growth. If formerly celebrated in a limited and patchy fashion, the practice took off in late Classical and Hellenistic times. Some twenty-one definite or possible cases are attested, with definite examples identified by unambiguous votive objects or ritual deposits.[66] While many of these assemblages remained on a fairly simple scale, some tombs experienced a significant degree of investment, witnessed in the use of specially made votive plaques, in the sacrifice of large animals, or in the addition of small shrines or ancillary buildings. For Messenia, this is seen most clearly at Voidokoilia (Fig. 4.7).[67]

We can suppose that such changes point to possible shifts in sponsorship, and thus in possible motivations for the ritual. Certainly a communal orientation remains appropriate, if in celebration of freedom rather than in resistance to subjugation. Yet control of the past no doubt was now more vigorously sought by certain groups within Messenian society, much as contemporary elite families strove to dominate civic memory in other parts of Greece. Carla Antonaccio, summing up the "wealth of evidence" from Messenia, remarked: "Thus tomb cult might have been an expression of resistance to external pressure, but it might also be indicative of competition between groups within

64. For civic inscriptions from Messenia, see *IG* V; Tod 1905; Valmin 1929; Wilhelm 1891.
65. Five Rivers: Coulson and Wilkie 1983: 337; Lukermann and Moody 1978: 110, no. 50 (Ayios Nikolaos, Classical/Hellenistic); Lukermann and Moody 1978: 109, no. 18 (Soudhes, Hellenistic). PRAP: D01 Gargaliani *Kanalos*: McDonald and Hope Simpson 1961: 237; M04 Gargaliani *Ayios Konstadtinos*: Davis 1998a: 278–80; see for both http://classics.lsa.umich.edu/PRAP.html.
66. Alcock (1991: 460–62, 465–66) identified eight definite, and ten possible, examples of individual tombs. To this list, two "definite" examples (Tragana 2; Ellenika/Thouria) and one "possible" (Antheia) should be added: Antonaccio 1995: 72, 79–80. *Definite*: (1) Kaminion Kremmidia; (2) Routsi; (3) Peristeria; (4) Tourliditsa; (5) Vathirema; (6) Voidokoilia; (7) Volimidia, Angelopoulos 2; (8) Volimidia, Angelopoulos 6; (9) Tragana 2; (10) Ellenika/Thouria. *Possible*: (1) "The Tholos at Kopanaki"; (2) Dhafni-Dara; (3) Karpophora (Akones); (4) Koukounara 4; (5) Koryphasion (Osmanaga); (6) Papoulia (Ay. Ioannis); (7) Mesiki/Psari; (8) "The Tholos at Vasiliko"; (9) Volimidia, Angelopoulos 10; (10) Volimidia, Kephalovrysos 2; (11) Antheia. See also Alcock 1998b.
67. Korres 1981/82: 394–97; 1988.

a community, played out in claims to the past." Tomb cult still drew people together to remember their past; such practices remained "sources of power and arenas for conflict," but the uses of that power, and the nature of those conflicts, did not go unaltered.[68]

One additional relevant activity, seen periodically in earlier times but more marked in the Hellenistic era, was the placement of new tombs within Bronze Age cemeteries, for example at Volimidia. An attractive explanation is that this phenomenon represents an annexation of ancestors, or of the heroic dead, by dominant families in Messenian cities. Burial in such venerated locales, affirming authority through proximity, would operate in parallel to elite claims supported by tomb cult. Again, such behavior fits within a wider constellation of contemporary practice, reinforcing the notion that Messenia, after an anomalous period, had resumed a more "normal" Greek course of development.[69]

Imagining community

On the face of it, all these alterations imply radical shifts in the workings of social memory. Most obviously, there were more avenues for its expression – liberation allowed far greater public display and new forms of celebration. Groups "remembering" within this landscape not only were transformed from a servile to a free population, they also multiplied, not least with the development of individual civic identities joining the umbrella category of Messenian. As in the previous period (and now far more clearly), it is possible to tease out a diversity of memory communities simultaneously in play. Nevertheless, certain overarching emphases are manifest in the period's commemorative behavior, visible through acts of both commission and omission. We can observe these both through material evidence, and – with due caution – in Book IV of Pausanias.

One conspicuous memorial choice, for example, was an adamant declaration of the heroism of the pre-conquest past. This theme was struck at the very foundation of the region's preeminent new center, Messene:

> To Epaminondas the site on which the city of Messene now stands appeared the most suitable, and he accordingly desired the seers to inquire whether the gods would be willing to take up their abode there. Being informed by them that the omens were propitious he prepared to found the

---

68. Morris 1988: 758; the quotation by Antonaccio is 1995: 142.
69. Alcock 1991: 461–62; Antonaccio 1995: 102; McDonald and Hope Simpson 1972: 144. On similar activity in Hellenistic Crete, see pp. 115–16.

city. He ordered stones to be brought, and he sent for men who were skilled in laying out streets, building houses and sanctuaries, and erecting city walls. When all was ready, the victims being furnished by the Arcadians, Epaminondas and the Thebans sacrificed to Dionysos and Ismenian Apollo in the customary way; the Argives sacrificed to Argive Hera and Nemean Zeus; and the Messenians sacrificed to Zeus of Ithome and to the Dioscuri, while their priests sacrificed to the Great Goddesses and Caucon. They also joined in calling upon the heroes to come and dwell with them, chiefly Messene, daughter of Triopas, and next to her Eurytus and Aphareus and his children, and of the Heraclids they invited Cresphontes and Aepytus; but loudest of all was the cry for Aristomenes, and the whole people joined in it. Thus the day was spent in sacrifice and prayer. But on the following days they proceeded to rear the circuit wall, and to build houses and sanctuaries within it. They worked to the music of Boeotian and Argive flutes alone . . . To the capital they gave the name of Messene, but they founded other towns also.   (Pausanias 4.27.5–7)

As necessary to the construction of the city as the circuit walls and houses was this call for the return of former kings, queens, and heroes.[70] Such a description could, of course, reflect later versions of "what should have happened" at this critical moment, but stress on these particular key figures is supported by other monuments reported in the city – not least a heroön and other dedications to Aristomenes, who was worshipped with the sacrifice of bulls.[71]

Archaeological evidence from the most thoroughly excavated sector of Messene also vehemently asserts this particular representation of the past. The well-known architectural complex of the Asklepieion received that particular name only in early imperial times; before that the precinct was dedicated to the region's first queen and eponymous heroine, Messene, whose temple stood in its open middle (Fig. 4.10). This complex has been dated to the late third and early second centuries BC, approximately 150 years after the city's foundation. A very clear programmatic thrust dictates the organization of select elements within this space; in the words of the excavator, Themelis:

---

70. Diodorus (15.67.1) implies that the much-admired walls were built with incredible rapidity in eighty-five days. While in absolute terms this claim is most unlikely, quick, "all hands on deck" construction projects can serve as a unifying disciplinary force; this would allow the Messenians, with the help of their allies, to display themselves as a free people in both active and monumental terms: see Paynter and McGuire 1991: 9.
71. Pausanias 4.14.7, 32.3; *SEG* 23.207.13; Habicht 1985: 58; Zunino 1997: 268–74. For recent findings from the Heroön of Aristomenes, *Ergon* 1998: 39–50; *AR* 1998–99: 47.

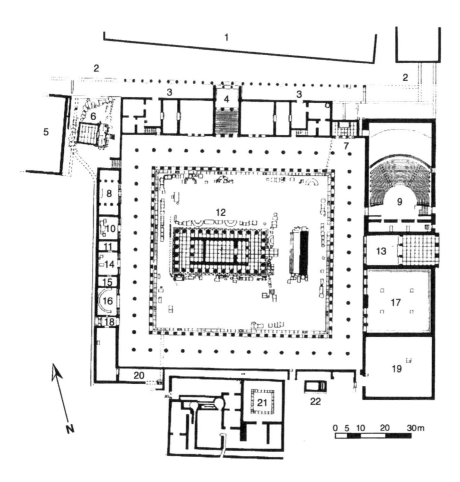

1. South side of Agora
2. Late Roman stoa
3. Sebasteion
4. North propylon
5. Hero sanctuary Ω-Ω
6. Temple of Artemis Orthia
7. Room of Asklepios and his sons
8. Cult room of Artemis

9. Odeion
10. Room of Tyche
11. Room of Epaminondas
12. Temple of Messene
13. East propylon
14. Room of Thebes
15. Room of Herakles
16. Room of Apollo and the Muses

17. Assembly hall
18. West entrance
19. Archive house?
20. Latrines
21. Bath complex
22. Heroon of Damophon

Fig. 4.10 Plan of the Asklepieion at Messene.

Its aim was to declare that, based on common race and tradition, the inhabitants of Messenia were a distinct ethnical unity in the Peloponnese. For this purpose stories about the deep roots of Messenian history in the pre-Dorian and Dorian past were invented and illustrated in the wall paintings of the Messene temple and in the sculptural decoration of the rooms around the stoas.

This sculptural decoration was said by Pausanias to be the work of Damophon of Messene, whose family line can be traced in the city's inscriptional record. Damophon was responsible for images representing, again in the words of Themelis, "deities, personifications and heroised mortals referring to the glorious past of the land and to the historical event of the refounding of the city by the Thebans in 369 BC."[72] These figures included Asklepios and his sons (members of one pre-Dorian royal Messenian lineage) in one location, while along the west side of the complex (in a series of rectangular roofed niches) stood statues of Apollo and the Muses, the personified city of Thebes (flanked by Theban Heracles and the Theban general Epaminondas), Tyche, and Artemis Phosphoros (Fig. 4.10). Fragments of most of these have been recovered (in the order outlined by Pausanias) through excavation, except for the Epaminondas, which was made of iron and not the work of Damophon. Other associated images reinforced the same commemorative stresses. Kresphontes, who won Messenia by lot at the time of the Dorian invasion, was depicted in a painting within the Messene temple, together with thirteen members of the pre-Dorian royal kindred; the thirteen again included Asklepios, who is here unambiguously presented in his role as legendary Messenian king, rather than as god of healing.[73] All in all, the precinct of the Asklepieion served as a kind of gallery of public memory for the residents of the community, for the Messenian population more generally, and for any others who would visit this regional center.[74]

Themelis pinpoints the genesis of this memorial space to a moment following in the wake of an anti-oligarchic revolt, democratic constitutional reform, the defeat of Philip V, and the revival of a Messenian federal organization. These events all led to "a refreshed consciousness of a distinctive Messenian nationality."[75] No doubt he is correct in seeking specific motivations for this spectacular act of self-conscious self-promotion. We do not yet know enough to determine the outlines of Messene's cityscape in the decades

72. Themelis 1994b, quotations at 30. It has been suggested that Damophon's grandfather was Boeotian by birth, coming to Messene at the time of the foundation.
73. Themelis 1994b: 4–5 and n. 9 on the problems of reconciling the construction of the Messene temple with the supposed artist of the painting, Omphalion; Themelis 1993: 25. Descent from Kresphontes was claimed by the "council of Oupesia's Gerousia," state officials responsible for the temple and cult of Artemis Orthia (attested in the imperial period): Themelis 1994a. On the organization of the Asklepieion: Themelis 1993; 1994a; 1994b. On Asklepios, see Zunino 1997: 281–84; for other Messenian "Eroi nazionale," 257–74.
74. Habicht 1985: 36–63. Felten (1983: 84–93, at 93) remarks on this "political" presentation of Asklepios, calling the space a "Staatsheiligtum," in line with developments at other newly created early Hellenistic sites such as Megalopolis.
75. Themelis 1994b: 29.

immediately after the foundation. Nevertheless, it seems inherently likely that – from the very start – adherence to this particular body of ancient tradition formed a central part of the city's self-representation. Evidence for this includes the immediate rebuilding of the hero cult at Sanctuary Ω-Ω, on the northwest edge of the Asklepieion and arguably dedicated to the Dioscouri and to Leucippus (who also appears in paintings of the Messene temple). Representations of Messene, Epaminondas, and Aristomenes are numbered among excavated statues which Themelis believes predate Damophon.[76] The commemorative density of Messene's thoughts – in public terms at least – positively gravitated to the pre-conquest age and to the moment of liberation. Other elements, such as remembrance of the exilic period, were surely present – Zeus Ithomatas, with his cult image made in exile, was after all a principal civic deity. But these seem overpowered by emphasis on the "before" and the "after" of Spartan domination.[77]

The Asklepieion stands, of course, in the primary city and political leader of the region; Messene's commemorative priorities would undoubtedly have proved generally influential. Yet that polity had a trajectory of its own, and its own particular problems to confront. Keeping in mind its mixed population, such a concocted community would need above all to remember and to celebrate what brought them together as a body – and that would be the act and fact of foundation. Stress in the Asklepieion on Thebes (Theban Heracles, Epaminondas) would, among other things, bind together potentially disparate elements. Messene's status as an independent polis is also significant. The landmark of Ithome surely remained of more than just civic interest (as suggested by Pausanias' anecdote about Zeus Ithomatas and the Messenian claim to Lakonian Leuktra). Yet Ithome, rather than being recognized as home to a pan-Messenian shrine, now appears primarily as the acropolis of a specific city: the eponymous priest of Zeus Ithomatas dated the civic calendar; the god's image adorned civic coins (Fig. 4.8). The memories of Messene, though compelling in the age following liberation, should not be taken as equivalent to the memories of all other Messenians.

76. Themelis 1994b: 36–37; 1998: 183. A predilection for cults specific in some way to Messenia has been noted before: "Some of these cults had peculiar legends connecting them with the country and polemizing against myths which claimed them for other regions": Rose 1970: 676. These sentiments are echoed, if somewhat toned down, in a later summary of Messenian ritual practices, which speaks of "an evident wish to confer antiquity on cults": Jost 1996. For a thorough review, see Meyer 1978.
77. Remembrances of exile might also include bringing the cult of Artemis Laphria from Naupaktos (Pausanias 4.31.7), together with the decision (in the first half of the second century BC) to rework a dedication from "the Messenians" at Delphi, a dedication probably originally dating to the early fifth century BC: Jeffery 1990: 205.

As one moves outside Messene and away from Ithome, that impression of difference sharpens. With the emergence of other cities came a spectrum of civic cults and local traditions, if – admittedly – this can be better argued from Pausanias' account than from any extant archaeological evidence. By the second century AD, for example, people of the Pylos district in western Messenia apparently possessed a very detailed sense of local heritage:

> Pylus was founded by Pylus, son of Cleson: he brought from Megaris the Leleges, who at that time occupied it. But he did not enjoy the city which he had founded, being driven out by Neleus and the Pelasgians of Iolcus. So he withdrew to the neighboring country and there occupied Pylus in Elis. But Neleus, after he became king, raised the repute of Pylus so high that Homer calls it the city of Neleus. Here there is a sanctuary of Athena called Coryphasian, and a house called the house of Nestor, and in it a painting of Nestor. His tomb is in the city: the tomb a little way from Pylus is said to be that of Thrasymedes. There is also in the city a cave, in which they say that the cows of Nestor and of Neleus before him were stalled. These cows must have been of Thessalian breed.
>
> (Pausanias 4.36.1–3)

The points of interest enumerated – Nestor's house, his image, his *mnema*, his cave, the tomb of his son Thrasymedes – are revealing.[78] Classical Pylos placed solid emphasis on the heroic past, but out of the broad genealogical sweep of Messenian history, attention appears trained on their own.

Drawing on this very mixed-assortment evidence, we can now envision different versions of the past being available to the communities of Hellenistic Messenia. If some strands emphasized the shared pre-conquest and post-liberation glories of "being Messenian," others were more attuned to localized landmarks and loyalties. Still other patterns of commemoration remained stubbornly fixed. Resistant to mitigation, for example, was the long-lived antipathy of Messenia and Sparta. Given their ongoing mutual detestation, no shared past could be agreed upon, and the two sides continued to "fight" over the land of Messenia, if now in more symbolic fashion. Contestations over territory went on well into Roman times, most famously over the Ager Dentheliates in the Taygetos mountain range where lay the important sanctuary of Artemis Limnatis. Both sides agreed that their bitter struggle began, once upon a time, at this sanctuary with murder, rape, and treachery – although memories of just "who started it" did not match up. Some six arbitrations are recorded on this border dispute, the last confirmed by the Roman

---

78. Baltsas 1987. Of all these monuments, only the "tomb of Thrasymedes" and the "cave of Nestor" have any proposed archaeological correlate.

Senate. Tacitus reports that the dispute was argued by the Spartans using the annals of tradition and the songs of poets. The Messenians fought back in kind and more:

> Against this claim, the Messenians adduced the ancient division of the Peloponnese among the descendants of Hercules, and that the Dentheliate territory in which the shrine stood had become the property of their king; and the memorials of that fact were still there, graven on rocks and in antique bronze . . . The decision was given in favor of Messene.
>
> (Tacitus, *Annales* 4.43)[79]

Silences and oblivion

Fervent post-liberation promotion of the past only abetted, of course, modern convictions about the "inventions" of that age. I am not arguing with the fact that this response was contingent upon altered political circumstances, nor can it be denied that liberation witnessed a critical juncture in Messenian self-conceptions. What can be queried is the assumption (and even more the grounds for the assumption) that the free population of Messenia inherited nothing from their predecessors in that land. Tales of the Messenian Wars or the hero worship of Aristomenes provided charismatic figures of pride and inspiring narratives of opposition. Such memories need hardly have been new in post-liberation times, however different the aspirations they fed. Knowing only the contexts, and not the content, of helot social memory, however, does not allow our speculations to wander much further.

The assumption that nothing was inherited, everything new created, is grounded, of course, in a general non-recognition of Messenia under Spartan domination. The silence of our sources conspires in that negation; as with the Greeks under Roman rule, or with Geary's medieval "phantoms of memory," ancient decisions about remembrance very much direct modern preconceptions. Messenia supplies, in fact, a classic case of memorial slippage and of the power of forgetfulness. The narrative of Pausanias, moving from one section of the *Messeniaka* to the next, effortlessly makes a chronological leap of some fifty Olympiads (664 BC to 464 BC), and thus hardly needs to mention the helots at all. The region's memorial landscape echoes this reticence.[80] The public face of Messene similarly highlights early kings and heroes of resistance, then "fast-forwards" to heroes of liberation; the commemorative

---

79. On Artemis Limnatis and the boundary arbitrations surrounding it: Pausanias 3.7.4; 4.4.2; 4.31.3; Strabo 8.362; Baladié 1980: 69; Breuillot 1985: 794; Cartledge and Spawforth 1989: 138–39; Kolbe 1904; Luraghi 2002; Malkin 1994: 34–35; Valmin 1930: 12–13, 27–32; see also *Ergon* 1988: 44–46.
80. Alcock 2001a. See Pausanias 4.23.4–26.3.

flurry that develops around the figures of Aristomenes and of Epaminondas elides the gap left in between. The long-lived sanctuary to Apollo Korynthos, whose votives previously possessed a "warlike" aspect, appears in Pausanias as a healing cult, relinquishing any formerly resistant overtones. Nothing suggests that Ithome's role as helot refuge was commemorated; instead, the mountain was honored as the acropolis of Messene and (together with countless other venues, not least on Crete) as the birthplace of the god Zeus. Indeed, as far as can be determined, nowhere were memories provoked of the epoch of helotage and rebellion. We see the net result of this failure to remember in our own loss of a chunk of Messenian history.

Given pervasive ancient attitudes to freedom and servitude, such an occlusion could be shrugged off as unsurprising. Yet that would simply perpetuate a grave mistake. At the very least, the phenomenon requires acknowledgment for the "willed forgetfulness" it represents, and future investigations of Messenia must take cognizance of such entrenched, but partial, perspectives. This includes a greater appreciation of the role played by monuments and the land itself in creating and promulgating certain remembrances at the expense of others, in fostering particular versions of the Messenian past.

*

With their checkered history of oppression and liberation, the Messenians are an exceptional case study in the dynamism of social memory. Helots, however, have already made one other appearance in contemporary memory studies. Pierre Vidal-Naquet, in his polemic against revisionist histories of the Holocaust, turns to this group of stigmatized and separate people, and in particular to the 2000 helots who (Thucydides tells us) were "made to disappear" by the Spartans. The passage quoted above (p. 157) is almost all that is known of this incident; as Vidal-Naquet put it, "only a slim thread of memory has come down to the Athenian historian." And yet, he argues, opacity or paucity of information should not end the story:

> In the Thucydides text I have just commented on, there is a little word that has not, to my knowledge, attracted the attention of the exegetes: the word *each*. When the Spartans opted to do away with the Helots who had distinguished themselves, their decision concerned a collectivity whose boundaries they themselves had fixed, with the participation of the victims, but each death was obviously individual. Each victim had his own history, and we will never know how death was administered, individually,

collectively or in small groups... Whatever the case, the sources at the
historian's disposal can not be bypassed, and it will remain for him to
interpret them.

He returns to this theme after discussing the lacunae and complexities of
historical testimony about Nazi activities, saying finally of the dead that "as
Thucydides said of the Messenians, we will never know how *each* one disappeared."[81] Vidal-Naquet's allusion can be taken in many ways, but he essentially insists on a refusal to accept the erasure, or the assassination, of memory
by subsequent forces, however seemingly powerful or determined. The two
episodes – distant as they are in time, space, and degree of trauma – together
reveal the critical vulnerability of memory and enjoin limitations on just how
much can be forgotten.

81. Vidal-Naquet 1992: quotations at 102, 109. Another study from the discipline of ancient history
   which draws analogies and inspiration from reactions to World War II memories is Lavelle's
   The Sorrow and the Pity (1993), named after the controversial 1971 film of the same name.

5

THREE SHORT STORIES ABOUT GREEK MEMORY

I claimed at the outset that too few students of Greek antiquity have pondered the workings of social memory within specific historical contexts; that they had yet to consider it as a dynamic expression of collective experience, as a point of likely internal contestation, and as a consequential element in decisions about present and future. With a heavy reliance on the archaeological evidence of landscape and of monuments, I have here attempted to get the ball rolling. To the smorgasbord of memory-tales recounted in chapter 1, we can thus now add, based on our case studies, three short stories about Greek memory.

IMPERIAL NOSTALGIA

"Graecia capta" was captivated by its own memories. The inhabitants of Achaia highlighted the past (and particularly the classical past) in many spheres of life, from urban architecture to public rhetoric, from the election of heroes to the promotion of cities. This observation is not entirely news. What separates my treatment (and certain other recent discussions) from past assessments of the *Graeculi* is recognition of the animated nature of this turn to the past. "Nostalgia" built up a reservoir of symbolic capital; shared respect for certain memories established effective networks of communication and negotiation, both among heterogeneous Greek populations and with Roman rulers.

Archaeological testimony makes a significant original contribution to this story. Upsetting developments reported in at least parts of the Achaian landscape include colonization, land reallocation, population displacement, and cult disruption. Regional survey quietly demonstrates the very real on-the-ground impact of these episodes. Such material disturbances promised similar dislocations in the social frameworks through which memory was channeled. Loss (or theft) of rural cult places is perhaps an especially sensitive indicator of the toll taken. Two conclusions emerge from a look at the Achaian land-scape. First, the imperial annexation of Achaia, while patently encouraging cultivation of the past in some quarters, also rooted it out in others. And sec-ond, acts of remembrance in this landscape are exposed as matters of effort and of selective reinforcement; there was nothing automatic or natural about Achaian commemorative patterns.

Provincial and civic elite families were, without question, the dominant agents behind promulgation of the past. Literary and epigraphic testimonia make that clear, but so too does the evidence for building and dedication of monuments and monumental complexes. Urban centers, such as the Agora or the heart of Sparta, at this time intensified their role as explicitly memo-rial spaces, taking on something of the character of a "museum." No single, approved version of the past, however, emerged from these spaces; rather, it is possible to trace expanding and often contradictory horizons of meaning. Monuments supported individual civic identities as well as feeding more pan-hellenic imaginings; both past antagonisms and past amities were kept alive. Also set within this same framework, however, were reminders of the current imperial situation, such as images of emperors or material signs of Roman patronage. In other words, monumental centers such as cities and sanctuaries came to embody a range of memorial stances, on which different memory communities – Greek or Roman, Athenian or Spartan, rich or poor – could differentially call, depending on circumstance, desire, or need. Elite patrons may have been principally responsible for the creation or maintenance of monuments, but – inscribed as they were in accessible and populous spaces – commemorative choices were plainly a matter for viewing and debate across a broad community.

Another example of such compound commemoration resides in one es-pecially charged set of memories – that revolving around the fifth-century BC Persian Wars. A constellation of meanings clung to those paradigmatic strug-gles, not least their symbolic appropriation by Rome to model the Parthian threat or their critical use as a yardstick by which to measure Hellenic decline. One particularly interesting memorial strain, however, was an inspiration to independence and insurgency. The notion of little Achaia mounting any serious opposition to Rome might seem laughable, but we must – as Jean Comaroff warns – beware of reducing resistance to "the zero-sum heroics of revolution successfully achieved."[1] Memories of the Persian Wars, while too compellingly authoritative to jettison, nevertheless became a tricky business.

1. Comaroff 1985: 261.

Compromise seems indicated here, signaled by elite interest in governing these sites of memory. Such control is manifest in the formal nature of battlefield commemoration and in the lack of any new battlefield monumentalization that might attract or inflame the unruly.

If certain channels of memories were nurtured, and others eradicated, still others were newly created through the juxtaposition of images, rituals, styles, and myths with variant pedigrees and (often, to our eyes) jarring discrepancies. Appreciation of early imperial "hybridity" has been hindered by the scholarly impulse to dissect places such as the Aphrodisian Sebasteion or the streets of Ephesus: "Greek" is counted as quite separate from "Roman," and Ephesian Artemis should not walk with Trajan. More helpful, perhaps, is to think of these places and spaces as they would have been experienced, and to consider the commemorative impact of such "in-between" zones. Hybrid versions of the past, born of their predecessors yet unlike any that had come before, allowed the elision of predicted frameworks of authority and hierarchy; the result was the creation of a new past for a newly ordered world.

One overriding commemorative impulse weaves through these various categories of evidence from the imperial east, and that is a bent toward nourishing an ongoing sense of cultural separation, without reaching too far into domains provoking outright confrontation. Such attitudes above all reflect elite concerns and priorities. Yet probably the most revelatory aspect of this entire story line is the sheer *diversity* of commemorative work going on in early Roman Achaia. Imperial nostalgia followed no one path, was the property of no single community. Adding to this already complicated picture is an argument for a growing *mobility* of memory. Textual and artistic sources speak of contemporary individuals who could strategically shift positions and juggle various roles, now emphasizing local connections, now aligning with the imperial center, and back again over the course of a career. I have hypothesized that social groups, such as cities or families, could similarly choose to present themselves in different guises, grounded in different accounts of the past. Corinth, for example, saw itself both as Roman colony and as antique Hellenic city; neither version was "false."

This mobility of memory, like other prevailing aspects of Greek commemorative practice, grew directly out of the conditions and pressures of empire; uses of the past now had to accommodate crucial rewritings (sometimes welcome, sometimes disturbing) of political, social, and geographical boundaries. Just how memory managed to serve so many different imperatives in the early imperial east is at least partially revealed for us in the complex elasticities of memorial practice and memorial space.

TWO CRETAN PROSPECTS

Residents of the warring city-states of Hellenistic Crete took good care of their memories. An attachment to the past was signaled in numerous, archaeologically visible ways: votives placed at ancient sites, graves nestled adjacent to older tombs, superimposition of new buildings on preexisting structures, a return to ancient grottoes, or the employment of antique symbols. The agency at work in certain of these cases is not far to seek, for example when cities, led by particular dominant families, took the formal decision to adopt ancient sanctuaries as their own and, if necessary, to fight for them. Other practices would seem to spring from more informal, popular roots. Apparently binding these commemorative acts together, however, was a concern for stability and security, a concern invested in local landmarks and monuments. Such anxiety accords well with the island's notorious political dissensions, and regional surveys attest even more directly to how political remapping – with the expansion of some cities and the decline of others – affected the whole of the settled landscape.

But links to the past snapped in the early years of Roman rule, with the termination of much of this commemorative activity. To some extent this may reflect direct central interventions; Crete had not been an easy conquest, and aspects of antiquity that abetted military prowess (such as the initiatory shrine of Glaukos at Knossos) would no longer have been welcome. More fundamental, however, were developments on the island itself (now forming half of an imperial province with North African Cyrenaica). Prominent Cretan families, increasingly engaged in far-flung networks of commerce, patronage, and ritual practice, had less interest in fostering purely parochial remembrances. With the passing of the competitive days of Cretan cities, large and self-assured polities such as Gortyn felt less need to cultivate ties to their rural hinterlands. A stable political landscape, and one where significant decisions were normally taken by aloof powers, left little scope for narrowly based appeals to the past.

We can qualify somewhat this schematic presentation of the "before" and "after" of Hellenistic and Roman Crete. First, certain brands of Cretan memory did continue to possess influence and authority within the empire. Cretans could assert insular pride and claims to consideration through the island's ties to Minos, to the Trojan War, and to the birth (and, more controversially, death) of Zeus. Such celebrated myths established contact and opened conversations across the empire – much as we have seen happening with select aspects of the past in the case of Roman Greece. The Cretan past was thus by no means abandoned following the Hellenistic period, but particular elements – those with a high-profile, broad-spectrum appeal – were now groomed and emphasized. A second qualification lies in the sphere of cave cult. According to the general model just outlined, ritual activity in ancient caves might be predicted to end at the same time as the modest veneration of rural landmarks or ancient tombs. Instead, cave cult seemingly reaches its high point in the Roman period, and not all of this activity can be explained away by reference to illustrious figures such as Zeus or Minos. An alternative form of commemoration here survives, one that bucks other visible trends but whose interpretation remains uncertain.

Only in very recent years has historic Crete, overshadowed by the modern power of the island's prehistoric past, begun to receive the attention it deserves. One legacy of this state of affairs is the entrenched image of a Crete in eternal thrall to its Minoan heritage. Such a presupposition had become very easy to doubt, but now we can actually begin to see just how inventively the Cretan past was treated over time. A pattern emerges in unmistakable fashion: the past clearly "haunted" the present in two very distinct ways, in the two very distinct societies of Hellenistic and Roman Crete.

MULTIPLE MESSENIANS

Discussion of the Messenians also broke into two broad temporal components: first, the period when the region lay under Spartan control, and then the subsequent, post-liberation epoch. In the former period, when they labored under coercive forms of exploitation, helots (at least in some areas) settled in clustered units; they were involved in regional and local sanctuaries; they made ritual offerings at tombs that, whatever their precise associations, must have appeared ancient. All these places provided opportunities for communal practice and mutual support, as well as for the transmission of memories. Only the contexts for such transmission survive to be examined; the reticence of our sources leaves us no sense of the focus or content of what was said or thought about the past.

Despite their oppressed status and the silence imposed on them, we cannot presume that all helots remembered alike; varied memory communities can, tentatively, be argued to be at work. Status differences, if constrained by circumstances, did mark the body of Messenians. Votive offerings or signs of feasting at tomb cults and sanctuaries suggest that display and commensality helped to shape such distinctions, raising implications about the control of social memory even in this "flattened" society. The possibility of different strands of memory may help account for faint glimpses of disunity among helots. Certainly, other residents of the region (notably the Spartans themselves) possessed variant understandings of the Messenian past, divergent understandings that fed remarkably long-lived hostilities and resentments.

Orbiting around their homeland were the dispossessed Messenians of the diaspora, those who had fled at various points in the long struggle with Sparta and whose families endured decades or even centuries of exile. The majority of evidence about this diaspora community long postdates that exile, and tales of their steadfastness no doubt improved in the telling. Nevertheless, signs of adherence to Messenia and to being *hoi Messenioi* are manifest in this group's cult choices, in preservation of their name and dialect, in ongoing opposition to Sparta, in their ultimate return home. Versions of the Messenian past, complete with accretions and alterations, surely evolved among these people *in absentia*. With the liberation of Messenia, the admixture of returned exiles and freed helots must have proved something of a commemorative shock, adding to all the other wondrous changes and confusions faced by the region at that time.

Claims about the Messenian past advanced following the liberation of 370/369 BC have frequently been dismissed as an invented pseudo-history. Many historians have taken for granted that nothing links helot memories (if such things, indeed, are even allowed to have existed) with this newly crafted past. I have great misgivings about that supposition and, more particularly, about the grounds on which it is based. Although certainty on the matter is impossible, that rupture may not have been quite so unbridgeable, and threads of memory may well have connected helot remembrance with what was selected for display in the Hellenistic Asklepieion of Messene.

That is a long way from saying that liberation did not work dramatic transformations in patterns of Messenian memory. The radical changes that ensued, in all aspects of life, would have required highly imaginative commemorative responses. In their quest for political acceptance and social affirmation, the Messenians had to make public and unequivocal where they stood in relation to other Greek genealogies and pantheons, to declare what was worthy about "being Messenian." In the central foundation of Messene itself, a sense of communal identity was particularly needed to bind together its newly mixed population. The public memorial space of the Asklepieion articulated these necessary narratives, with homage firmly trained upon early Messenian kings and heroes and upon Theban liberators. Elsewhere in Messenia the development of new polities, such as Pylos, simultaneously required reorientation in aid of more local loyalties, leading to the regional development of a far richer, more diverse commemorative landscape. Forgetfulness was everywhere part and parcel of these restructurings. "Bad memories" – anything recalling the lack of independence and the fact of territorial dispossession – were dropped, or at least received no visible formal commemoration. Continued antagonism with Sparta none the less suggests that these memories, if "disremembered," were never entirely erased.

These conjectures about the long-silent Messenians challenge many former approaches to this difficult subject. Adopting social memory as the lens through which to view these peoples not only evades the (insoluble) problem of recovering their "true" history, but shatters their image as an undifferentiated, impenetrable subject population. Recognizing the later filters placed upon their history by the Messenians themselves (above all their stern occlusion of the Spartan past) should prevent us from following blindly in their footsteps and seeing only what they wished to be seen. The landscape and monuments of Messenia reveal phantoms once thought best forgotten, for reasons we should no longer accept.

*

These three short stories, of course, only propose a starting point for the study of social memory in the ancient Greek world. Moreover – since one of the blessings of archaeology is the continual expansion of our data base – future additional evidence will certainly refine, or perhaps undercut, the interpretations of Achaia, Crete, and Messenia I have presented here. Still, they serve to illustrate how we can strengthen our grasp on "uses of the past in the past," and more particularly how we can access a broader spectrum of memorial stances and practices by taking full advantage of available material evidence.

If such a demonstration was the central mission of this book, I would also note several other positive outcomes. First has been the pleasure of prodding classical archaeology along non-traditional paths. Second are the fresh questions provoked, and unaccustomed data sets employed, when social memory becomes a target for investigation. And third is the salutary reminder of just how far memorious interventions in the past irrevocably affect our understandings in the present.

The most direct precursors to this book lie in two quite distinct areas: in the archaeology of prehistoric European monuments, and in the anthropology of marginalized, often dispossessed peoples. The Mediterranean world may seem, at first blush, an odd place for the two fields to intersect. Recent critique has certainly castigated classical archaeology for its traditionally conservative, elitist orientation, for its absorption with facts far removed from the daily lives (let alone memories) of antiquity.[2] Such attacks, however, only point to some healthy soul-searching, and since the 1980s or so classical archaeologists have attempted to use their undeniably rich data in more sophisticated ways. In that spirit, I would argue that the perspective offered by a concern for social memory is healthy for the field, in that it expands the scope and range of questions we think fit to ask.

That perspective also forces us to reconsider the deployment of our evidence. Looking back over the diverse types of archaeological data utilized in this study, it is clear that many entrenched divisions have fallen by the wayside. Categories usually kept carefully segregated have been juxtaposed and jointly interrogated: regional settlement patterns with tombs, urban artistic programs with minor rural shrines, streets with battlefields, centuriation with portraiture. Since memories are invested in all of these places, how can – and why should – they be kept in isolation? I earlier contended that a focus on memory does not require entirely novel sources of information. What it does demand is an extra turn of the kaleidoscope, bringing heterogeneous relevant elements into unforeseen but enlightening conjunctions.

Finally, the study of social memory carries with it some inescapable consequences. The way in which "the past is modeled, invented, reinvented, and reconstructed by the present" – my quotation from Jan Assmann at this book's very beginning – has been, and will always remain, a continuous process, continually reshaping in turn the evidence on which we often unquestioningly rely. Tacitly or explicitly, we acknowledge our loss of innocence, and it is no longer possible to evade the issue, ignoring or downplaying the vital force of social memory. One way forward is to turn for guidance to the matrix through which memory works, to the commemorative framework of landscape and of monuments.

2. For recent critiques of the discipline of classical archaeology, see Dyson 1998; Morris 1994; 2000; Shanks 1996; Snodgrass 1987.

BIBLIOGRAPHY

Abercrombie, T. A. (1998) *Pathways of Memory and Power: Ethnography and History among an Andean People*, Madison.

Ager, S. (1994) Hellenistic Crete and KOINODIKION, *JHS* 114: 1–18.

Alcock, S. E. (1991) Tomb cult and the post-classical polis, *AJA* 95: 447–67.

(1993) *Graecia Capta: The Landscapes of Roman Greece*, Cambridge.

(1994a) Breaking up the Hellenistic world: survey and society, in I. Morris, ed., *Classical Greece: Ancient Histories and Modern Archaeologies*, 171–90. Cambridge.

(1994b) Minding the gap in Hellenistic and Roman Greece, in S. E. Alcock and R. Osborne, eds., *Placing the Gods: Sanctuaries and Sacred Space in Ancient Greece*, 247–61. Oxford.

(1996) Landscapes of memory and the authority of Pausanias, in J. Bingen, ed., *Pausanias historien* (EntrHardt 41), 241–76. Vandœuvres.

(1997) Greece: a landscape of resistance?, in D. J. Mattingly, ed., *Dialogues in Roman Imperialism: Power, Discourse and Discrepant Experience in the Roman Empire*, 103–15. Ann Arbor.

(1998a) Liberation and conquest: Hellenistic and Roman Messenia, in J. L. Davis, ed., *Sandy Pylos: An Archaeological History from Nestor to Navarino*, 179–91. Austin.

(1998b) Power from the dead: tomb cult in postliberation Messenia, in J. L. Davis, ed., *Sandy Pylos: An Archaeological History from Nestor to Navarino*, 199–204. Austin.

(1999) The pseudo-history of Messenia unplugged, *TAPA* 129: 333–41.

(2000) Classical order and the uses of nostalgia, in J. Richards and M. Van Buren, eds., *Order, Legitimacy and Wealth in Early States*, 110–19. Cambridge.

(2001a) The peculiar Book IV and the problem of the Messenian past, in S. E. Alcock, J. F. Cherry, and J. Elsner, eds., *Pausanias: Travel and Memory in Roman Greece*, 142–53. New York.

(2001b) The reconfiguration of memory in the eastern Roman empire, in S. E. Alcock, T. N. D'Altroy, K. D. Morrison, and C. M. Sinopoli, eds., *Empires: Perspectives from Archaeology and History*, 323–50. Cambridge.

(forthcoming) Four colonies and some questions: convergences, divergences and identity politics, in G. Stein, ed., *The Archaeology of Colonization in Cross-Cultural Perspective* (School of American Research Advanced Seminar). Santa Fe.

Alcock, S. E., Berlin, A., Harrison, A., Heath, S., and Spencer. N. (in prep.) The Pylos Regional Archaeological Project. Part IV: Historic Messenia, Geometric to Late Roman, *Hesperia*.

Alcock, S. E., Cherry, J. F., and Davis, J. L. (1994) Intensive survey, agricultural practice and the classical landscape of Greece, in I. Morris, ed., *Classical Greece: Ancient Histories and Modern Archaeologies*, 137–90. Cambridge.

Alcock, S. E. and Osborne, R., eds. (1994) *Placing the Gods: Sanctuaries and Sacred Space in Ancient Greece*, Oxford.

Alcock, S. E. and Van Dyke, R., eds. (in prep.) *The Archaeology of Memory*, Malden, MA.

Alexiou, S. (1972) Anaskaphai eis Agia Pelagian Irakleiou, *AAA* 5: 230–44.

Alonso, A. M. (1988) The effects of truth: re-presentations of the past and the imagining of community, *Journal of Historical Sociology* 1: 33–58.

Amandry, P. (1980) Sur les concours Argiens, in *Etudes Argiennes* (*BCH* Supplément 6), 211–53. Paris.

Anderson, B. (1991) *Imagined Communities: Reflections on the Origins and Spread of Nationalism* (revised edn), London.

Anderson, G. (1993) *The Second Sophistic: A Cultural Phenomenon in the Roman Empire*, London.

Andrei, O. (1984) *A. Claudius Charax di Pergamo: interessi antiquari e antichità cittadine nell'età degli Antonini*, Bologna.

Antonaccio, C. M. (1994) Placing the past: the Bronze Age in the cultic topography of Early Greece, in S. E. Alcock and R. Osborne, eds., *Placing the Gods: Sanctuaries and Sacred Space in Ancient Greece*, 79–104. Oxford.

   (1995) *An Archaeology of Ancestors: Tomb Cult and Hero Cult in Early Greece*, Lanham, MD.

Appadurai, A. (1981) The past as a scarce resource, *Man* 16: 201–19.

   (1988) Introduction: place and voice in anthropological theory, *Cultural Anthropology* 3: 16–20.

Arafat, K. (1996) *Pausanias' Greece: Ancient Artists and Roman Rulers*, Cambridge.

Arditti, R. (1999) *Searching for Life: The Grandmothers of the Plaza de Mayo and the Disappeared Children of Argentina*, Berkeley.

Asheri, D. (1983) La diaspora e il ritorno dei Messeni, in E. Gabba, ed., *Tria Corda: Scritti in onore di Arnaldo Momigliano*, 27–42. Como.

Ashmore, W. and Knapp, A. B., eds. (1999) *Archaeologies of Landscape: Contemporary Perspectives*, Oxford.

Assmann, A. (1996) Texts, traces and trash: the changing media of cultural memory, *Representations* 56: 123–34.

Assmann, A., Assmann, J., and Hardmeier, C., eds. (1983) *Schrift und Gedächtnis: Beiträge zur Archäologie der literarischen Kommunikation*, Munich.

Assmann, J. (1988) Stein und Zeit. Das monumentale Gedächtnis der alt-ägypt. Kultur, in J. Assmann and T. Hölscher, eds., *Kultur und Gedächtnis*, 9–19. Frankfurt am Main.

   (1992) *Das kulturelle Gedächtnis: Schrift, Erinnerung und politische Identität in frühen Hochkulturen*, Munich.

   (1995) *Stein und Zeit: Mensch und Gesellschaft im alten Ägypten*, Munich.

   (1997) *Moses the Egyptian: The Memory of Egypt in Western Monotheism*, Cambridge, MA.

Assmann, J. and Hölscher, T., eds. (1988) *Kultur und Gedächtnis*, Frankfurt am Main.

Auberger, J. (1992a) Pausanias et les Messéniens: une histoire d'amour!, *Revue des études anciennes* 94: 187–97.

   (1992b) Pausanias romancier? Le témoignage du Livre IV, *Dialogues d'histoire ancienne* 18: 257–80.

Azaryahu, M. (1993) From remains to relics: authentic monuments in the Israeli landscape, *History and Memory* 5: 82–103.

Bachelard, G. (1964) *The Poetics of Space*, trans. by M. Jolas, Boston.

Bahloul, J. (1996) *The Architecture of Memory: A Jewish-Muslim Household in Colonial Algeria*, Cambridge.

Baines, J. and Yoffee, N. (1998) Order, legitimacy and wealth in ancient Egypt and Mesopotamia, in G. Feinman and J. Marcus, eds., *The Archaic State: A Comparative Perspective*, 199–260. Santa Fe.

Baker, F. (1988) Archaeology and the heritage industry, *Archaeological Review from Cambridge* 7.2: 141–44.

Baker, K. M. (1985) Memory and practice: politics and the representation of the past in eighteenth century France, *Representations* 11: 134–64.

Baladié, R. (1980) *Le Péloponnèse de Strabon: étude de géographie historique*, Paris.

Baldassari, P. (1995) Augusto soter: ipotesi su monopteros dell'Acropolis ateniese, *Ostraka* 4.1: 69–84.

Baldwin Bowsky, M. (1989) Portrait of a polis: Lato pros Kamara (Crete) in the late second century BC, *Hesperia* 58: 331–47.

 (1994) Cretan connections: the transformation of Hierapytna, *Cretan Studies* 4: 1–44.

 (1999) The business of being Roman: the prosopographical evidence, in A. Chaniotis, ed., *From Minoan Farmers to Roman Traders: Sidelights on the Economy of Ancient Crete*, 305–47. Stuttgart.

Baltsas, C. (1987) *Pylos: Navarino, Niokastro, Anaktoro Nestoros*, Athens.

Banti, L. (1941–43) I culti Minoici e Greci di Haghia Triada, *ASAtene* 3–5: 9–74.

Barber, R. (1999) *A Guide to Rural Attika*, Edinburgh.

Barkan, E. (2000) *The Guilt of Nations: Restitution and Negotiating Historical Injustices*, New York.

Barrett, J. C., Bradley, R., and Green, M. (1991) *Landscape, Monuments and Society: The Prehistory of Cranborne Chase*, Cambridge.

Bartlett, F. C. (1932) *Remembering*, Cambridge.

Basso, K. and Feld, S. (1996) *Senses of Place*, Santa Fe.

Bastide, R. (1970) Mémoire collective et sociologie du bricolage, *L'Année sociologique* 21: 65–108.

 (1978) *The African Religions of Brazil: Toward a Sociology of the Interpenetration of Civilizations*, trans. H. Sebba, Baltimore.

Battaglia, D. (1992) The body in the gift: memory and forgetting in Sabarl mortuary exchange, *American Ethnologist* 19: 3–18.

Bauslaugh, R. A. (1990) Messenian dialect and dedications of the "Methanioi," *Hesperia* 59: 661–68.

Beard, M. (1987) A complex of times: no more sheep on Romulus' birthday, *PCPS* 33: 1–15.

Beard, M. and Henderson, J. (2001) *Classical Art: From Greece to Rome* (Oxford History of Art), Oxford.

Bender, B. (1992) Theorizing landscape, and the prehistoric landscapes of Stonehenge, *Man* 27: 735–55.

 ed. (1993) *Landscape: Politics and Perspectives*, Oxford.

Benjamin, A. and Raubitschek, A. (1959) Arae Augusti, *Hesperia* 28: 65–85.

Benjamin, W. (1968) Theses on the philosophy of history, in *Illuminations*, trans. H. Zohn, 253–64. New York.

Bennet, J. (1990) Knossos in context: comparative perspectives on the Linear B administration of LM II–III Crete, *AJA* 94: 193–211.

Ben-Yehuda, N. (1995) *The Masada Myth: Collective Memory and Mythmaking in Israel*, Madison.

Bérard, C. (1982) Récupérer la mort du prince: héroïsation et formation de la cité, in G. Gnoli and J.-P. Vernant, eds., *La mort, les morts dans les sociétés anciennes*, 89–105. Cambridge.

Bergemann, J. (1998) *Die römische Kolonie von Butrint und die Romanisierung Griechenlands*, Munich.

Bergmann, B. (1994) The Roman house as memory theater: the House of the Tragic Poet in Pompeii, *Art Bulletin* 76: 225–56.

Beschi, L. (1974) Adriano e Creta, *Antichità Cretesi: studi in onore di Doro Levi*, vol. II, 219–26. Catania.

Bhabha, H. K. (1985) Signs taken for wonders: questions of ambivalence and authority under a tree outside Delhi, May 1817, *Critical Inquiry* 12: 144–65.

(1994) *The Location of Culture*, London and New York.

Bikerman, E. (1952) Origines gentium, *CP* 47: 65–81.

Binder, W. (1969) *Der Roma-Augustus Monopteros auf der Akropolis in Athen und sein typologischer Ort*, Stuttgart.

Bingham, A. (1995) Crete's Roman past, *History Today* 45: 4–5.

Black, D. W., Kunze, D., and Pickles, J., eds. (1989) *Commonplaces: Essays on the Nature of Place*, Lanham, MD.

Blackman, D. and Branigan, K. (1975) An archaeological survey on the south coast of Crete, between the Ayiofarango and Chrisostomos, *BSA* 70: 17–36.

(1977) An archaeological survey of the lower catchment of the Ayiofarango valley, *BSA* 72: 13–84.

(1982) The excavation of an Early Minoan tholos tomb at Ayia Kyriaki, Ayiofarango, southern Crete, *BSA* 77: 1–57.

Bloch, M. (1977) The past and the present in the past, *Man* 12: 278–92.

Boardman, J. (1961) *The Cretan Collection in Oxford: The Dictaean Cave and Iron Age Crete*, Oxford.

Boatwright, M. (1983) Further thoughts on Hadrianic Athens, *Hesperia* 52: 173–76.

(2000) *Hadrian and the Cities of the Roman Empire*, Princeton.

Boffo, L. (1988) Epigrafi di città greche: un'espressione di storiografia locale, in L. Boffo, ed., *Studi di Storia e Storiografia Antiche per Emilio Gabba*, 9–48. Pavia.

Bohannan, L. A. (1952) A genealogical charter, *Africa* 22: 301–15.

Borg, A. (1991) *War Memorials*, London.

Borofsky, R. (1987) *Making History: Pukapukan and Anthropological Constructions of Knowledge*, Cambridge.

Bosanquet, R. C. (1939–40) Dicte and the temples of Dictaean Zeus (with revisions by R. W. Hutchinson), *BSA* 40: 60–77.

Bourguet, M.-N., Valensi, L., and Wachtel, N., eds. (1990) *Between Memory and History*, London.

Bousquet, J. (1938) Le temple d'Aphrodite et d'Arès à Sta Lenikà (Crète orientale), *BCH* 62: 386–408.

Bowen, A. (1992) *Plutarch, The Malice of Herodotus (de Malignitate Herodoti)*, Warminster.

Bowersock, G. W. (1961) Eurycles of Sparta, *JRS* 51: 111–18.

(1964) Augustus on Aegina, *CQ* 14: 120–21.

(1965) *Augustus and the Greek World*, Oxford.

(1969) *Greek Sophists in the Roman Empire*, Oxford.

ed. (1974) *Approaches to the Second Sophistic*, University Park, PA.

(1984) Augustus and the East: the problem of the succession, in F. Millar and E. Segal, eds., *Caesar Augustus: Seven Aspects*, 169–88. Oxford.

Bowie, E. L. (1974) The Greeks and their past in the Second Sophistic, in M. I. Finley, ed., *Studies in Ancient Society*, 166–209. London (= *PastPres* 46 [1970]: 3–41).

(1982) The importance of sophists, *Yale Classical Studies* 27: 29–59.

(1996) Past and present in Pausanias, in J. Bingen, ed., *Pausanias historien* (EntrHardt 41), 207–39. Vandœuvres.

Brady, J. E. and Ashmore, W. (1999) Mountains, caves, water: ideational landscapes of the Ancient Maya, in W. Ashmore and A. B. Knapp, eds., *Archaeologies of Landscape: Contemporary Perspectives*, 124–45. Oxford.

Bradley, R. (1987) Time regained: the creation of continuity, *Journal of the British Archaeological Association* 140: 1–17.

(1990) *Monuments and the Monumental* (= *World Archaeology* 22.2), London.

(1993) *Altering the Earth: The Origins of Monuments in Britain and Continental Europe* (Society of Antiquaries of Scotland Monograph Series 8), Edinburgh.

(1998) *The Significance of Monuments: On the Shaping of Human Experience in Neolithic and Bronze Age Europe*, London.

Bradley, R. and Williams, H., eds. (1998) *The Past in the Past: The Reuse of Ancient Monuments* (= *World Archaeology* 30.1), London.

Branigan, K. (with contributions by T. Carter and P. O'Connor) (1998) Prehistoric and early historic settlement in the Ziros region, eastern Crete, *BSA* 93: 23–90.

Braun, T. (1994) Khrestous poiein, *Classical Quarterly* 44: 40–45.

Braund, D. (1997) Greeks and barbarians: the Black Sea region and Hellenism under the early empire, in S. E. Alcock, ed., *The Early Roman Empire in the East*, 121–36. Oxford.

Brenk, F. E. (1987) An imperial heritage: the religious spirit of Plutarch of Chaironeia, *ANRW* II.36.1: 248–349.

Breuillot, M. (1985) L'eau et les dieux de Messène, *Dialogues d'histoire ancienne* 11: 789–804.

Brewer, D. (2001) *The Flame of Freedom: The Greek War of Independence, 1821–1833*, London.

Briscoe, J. (1974) Rome and the class struggle in the Greek states: 200–146 BC, in M. I. Finley, ed., *Studies in Ancient Society*, 53–73. London (= *PastPres* 36 [1967]: 3–20).

Brumfiel, E. M. (2000) The politics of high culture: issues of worth and rank, in J. Richards and M. Van Buren, eds., *Order, Legitimacy and Wealth in Early States*, 131–39. Cambridge.

Brunt, P. A. (1994) The bubble of the Second Sophistic, *Bulletin of the Institute of Classical Studies of the University of London* 39: 25–52.

Burke, P. (1989) History as social memory, in T. Butler, ed., *Memory: History, Culture and the Mind*, 97–113. Oxford.

Cadogan, G. (1977–78) Pyrgos, Crete, 1970–77, *Archaeological Reports* 24: 70–84.

(1981) A probable shrine in the country house at Pyrgos, in R. Hägg and N. Marinatos, eds., *Sanctuaries and Cults in the Aegean Bronze Age* (Proceedings of the First International Symposium at the Swedish Institute in Athens, 12–13 May, 1980), 169–71. Lund.

(1992) Myrtos-Pyrgos, in J. W. Myers, E. E. Myers, and G. Cadogan, eds., *The Aerial Atlas of Ancient Crete*, 202–9. London.

Callaghan, P. J. (1978) KRS 1976: excavations at a shrine of Glaukos, Knossos, *BSA* 73: 1–30.

(1981) The Little Palace Well and Knossian pottery of the late third and second century B.C., *BSA* 76: 35–58.

(1992) Archaic to Hellenistic pottery, in L. H. Sackett, ed., *Knossos From Greek City to Roman Colony: Excavations at the Unexplored Mansion* II, 89–136. Oxford.

(1994) Archaic, Classical and Hellenistic Knossos – a historical summary, in D. Evely, H. Hughes-Brock, and N. Momigliano, eds., *Knossos: A Labyrinth of History. Papers in Honour of Sinclair Hood*, 135–40. Oxford.

Callaghan, P. J., Catling, H. W., Catling, E. A., and Smyth, D. (1981) Knossos 1975: Minoan *paralipomena* and post-Minoan remains, *BSA* 76: 83–107.

Camp, J. M. (1986) *The Athenian Agora: Excavations in the Heart of Classical Athens*, London. (Updated edn 1992.)

Carroll, K. K. (1982) *The Parthenon Inscription*, Durham, NC.

Carruthers, M. (1990) *The Book of Memory: A Study of Memory in Medieval Culture*, Cambridge.

Carruthers, M. and Ziolkowski, J. M. (forthcoming) *The Medieval Craft of Memory: An Anthology of Words and Pictures*, Philadelphia.

Carsten, J. (1995) The politics of forgetting: migration, kinship and memory on the periphery of the southeast Asian state, *Journal of the Royal Anthropological Institute* n.s. 1: 317–35.

Cartledge, P. A. (1979) *Sparta and Lakonia: A Regional History c. 1300–362 BC*, London. (Reprinted with corrections and additions 2001.)

(1987) *Agesilaos and the Crisis of Sparta*, Baltimore. (Reprinted 2000.)

(1991) Richard Talbert's revision of the Spartan–Helot struggle: a reply, *Historia* 40: 379–81.

(1997) *The Greeks: A Portrait of Self and Others*, Oxford and New York.

(2001) Rebels & sambos in Classical Greece: a comparative view, in *Spartan Reflections*, 127–52. London. (Originally published 1985.)

Cartledge, P. A. and Spawforth, A. (1989) *Hellenistic and Roman Sparta: A Tale of Two Cities*, London.

Casey, E. S. (1987) *Remembering: A Phenomenological Study*, Bloomington.

(1993) *Getting Back into Place: Toward a Renewed Understanding of the Place-World*, Bloomington.

Catling, H., Ridley, C., Carington Smith, J., Smyth, D., and Dunn, A. W. (1982) Knossos 1978: Roman finds at the Venezeleion, *BSA* 77: 59–64.

Cavanagh, W. G. and Curtis, M., eds., with J. N. Coldstream and A. W. Johnston, co-eds. (1998) *Post-Minoan Crete. Proceedings of the First Colloquium on Post-Minoan Crete held by the British School at Athens and the Institute of Archaeology, University College London, 10–11 November 1995* (British School at Athens Studies 2), London.

Cavanagh, W. G. and Walker, S., eds. (1998) *Sparta in Laconia. Proceedings of the Nineteenth British Museum Classical Colloquium* (British School at Athens Studies 4), London.

Champlin, E. (1981) Serenus Sammonicus, *HSCP* 85: 189–212.

Chaniotis, A. (1988a) Habgierige Götter, habgierige Städte. Heiligumsbesitz und Gebietanspruch in den kretischen Staatsverträgen, *Ktema* 13: 21–39.

(1988b) *Historie und Historiker in den griechischen Inschriften*, Stuttgart.

(1988c) Vinum Creticum excellens: Zum Weinhandel Kretas, *Münstersche Beiträge zur antiken Handelsgeschichte* 7: 62–89.

(1995a) City and sanctuary in Classical and Hellenistic Crete: an epigraphic survey. Paper presented at 'Post-Minoan Crete. Proceedings of the First Colloquium on Post-Minoan Crete' held by the British School at Athens and the Institute of Archaeology, University College London, 10–11 November 1995.

(1995b) Problems of "pastoralism" and "transhumance" in Classical and Hellenistic Crete, *Orbis Terrarum* 1: 39–89.

(1996) *Die Verträge zwischen kretischen Städten in hellenistischer Zeit*, Stuttgart.

ed. (1999a) *From Minoan Farmers to Roman Traders: Sidelights on the Economy of Ancient Crete*, Stuttgart.

(1999b) Milking the mountain: economic activities on the Cretan uplands in the Classical and Hellenistic period, in A. Chaniotis, ed., *From Minoan Farmers to Roman Traders: Sidelights on the Economy of Ancient Crete*, 181–220. Stuttgart.

Cherry, J. F. (2001) Travel, nostalgia and Pausanias's Giant, in S. E. Alcock, J. F. Cherry, and J. Elsner, eds., *Pausanias: Travel and Memory in Roman Greece*, 247–55. New York.

Chippindale, C. (1993) Ambition, deference, discrepancy, consumption: the intellectual background to a post-processual archaeology, in N. Yoffee and A. Sherratt, eds., *Archaeological Theory: Who Sets the Agenda?*, 27–36. Cambridge.

(1994) *Stonehenge Complete*, New York.

Chippindale, C., Devereux, P., Fowler, P., Jones, R., and Sebastian, T., eds. (1990) *Who Owns Stonehenge?*, London.

Clifford, J. (1994) Diasporas, *Cultural Anthropology* 9: 302–38.

Clinton, K. (1989) The Eleusinian Mysteries: Roman initiates and benefactors, second century B.C. to A.D. 267, *ANRW* II.18.2: 1499–1539.

(1997) Eleusis and the Romans: Late Republic to Marcus Aurelius, in M. Hoff and S. Rotroff, eds., *The Romanization of Athens*, 161–81. Oxford.

Cohen, A. (1995) Alexander and Achilles – Macedonians and "Mycenaeans," in J. B. Carter and S. P. Morris, eds., *The Ages of Homer: A Tribute to Emily Townsend Vermeule*, 483–505. Austin.

Cohen, A. P. (1985) *The Symbolic Construction of Community*, London.

Coldstream, J. N. (1973) *Knossos: The Sanctuary of Demeter* (BSA Supplement 8), Oxford.
(1976) Hero cults in the age of Homer, *JHS* 96: 8–17.
(1998) Minos Redivivus: some nostalgic Knossians of the ninth century BC (a summary), in W. G. Cavanagh and M. Curtis, eds., with J. N. Coldstream and A. W. Johnston, co-eds., *Post-Minoan Crete. Proceedings of the First Colloquium on Post-Minoan Crete held by the British School at Athens and the Institute of Archaeology, University College London, 10–11 November 1995*, 58–61. (British School at Athens Studies 2), London.

Coldstream, J. N. and Catling, H. W., eds. (1996) *Knossos North Cemetery: Early Greek Tombs* (BSA Supplement 28; 4 vols.), London.

Coleman, J. (1992) *Ancient and Medieval Memories: Studies in the Reconstruction of the Past*, Cambridge.

Coleman, K. M. (1993) Launching into history: aquatic displays in the early empire, *JRS* 83: 48–74.

Collard, A. (1989) Investigating "social memory" in a Greek context, in E. Tonkin, M. McDonald, and M. Chapman, eds., *History and Ethnicity*, 89–103. London.

Comaroff, J. (1985) *Body of Power, Spirit of Resistance: The Culture and History of a South African People*, Chicago.

Confino, A. (1997) Collective memory and cultural history: problems of method, *American Historical Review* 102: 1386–1404.

Connerton, P. (1989) *How Societies Remember*, Cambridge.

Cook, A. B. (1914) *Zeus: A Study in Ancient Religion* I, Cambridge. (Reprinted 1964.)
(1940) *Zeus: A Study in Ancient Religion* II, Cambridge. (Reprinted 1964.)

Coulson, W. D. E. and Wilkie, N. (1983) Archaic to Roman times: the site and environs, in W. A. McDonald, W. D. E. Coulson, and J. Rosser, eds., *Excavations in Nichoria in Southwest Greece, III: Dark Age and Byzantine Occupation*, 332–50. Minneapolis.

Coulton, J. J. (1983) The buildings of Oinoanda, *PCPS* 29: 1–20.

Crane, S. (1997) Writing the individual back into collective memory, *American Historical Review* 102: 1372–85.

Crawford, M. H. (1978) Greek intellectuals and the Roman aristocracy in the first century BC, in P. Garnsey and C. R. Whittaker, eds., *Imperialism in the Ancient World*, 193–207. Cambridge.

Cronon, W. (1983) *Changes in the Land: Indians, Colonists and the Ecology of New England*, New York.

Crossland, Z. (2000) Buried lives: forensic archaeology and the disappeared in Argentina, *Archaeological Dialogues* 7: 146–59.

Crowther, C. (1988) A note on Minoan Dikta, *BSA* 83: 37–44.

Cucuzza, N. (1997) Considerazioni su alcuni culti nella Messarà di epoca storica e sui rapporti territoriali fra Festòs e Gortina, *Atti dell'Accademia Nazionale dei Lincei. Rendiconti* 9.8: 63–93.

Culley, G. R. (1975) The restoration of sanctuaries in Attica: *IG*, II(2), 1035, *Hesperia* 44: 207–23.
(1977) The restoration of sanctuaries in Attica, II. The structure of *IG*, II(2), 1035 and the topography of Salamis, *Hesperia* 46: 282–98.

Curty, O. (1995) *Les parentés légendaires entre cités grecques*, Geneva.

D'Agata, A.-L. (1997) The shrines on the Piazzale dei Sacelli at Ayia Triadha. The LM IIIC and SM material: a summary, in J. Driessen and A. Farnoux, eds., *La Crète Mycénienne* (*BCH* Supplément 30), 85–100. Athens.

(1998) Changing patterns in a Minoan and post-Minoan sanctuary: the case of Agia Triada, in W. G. Cavanagh and M. Curtis, eds., with J. N. Coldstream and A. W. Johnston, co-eds., *Post-Minoan Crete. Proceedings of the First Colloquium on Post-Minoan Crete held by the British School at Athens and the Institute of Archaeology, University College London, 10–11 November 1995*, 19–26. (British School at Athens Studies 2), London.

Dagron, G. (1984) *Constantinople imaginaire: études sur le recueil des Patria*, Paris.

Daly, L. W. (1950) Roman study abroad, *AJP* 71: 40–58.

Darian-Smith, K. and Hamilton, P., eds. (1994) *Memory and History in Twentieth Century Australia*, Melbourne and New York.

Dascalakis, A. (1962) *Problèmes historiques autour de la bataille des Thermopyles*, Paris.

Davaras, C. (1971) Excavations at Stylos, district of Apokoronas, *AAA* 4: 42–44.

Daverio Rocchi, G. (1988) *Frontiera e confini nella Grecia antica*, Rome.

David, E. (1989) Laughter in Spartan society, in A. Powell, ed., *Classical Sparta: Techniques behind Her Success*, 1–25. London.

Davies, J. (1993) War memorials, in D. Clark, ed., *The Sociology of Death*, 112–28. Oxford.

Davies, J. K. (1984) Cultural, social and economic features of the Hellenistic world, in F. W. Walbank, A. E. Astin, M. W. Frederiksen, and R. M. Ogilvie, eds., *The Cambridge Ancient History, VII.I: The Hellenistic World* (second edition), 257–320. Cambridge.

Davies, P. (2000) *Death and the Emperor: Roman Imperial Funerary Monuments from Augustus to Marcus Aurelius*, New York.

Davis, J. (1996) *The Landscape of Belief: Encountering the Holy Land in Nineteenth-Century American Art and Culture*, Princeton.

Davis, J. L. (1998a) From Pausanias to present, in J. L. Davis, ed., *Sandy Pylos: An Archaeological History from Nestor to Navarino*, 273–91. Austin.

(1998b) Glimpses of Messenia past, in J. L. Davis, ed., *Sandy Pylos: An Archaeological History from Nestor to Navarino*, xxix–xliii. Austin.

ed. (1998c) *Sandy Pylos: An Archaeological History from Nestor to Navarino*, Austin.

Davis, J. L., Alcock, S. E., Bennet, J., Lolos, Y. G., and Shelmerdine, C. W. (1997) The Pylos Regional Archaeological Project. Part I: Overview and the archaeological survey, *Hesperia* 66: 391–494.

Davis, N. Z. and Starn, R. (1989) Introduction (Special Issue: Memory and Counter-Memory), *Representations* 26: 1–6.

Dawkins, R. M., Hawes, C. H., and Bosanquet, R. C. (1904–5) Excavations at Palaikastro IV, *BSA* 11: 258–308.

Den Boer, W. (1956) Political propaganda in Greek chronology, *Historia* 5: 162–77.

Di Vita, A. (1988) *Gortina* I, Rome.

(1992) Gortyn, in J. W. Myers, E. E. Myers, and G. Cadogan, eds., *The Aerial Atlas of Ancient Crete*, 96–103. London.

Di Vita, A. and La Regina, A., eds. (1984) *Creta Antica: cento anni di archeologia italiana (1884–1984)*, Rome.

Dinsmoor, W. B. (1920) The monument of Agrippa at Athens (abstract), *AJA* 24: 83.

(1940) The temple of Ares at Athens, *Hesperia* 9: 1–52.

Dinsmoor, W. B., Jr. (1974) The temple of Poseidon: a missing sima and other matters, *AJA* 78: 211–38.

(1982) Anchoring two floating temples, *Hesperia* 51: 410–52.

Dodwell, E. (1821) *Views in Greece, From Drawings by Edward Dodwell*, London.

Doukellis, P. (1988) Cadastres romains en Grèce: traces d'un réseau rural à Actia Nicopolis, *Dialogues d'histoire ancienne* 14: 159–66.

(1990) Actia Nicopolis: idéologie impériale, structures urbaines et développement régional, *JRA* 3: 399–406.

(1994) Le territoire de la colonie romaine de Corinthe, in L. Mendoni and P. Doukellis, eds., *Structures rurales et sociétés antiques. Actes du colloque de Corfou (14–16 mai 1992)*, 359–90. Paris.

Dryden, J. (1962) *Plutarch, The Lives of the Noble Grecians and Romans*, trans. J. Dryden and rev. A. H. Clough, New York. (Reprint, original publication 1864.)

Dubuisson, M. (1991) Graecus, graeculus, graecari: l'emploi péjoratif du nom des grecs en latin, in S. Saïd, ed., *HELLENISMOS: quelques jalons pour une histoire de l'identité grecque*, 315–35. Leiden.

Duby, G. and Lardreau, G. (1980) *Dialogues*, Paris.

Ducat, J. (1974) Le mépris des Hilotes, *Annales: Economie, Sociétés, Civilisations* 29: 1451–64.

(1978) Aspects de l'hilotisme, *Ancient Society* 9: 5–46.

(1990) *Les hilotes* (*BCH* Supplément 20), Athens.

Ducrey, P. (1970) Nouvelles remarques sur deux traités attalides avec des cités crétoises, *BCH* 94: 637–59.

Dyson, S. L. (1998) *Ancient Marbles to American Shores*, Philadelphia.

Eco, U. (1986) *Travels in Hyperreality*, London.

Edmonds, M. (1999) *Ancestral Geographies of the Neolithic: Landscapes, Monuments and Memory*, London.

Edwards, C. (1996) *Writing Rome: Textual Approaches to the City*, Cambridge.

Edwards, D.R. (1996) *Religion and Power: Pagans, Jews and Christians in the Greek East*, Oxford.

Eisner, R. (1991) *Travelers to an Antique Land: The History and Literature of Travel to Greece*, Ann Arbor.

Elsner, J. (1992) Pausanias: a Greek pilgrim in the Roman world, *PastPres* 135: 3–29.

(1995) *Art and the Roman Viewer: The Transformation of Art from the Pagan World to Christianity*, Cambridge.

(1997) The origins of the icon: pilgrimage, religion and visual culture in the Roman East as "resistance" to the centre, in S. E. Alcock, ed., *The Early Roman Empire in the East*, 178–99. Oxford.

Engels, D. (1990) *Roman Corinth: An Alternative Model for the Classical City*, Chicago.

Erdemgil, S. (1986) *Ephesus*, Istanbul.

Erickson, B. L. (2000) Late Archaic and Classical Crete: island pottery styles in an age of historical transition, *c.* 600–400 B.C. Unpublished Ph.D thesis, The University of Texas at Austin.

Etienne, R. and Piérart, M. (1975) Un décret du koinon des Hellènes à Platées en l'honneur de Glaucon, fils d'Etéoclès, d'Athènes, *BCH* 99: 51–75.

Erim, K. (1986) *Aphrodisias, City of Venus Aphrodite*, New York.

Evans, A. (1921) *The Palace of Minos: A Comparative Account of the Successive Stages of the Early Cretan Civilization as Illustrated by the Discoveries, I: The Neolithic and Early and Middle Minoan Ages*, New York. (Reprinted 1964.)

(1928) *The Palace of Minos: A Comparative Account of the Successive Stages of the Early Cretan Civilization as Illustrated by the Discoveries, II. I: Fresh Lights on Origins and External Relations: The Restoration in Town and Palace after Seismic Catastrophe towards Close of MM III, and the Beginnings of the New Era*, New York. (Reprinted 1964.)

Eves, R. (1996) Remembrance of things past: memory, body and the politics of feasting in New
        Ireland, Papua, New Guinea, *Oceania* 66: 266–77.
Fabian, J. (1983) *Time and the Other: How Anthropology Makes its Object*, New York.
Faklaris, P. (1990) *Archaia Kunouria*, Athens.
Fara, P. and Patterson, K., eds. (1998) *Memory*, Cambridge.
Farrell, J. (1997) The phenomenology of memory in Roman culture, *Classical Journal* 92:
        373–83.
Faure, P. (1964) *Fonctions des cavernes crétoises*, Paris.
Favro, D. (1993) Reading the Augustan city, in P. Holliday, ed., *Narrative and Event in Ancient
        Art*, 230–50. New York.
    (1996) *The Urban Image of Augustan Rome*, Cambridge.
    (1999) The city is a living thing: the performative role of an urban site in ancient Rome,
        the Vallis Murcia, in B. Bergmann and C. Kondoleon, eds., *The Art of Ancient Spec-
        tacle* (Studies in the History of Art 56; Center for Advanced Study in the Visual Arts
        Symposium Papers 34), 205–19. New Haven and London.
Felten, F. (1983) Heiligtümer oder Märkte?, *Antike Kunst* 26: 84–105.
Fentress, J. and Wickham, C. (1992) *Social Memory*, Oxford.
Ferrary, J.-L. (1988) *Philhellénisme et impérialisme: aspects idéologiques de la conquête romaine
        du monde hellénistique*, Paris and Rome.
Figueira, T. (1999) The evolution of the Messenian identity, in S. Hodkinson and A. Powell,
        eds., *Sparta: New Perspectives*, 211–44. London.
Finley, G. (1857) *Greece Under the Romans*, second edn, Edinburgh.
Finley, M. (1965) Myth, memory and history, *History and Theory* 4: 281–302.
Fisher, N. (1989) Drink, hybris and the promotion of harmony, in A. Powell ed., *Classical
        Sparta: Techniques behind Her Success*, 26–50. London.
Flashar, M. (1996) Die Sieger von Marathon: zwischen Mythos und Vorbildlichkeit, in
        M. Flashar, H.-J. Gehrke, and E. Heinrich, eds., *Retrospektive: Konzepte von Vergangenheit
        in der griechisch-römischen Antike*, 63–85. Munich.
Förtsch, R. (1998) Spartan art: its many different deaths, in W. G. Cavanagh and S. Walker, eds.,
        Sparta in Laconia. Proceedings of the 19th British Museum Classical Colloquium (British
        School at Athens Studies 4), 48–54. London.
Fossey, J. M. (1988) *Topography and Population of Ancient Boeotia*, Chicago.
Foucault, M. (1977) *Language, Counter-Memory, Practice*, ed. D. F. Bouchard, Ithaca.
Foxhall, L. (1995) Monumental ambitions: the significance of posterity in Greece, in N. Spencer,
        ed., *Time, Tradition and Society in Greek Archaeology: Bridging the 'Great Divide'*, 132–49.
        London.
Frantz, A. (1988) *The Athenian Agora, XXIV: Late Antiquity: AD 267–700*, Princeton.
Frazer, J. G. (1898a) *Pausanias's Description of Greece, I: Translation*, London. (Reprinted 1965.)
    (1898b) *Pausanias's Description of Greece, III: Commentary on Books II–V*, London. (Reprinted
        1965.)
Frazer, R. M., Jr. (1966) *The Trojan War: The Chronicles of Dictys of Crete and Dares the Phrygian*,
        Bloomington.
Freud, S. (1985) *Civilisation, Society and Religion*, trans. Albert Dickson, London.
Friedlander, S. (1993) *Memory, History and the Extermination of the Jews of Europe*, Bloomington.
Fröhlich, P. (1999) Les institutions des cités de Messénie à la Basse époque hellénistique, in
        J. Renard, ed., *Le Péloponnèse: archéologie et histoire*, 229–42. Rennes.
Frost, F. J. and Hadjidaki, E. (1990) Excavations at the harbor of Phalasarna in Crete: the 1988
        season, *Hesperia* 59: 513–27.
Funkenstein, A. (1993) *Perceptions of Jewish History*, Los Angeles.

Fuqua, C. (1981) Tyrtaeus and the cult of heroes, *Greek, Roman and Byzantine Studies* 22: 215–26.

Galli, M. (forthcoming) Pepaideumenoi am "Ort des Heiligen": Euergetische Initiativen und Kommunikationsformen in griechischen Heiligtümern zur Zeit der Zweiten Sophistik, in C. Reusser, ed., *Griechenland in der Kaiserzeit: Neue Funde und Forschungen zu Skulptur, Architektur und Topographie* (Hefte des archäologischen Seminars der Universität Bern 4), 43–70. Zurich.

Garnsey, P. (1998) Where did Italian peasants live?, in P. Garnsey, *Cities, Peasants and Food in Classical Antiquity: Essays in Social and Economic History* (ed. and with addenda by W. Scheidel), 107–33. Cambridge.

Geagan, D. (1979a) Roman Athens: some aspects of life and culture I. 86 BC – AD 267, *ANRW* II.7.1: 371–437.

    (1979b) Tiberius Claudius Novius, the Hoplite generalship and the Epimeleteia of the free city of Athens, *AJP* 100: 279–87.

    (1997) The Athenian elite: Romanization, resistance and the exercise of power, in M. Hoff and S. Rotroff, eds., *The Romanization of Athens*, 19–32. Oxford.

Geary, P. (1994) *Phantoms of Remembrance: Memory and Oblivion at the End of the First Millennium*, Princeton.

Gedi, N. and Elam, Y. (1996) Collective memory – what is it?, *History and Memory* (Fall 1996): 30–50.

Gehrke, H.-J. (2001) History and collective identity: uses of the past in ancient Greece and beyond, in N. Luraghi, ed., *The Historian's Craft in the Age of Herodotus*, 286–313. Oxford.

    (forthcoming) Marathon als Mythos: Von Helden und Barbaren, in G. Krumeich and S. Brandt, eds., *Schlachtenmythen*.

Genière, J. de la and Erim, K., eds. (1987) *Aphrodisias de Carie*, Paris.

Genovese, E. (1974) *Roll, Jordan, Roll: The World the Slaves Made*, New York.

Gillis, J. R., ed. (1994a) *Commemorations: The Politics of National Identity*, Princeton.

    (1994b) Memory and identity: the history of a relationship, in J. R. Gillis, ed., *Commemorations: The Politics of National Identity*, 3–24. Princeton.

Giovannini, A. (1978) *Rome et la circulation monétaire en Grèce au IIe siècle avant Jésus-Christ*, Basel.

Gleason, M. W. (1995) *Making Men: Sophists and Self-Presentation in Ancient Rome*, Princeton.

Gombrich, E. H. (1970) *Aby Warburg: An Intellectual Biography*, Chicago.

Gondicas, D. (1988) *Recherches sur la Crète occidentale: de l'époque géométrique à la conquête romaine. Inventaire des sources archéologiques et textuelles, position du problème*, Amsterdam.

Gonick, L. (1989) *The Cartoon History of the Universe: From the Big Bang to Alexander the Great*, New York and London.

Gonzales-Berry, E. and Maciel, D. R., eds. (2000) *The Contested Homeland: A Chicano History of New Mexico*, Albuquerque.

Goody, J. and Watt, I. (1968) The consequences of literacy, in J. Goody, ed., *Literacy in Traditional Societies*, 27–68. Cambridge. (First published 1962–63.)

Graindor, P. (1927) *Athènes sous Auguste*, Cairo.

Grundy, G. B. (1894) *The Topography of the Battle of Plataea*, London.

Grütter, H. T. (1997) Die athenische Demokratie als Denkmal und Monument: Überlegungen zur politischen Ikonographie im 5. Jahrhundert, in W. Eder and K.-J. Hölkeskamp, eds., *Volk und Verfassung in vorhellenistischen Griechenland*, 113–32. Stuttgart.

Guest-Papamanoli, A. and Lambraki, A. (1980) Les grottes de Léra et de l'Arkoudia en Crète, *ArchDelt* 31: 178–243.

Guldager Bilde, P., Nielsen, I., and Nielsen, M. (1993) *Aspects of Hellenism in Italy: Towards a Cultural Unity?* (*Acta Hyperborea* 5), Copenhagen.

Gurahian, J. (1990) In the mind's eye: collective memory and Armenian village ethnographies, *Armenian Review* 43: 19–29.

Habicht, C. (1985) *Pausanias' Guide to Ancient Greece*, Berkeley.

    (1996) Salamis in der Zeit nach Sulla, *Zeitschrift für Papyrologie und Epigraphik* 111: 79–87.

    (1997) Roman citizens in Athens (228–31 B.C.), in M. Hoff and S. Rotroff, eds., *The Romanization of Athens*, 9–17. Oxford.

Habinek, T. and Schiesaro, A., eds. (1997) *The Roman Cultural Revolution*, Cambridge.

Haggis, D. C. (1996a) Archaeological survey at Kavousi, East Crete: preliminary report, *Hesperia* 65: 373–432.

    (1996b) The port of Tholos in eastern Crete and the role of a Roman horreum along the Egyptian "corn route," *Oxford Journal of Archaeology* 15: 183–209.

Halbwachs, M. (1925) *Les cadres sociaux de la mémoire*, Paris. (Reprinted 1976.)

    (1941) *La topographie légendaire des évangiles en terre sainte: étude de mémoire collective*, Paris.

    (1950) *Mémoires collectives*, Paris.

    (1992) *On Collective Memory*, ed., trans. and with an introduction by L. A. Coser, Chicago.

Hall, C. (1998) "Turning a blind eye": memories of empire, in P. Fara and K. Patterson, eds., *Memory*, 27–46. Cambridge.

Hall, J. M. (1995a) How Argive was the "Argive" Heraion?, *AJA* 99: 577–613.

    (1995b) The role of language in Greek ethnicities, *PCPS* 41: 83–100.

    (1997) *Ethnic Identity in Greek Antiquity*, Cambridge.

    (2000) Sparta, Lakedaimon and the nature of Perioikic dependency, in P. Flensted-Jensen, ed., *Further Studies in the Ancient Greek Polis* (Historia Einzelschrift 139), 73–89. Stuttgart.

Hall, M. (2001) Social archaeology and the theatres of memory, *Journal of Social Archaeology* 1: 50–61.

Hamilakis, Y. (1998) Eating the dead: mortuary feasting and the politics of memory in the Aegean Bronze Age societies, in K. Branigan, ed., *Cemetery and Society in the Aegean Bronze Age*, 115–32. Sheffield.

Hammond, N. G. L. (1968) The campaign and the battle of Marathon, *JHS* 88: 13–57.

Hanson, V. D. (1999) *The Soul of Battle*, New York.

Harbison, R. (1991) *The Built, the Unbuilt and the Unbuildable: In Pursuit of Architectural Meaning*, Cambridge, MA.

Harder, A. (1985) *Euripides' Kresphontes and Archelaos: Introduction, Text and Commentary*, Leiden.

Harrison, A. and Spencer, N. (1998) After the palace: the early "history" of Messenia, in J. L. Davis, ed., *Sandy Pylos: An Archaeological History from Nestor to Navarino*, 147–62. Austin.

Harrison, E. B. (1960) New sculpture from the Athenian agora, 1959, *Hesperia* 29: 369–92.

    (1972) The south frieze of the Nike temple and the Marathon painting in the Painted Stoa, *AJA* 76: 353–78.

Harrison, G. (1988) Background to the first century of Roman rule in Crete, *Cretan Studies* 1: 125–55.

    (1991) Changing patterns in land tenure and land use in Roman Crete, in G. Barker and J. Lloyd, eds., *Roman Landscapes: Archaeological Survey in the Mediterranean Region* (Archaeological Monographs of the British School at Rome 2), 115–21. London.

    (1993) *The Romans and Crete*, Amsterdam.

Hartswick, K. (1990) The Ares Borghese reconsidered, *Revue Archéologique* n.s. 2: 227–83.

Harvey, D. (1979) Monument and myth, *Annals of the Association of American Geographers* 69: 362–81.

Hass, K. A. (1998) *Carried to the Wall: American Memory and the Vietnam Veterans Memorial*, Berkeley.

Hatzfeld, J. (1919) *Les trafiquants italiens dans l'Orient hellénique*, New York. (Reprinted 1974.)

Hauvette, M. A. (1892) Marathon, *Nouvelles Archives des Missions Scientifiques et Littéraires* 2: 326–44.

Haverkamp, A. and Lachmann, R., eds. (1991) *Gedächtniskunst: Raum, Bild, Schrift: Studien zur Mnemotechnik*, Frankfurt am Main.

Hayden, B. J. (1995) Rural settlement of the Orientalizing through Early Classical period: the Meseleroi Valley, Eastern Crete, *Aegean Archaeology* 2: 93–144.

Hayden, B. J., Moody, J. A., and Rackham, O. (1992) The Vrokastro Survey Project, 1986–89: research design and preliminary results, *Hesperia* 61: 293–353.

Hayden, D. (1995) *The Power of Place: Urban Landscapes as Public History*, Cambridge, MA.

Hayes, A. C. (1974) *The Four Churches of Pecos*, Albuquerque.

Healy, C. (1997) *From the Ruins of Colonialism: History as Social Memory*, Cambridge.

Helbig, W. (1895) *Guide to the Collections of Classical Antiquities in Rome, I*, trans. J. and F. Muirhead, Leipzig.

Henige, D. P. (1982) *Oral Historiography*, London.

Henrichs, A. (1995) Graecia capta: Roman views of Greek culture, *HSCP* 97: 243–61.

Herzfeld, M. (1982) *Ours Once More: Folklore, Ideology and the Making of Modern Greece*, Austin.

(1987) *Anthropology through the Looking-Glass: Critical Ethnography in the Margins of Europe*, Cambridge.

(1991) *A Place in History: Social and Monumental Time in a Cretan Town*, Princeton.

Higbie, C. (1997) The bones of a hero, the ashes of a politician: Athens, Salamis, and the usable past, *Classical Antiquity* 16: 278–307.

Hill, J. D., ed. (1988) *Rethinking History and Myth: Indigenous South American Perspectives on the Past*, Urbana.

Hirsch, E. and O'Hanlon, M. (1995) *The Anthropology of Landscape: Perspectives on Place and Space*, Oxford.

Hobsbawm, E. J. (1972) The social function of the past, *PastPres* 55: 3–17.

Hobsbawm, E. J. and Ranger, T., eds. (1983) *The Invention of Tradition*, Cambridge.

Hodkinson, S. (1992) Sharecropping and Sparta's economic exploitation of the helots, in J. M. Sanders, ed., *PHILOLAKON: Lakonian Studies in Honour of Hector Catling*, 123–34. London.

(2000) *Property and Wealth in Classical Sparta*, London and Swansea.

(n.d.) Subsistence, patronage and communal organisation. Unpublished paper.

Hoff, M. (1988) The Roman Agora at Athens. Unpublished Ph.D. thesis, Boston University.

(1989a) Civil disobedience and unrest in Augustan Athens, *Hesperia* 59: 267–76.

(1989b) The early history of the Roman Agora at Athens, in S. Walker and A. Cameron, eds., *The Greek Renaissance in the Roman Empire*, 1–8. London.

(1994) The so-called Agoranomion and the imperial cult in Julio-Claudian Athens, *Archäologischer Anzeiger*: 93–117.

(1996) The politics and architecture of the Athenian Imperial Cult, in A. Small, ed., *Subject and Ruler: The Cult of the Ruling Power in Classical Antiquity* (*JRA* Supplement 17), 185–200. Ann Arbor.

(1997) *Laceratae Athenae*: Sulla's siege of Athens in 87/6 B.C. and its aftermath, in M. Hoff and S. Rotroff, eds., *The Romanization of Athens*, 33–51. Oxford.

Hoff, M. and Rotroff, S., eds. (1997) *The Romanization of Athens*, Oxford.

Hogarth, D. G. (1899–1900) The Dictaean Cave, *BSA* 6: 94–116.

Hölscher, T. (1974) Die Nike der Messenier und Naupaktier in Olympia, *Jahrbuch des deutschen archäologischen Instituts* 89: 70–111.

Hood, S. and Smyth, D. (1981) *Archaeological Survey of the Knossos Area* (*BSA* Supplementary Volume 14), second edn, London.

Hope Simpson, R. and Betancourt, P. (1990) Intensive survey of Pseira Island, Crete, *AJA* 94: 322 (abstract).

Hope Simpson, R. and Dickinson, O. T. P. K. (1979) *A Gazetteer of Aegean Civilisation in the Bronze Age I: The Mainland and Islands*, Göteborg.

Hope Simpson, R. *et al.* (1995) The archaeological survey of the Kommos area, in J. W. Shaw and M. C. Shaw, eds., *Kommos I: The Kommos Region and Houses of the Minoan Town. Part I*, 325–402. Princeton.

Hutton, P. (1993) *History as an Art of Memory*, Hanover, NH.

(1994) Review of J. Le Goff, *History and Memory* (1992) and P. Vidal-Naquet, *Assassins of Memory* (1992). *History and Theory* 33: 95–107.

Huxley, G. L. (1962) *Early Sparta*, Cambridge, MA.

(1968) *Minoans in Greek Sources, A Lecture*, Belfast.

(1994) On Knossos and her neighbours (7th century to mid-4th century BC), in D. Evely, H. Hughes-Brock, and N. Momigliano, eds., *Knossos: A Labyrinth of History. Papers in Honour of Sinclair Hood*, 123–33. Oxford.

Huyssen, A. (1994) Monument and memory in a postmodern age, in J. E. Young, ed., *The Art of Memory: Holocaust Memorials in History*, 9–17. Munich.

(1995) *Twilight Memories: Marking Time in a Culture of Amnesia*, New York.

Ingold, T. (1993) The temporality of the landscape, *World Archaeology* 25: 152–74.

Irwin-Zarecki, I. (1994) *Frames of Remembrance: The Dynamics of Collective Memory*, New Brunswick, NJ.

Isager, S. (1998) The pride of Halicarnassos, *Zeitschrift für Papyrologie und Epigraphik* 123: 1–23.

Jacoby, F. (1944) Khrestous poiein: Aristotle fr. 592R, *Classical Quarterly* 38: 15–16.

Jacquemin, A. and Laroche, D. (1982) Notes sur trois piliers delphiques, *BCH* 106: 191–207.

Jaeger, M. (1997) *Livy's Written Rome*, Ann Arbor.

James, D. (1997) Meatpackers, Peronists, and collective memory: a view from the south, *American Historical Review* 102: 1404–12.

Jameson, F. (1985) Postmodernism and consumer society, in H. Foster, ed., *Postmodern Culture*, 111–25. London.

(1991) *Postmodernism or, the Cultural Logic of Late Capitalism*, Durham, NC.

Jameson, M. H., Runnels, C. N., and van Andel, T. H., eds. (1994) *A Greek Countryside: The Southern Argolid from Prehistory to the Present Day*, Stanford.

Jarman, N. (1993) Intersecting Belfast, in B. Bender, ed., *Landscape: Politics and Perspective*, 107–38. Oxford.

Jeffery, L. H. (1990) *The Local Scripts of Archaic Greece* (revised edn with a supplement by A. W. Johnston), Oxford.

Jones, A. H. M. (1963) The Greeks under the Roman empire, *Dumbarton Oaks Papers* 17: 3–19.

Jones, C. P. (1986) *Culture and Society in Lucian*, Cambridge, MA.

(1970) A leading family from Roman Thespiae, *HSCP* 74: 223–55.

(1971) *Plutarch and Rome*, Oxford.

(1978a) *The Roman World of Dio Chrysostom*, Cambridge, MA.

(1978b) Three foreigners in Attica, *Phoenix* 32: 222–34.

(1990) A new Lycian dossier establishing an artistic contest and festival in the reign of Hadrian, *JRA* 3: 484–88.

(1996a) The Panhellenion, *Chiron* 26: 29–56.

(1996b) Review of K. Arafat, *Pausanias' Greece: Ancient Artists and Roman Rulers*, *Echos du Monde Classique/Classical Views* 15: 458–62.

(1999a) A decree of Thyatira in Lydia, *Chiron* 29: 1–21.

(1999b) *Kinship Diplomacy in the Ancient World*, Cambridge, MA and London.

Jonker, G. (1995) *The Topography of Remembrance: The Dead, Tradition and Collective Memory in Mesopotamia*, Leiden.

Jost, M. (1985) *Sanctuaires et cultes d'Arcadie* (Ecole Française d'Athènes, Etudes Péloponnésiennes 9), Paris.

   (1996) Messenian cults and myths, in S. Hornblower and A. Spawforth, eds., *The Oxford Classical Dictionary*, third edn, 965. Oxford.

Kalpaxis, T., Schapp, A., and Viviers, D. (1995) Itanos (Crète orientale), *BCH* 119: 711–36.

Kaltsas, N. (1985) H archaïke oikia sto Kopanaki tes Messenias, *Archaiologike Ephemeris* 1983: 207–37.

Kammen, M. (1991) *Mystic Chords of Memory: The Transformation of Tradition in American Culture*, New York.

Kapetanopoulos, E. (1981) Salamis and Julius Nikanor, *Hellenika* 33: 217–37.

Karetsou, A. (1981) The peak sanctuary at Mt. Juktas, in R. Hägg and N. Marinatos, eds., *Sanctuaries and Cults in the Aegean Bronze Age* (Proceedings of the First International Symposium at the Swedish Institute in Athens, 12–13 May, 1980), 137–53. Lund.

Kennell, N. M. (1995) *The Gymnasium of Virtue: Education and Culture in Ancient Sparta*, Chapel Hill and London.

Kiechle, F. (1959) *Messenische Studien: Untersuchungen zur Geschichte der messenischen Kriege und der Auswanderung der Messenier*, Kallmünz.

King, L. W. (1910) *A History of Sumer and Akkad: An Account of the Early Races of Babylonia from Prehistoric Times to the Foundation of the Babylonian Monarchy*, London.

Kirschenblatt-Gimblett, B. (1998) *Destination Culture: Tourism, Museums and Heritage*, Berkeley and Los Angeles.

Klein, K. L. (2000) On the emergence of *memory* in historical discourse, *Representations* 69: 127–50.

Kleiner, D. (1983) *The Monument of Philopappos in Athens*, Rome.

Knaut, A. L. (1995) *The Pueblo Revolt of 1680: Conquest and Resistance in Seventeeth-Century New Mexico*, Norman.

Kokkou, A. (1971) Adrianeia erga eis tas Athenas, *ArchDelt* 24 (1970): 150–73.

Kolbe, W. (1904) Die Grenzen Messeniens in der ersten Kaiserzeit, *Mitteilungen des deutschen archäologischen Instituts, athenische Abteilung* 29: 364–78.

Konecny, A. (1998) Der Plataia-Survey 1996–97, *Jahreshefte des österreichischen archäologischen Instituts in Wien* 67: 53–62.

Konstan, D. (2001) The joys of Pausanias, in S. E. Alcock, J. F. Cherry, and J. Elsner, eds., *Pausanias: Travel and Memory in Roman Greece*, 57–60. New York.

Koonz, C. (1994) Between memory and oblivion: concentration camps in German memory, in J. R. Gillis, ed., *Commemorations: The Politics of National Identity*, 258–80. Princeton.

Koortbojian, M. (1995) *Myth, Meaning and Memory on Roman Sarcophagi*, Berkeley.

Korres, G. (1981/82) E problematike dia ten metagenesteran chresin ton mukenaikon taphon Messenias, *Praktika of the Second International Congress of Peloponnesian Studies*, 363–450. Athens.

   (1988) Evidence for a Hellenistic chthonian cult in the prehistoric cemetery of Voïdokilia in Pylos (Messenia), *Klio* 70: 311–28.

Koumanoudis, S. N. (1978) Marathoni, *AAA* 11: 232–44.

Kourou, N. and Karetsou, A. (1994) To iero tou Ermou Kranaiou sten Pato Amariou, in L. Rochetti, ed., *Sybrita: la valle di Amari tra Bronzo e Ferro* (*Incunabula Graeca* 96), 81–164.

Kraft, J. C., Rapp, G. R., Jr., Szemler, G. J., Tziavos, C., and Kase, E. W. (1987) The pass at Thermopylae, *Journal of Field Archaeology* 14: 181–98.

Kroll, J. (1997) Coinage as an index of Romanization, in M. Hoff and S. Rotroff, eds., *The Romanization of Athens*, 135–50. Oxford.

Küchler, S. (1987) Malangan: art and memory in a Melanesian society, *Man* n.s. 22: 238–55.

(1993) Landscape as memory: the mapping of process and its representation in a Melanesian society, in B. Bender, ed., *Landscape: Politics and Perspective*, 85–106. Oxford.

Küchler, S. and Melion, W., eds. (1991) *Images of Memory: On Remembering and Representation*, Washington, DC.

LaCapra, D. (1994) *Representing the Holocaust: History, Theory, Trauma*, Ithaca.

(1998) *History and Memory after Auschwitz*, Ithaca.

Lalonde, G. V. (1980) A hero shrine in the Athenian agora, *Hesperia* 49: 97–105.

Lamberton, R. (1997) Plutarch and the Romanizations of Athens, in M. Hoff and S. Rotroff, eds., *The Romanization of Athens*, 151–60. Oxford.

Lappin, E. (1999) The man with two heads, *Granta* 66 (Summer): 7–65.

La Rosa, V. (1984) Ceramiche del tipo Hadra da Festòs, in *Alessandria e il mondo ellenistico-romano. Studi in onore di Achille Adriani* (Studi e Materiali, Istituto di Archeologia Università di Palermo 6), 804–18. Rome.

(1992a) Ayia Triada, in J. W. Myers, E. E. Myers, and G. Cadogan, eds., *The Aerial Atlas of Ancient Crete*, 70–77. London.

(1992b) Phaistos, in J. W. Myers, E. E. Myers, and G. Cadogan, eds., *The Aerial Atlas of Ancient Crete*, 232–43. London.

(1993) Considerazioni sul sito di Haghia Triada in età ellenistico-romana, *ASAtene* 66–67: 259–75.

Larsen, J. A. O. (1938) Roman Greece, in T. Frank, ed., *An Economic Survey of Ancient Rome IV*, 259–498. Baltimore.

Larson, P. M. (1999) Reconsidering trauma, identity, and the African diaspora: enslavement and historical memory in nineteenth-century highland Madagascar, *William and Mary Quarterly* 56: 335–62.

LaTorre, G. F. (1993) Contributo preliminaire alla conoscenza del territorio di Gortina, *ASAtene* 66–67: 277–322.

Lavelle, B. M. (1993) *The Sorrow and the Pity: A Prolegomenon to a History of Athens under the Peisistratids, c. 560–510 B.C.* (Historia Einzelschriften 80), Stuttgart.

Layton, R., ed. (1994) *Who Needs the Past? Indigenous Values and Archaeology*, London and New York.

Lazenby, J. F. and Hope Simpson, R. (1972) Greco-Roman times: literary tradition and topographical commentary, in W. A. McDonald and G. R. Rapp, Jr., eds., *The Minnesota Messenia Expedition: Reconstructing a Bronze Age Regional Environment*, 81–99. Minneapolis.

Le Goff, J. (1992) *History and Memory*, trans. S. Rendall and E. Claman, New York. (Originally published 1988.)

Lebessi, A. (1983) E synecheia tes Kretomykenaïkes latreias: epibioseis kai anabioseis, *Archaiologike Ephemeris* 1981: 1–24.

(1992) Syme, in J. W. Myers, E. E. Myers, and G. Cadogan, eds., *The Aerial Atlas of Ancient Crete*, 268–75. London.

Lebessi, A. and Muhly, P. (1987) The sanctuary of Hermes and Aphrodite at Syme, Crete, *National Geographic Research* 3: 102–13.

(1990) Aspects of Minoan cult sacred enclosures: the evidence from the Syme sanctuary (Crete), *Archäologischer Anzeiger* (1990): 315–36.

Lebessi, A. and Reese, D. (1990) Recent and fossil shells from the Sanctuary of Hermes and Aphrodite, Syme Viannou, Crete, *Archaiologike Ephemeris* 1986: 183–88.

Lefebvre, H. (1991) *The Production of Space*, trans. D. Nicholson-Smith, Oxford.

Leigh Fermor, P. (1966) *Roumeli: Travels in Northern Greece*, Harmondsworth.

Leitao, D. (1995) The perils of Leukippos: initiatory transvestism and male gender ideology in the Ekdusia at Phaistos, *Classical Antiquity* 14: 130–63.

Levi, D. (1961–62a) Gli scavi a Festòs negli anni 1958–1960, *ASAtene* 39–40 (n.s. 23–24): 377–504.

    (1961–62b) La tomba a tholos di Kamilari presso a Festòs, *ASAtene* 39–40 (n.s. 23–24): 7–148.

    (1964) *The Recent Excavations at Phaistos* (Studies in Mediterranean Archaeology 11), Lund.

Levine, F. (1999) *Our Prayers Are in This Place: Pecos Pueblo Identity over the Centuries*, Albuquerque.

Lin, M. (1995) *Maya Lin: A Strong Clear Vision*, video produced by F. L. Mock and T. Sanders, directed by F. L. Mock. Santa Monica, CA.

Linenthal, E. T. (1995) *Preserving Memory: The Struggle to Create America's Holocaust Museum*, New York.

Linenthal, E. T., and Engelhardt, T., eds. (1996) *History Wars: The Enola Gay and Other Battles for the American Past*, New York.

Lipstadt, H. (1999) Thiepval in the age of the anti-monument, *Harvard Design Magazine* (Fall): 65–70.

Lowenthal, D. (1985) *The Past is a Foreign Country*, Cambridge.

    (1997) *The Heritage Crusade and the Spoils of History*, Cambridge.

Loyer, F. (1992) Le Sacré-Cœur de Montmartre, in P. Nora, ed., *Les lieux de mémoire III. Les France*, 450–73. Paris.

Lukermann, F. and Moody, J. (1978) Nichoria and vicinity: settlements and circulation, in G. Rapp, Jr. and S. E. Aschenbrenner, eds., *Excavations in Nichoria in Southwest Greece, I: Site, Environs and Techniques*, 78–112. Minneapolis.

Luraghi, N. (1994) Pausanias e la fondazione di Messene sullo stretto, *Rivista di Filologia e di Istruzione Classica* 122: 140–51.

    (2002) Becoming Messenian, *Journal of Hellenic Studies* 122.

    (in press) Rethinking Helotic slavery, in S. Hodkinson and A. Powell, eds., *All You Wanted to Know About Sparta But Never Dared to Ask*. London.

McAllister, M. H. (1959) The temple of Ares at Athens: a review of the evidence, *Hesperia* 28: 1–64.

McDonald, W. A. (1975) Excavations at Nichoria in Messenia: 1972–1973, *Hesperia* 44: 69–141.

    (1984) The Minnesota Messenia Survey: a look back, in A. L. Boegehold *et al.*, eds., *Studies Presented to Sterling Dow on his Eightieth Birthday*, 185–91. Durham, NC.

McDonald, W. A. and Hope Simpson, R. (1972) Archaeological exploration, in W. A. McDonald and G. R. Rapp, Jr., eds., *The Minnesota Messenia Expedition: Reconstructing a Bronze Age Regional Environment*, 117–47. Minneapolis.

McDonald, W. A. and Rapp, G. R., Jr. (1972) *The Minnesota Messenia Expedition: Reconstructing a Bronze Age Regional Environment*, Minneapolis.

MacGillivray, J. A. (2000) *Minotaur: Sir Arthur Evans and the Archaeology of the Minoan Myth*, New York.

MacGillivray, J. A. and Sackett, L. H. (1984) An archaeological survey of the Roussolakkos area at Palaikastro, *BSA* 79: 129–59.

McNeal, R. A. (1991) Archaeology and the destruction of the later Athenian acropolis, *Antiquity* 65: 49–63.

Macready, S. and Thompson, F. H., eds. (1987) *Roman Architecture in the Greek World* (Society of Antiquaries of London Occasional Papers 10), London.

Maier, C. (1993) A surfeit of memory?, *History and Memory* 5: 136–51.

Malkin, I. (1994) *Myth and Territory in the Spartan Mediterranean*, Cambridge.

Marangou-Lerat, A. (1996) *Le vin et les amphores de Crète de l'époque classique à l'époque impériale*, Paris.

Marinatos, S. (1940–41) The cult of the Cretan caves, *Review of Religion* 5: 129–36.

(1958) Grammáton didaskália, in E. Grumach, ed., *Minoica: Festschrift zum 80. Geburtstag von Johannes Sundwall*, 226–31. Berlin.

Matsuda, M. (1996) *The Memory of the Modern*, New York and Oxford.

Mavrigiannaki, K. (1972) Topografia Cretese: Stylos Apokoronou, *Studi micenei ed egeo-anatolici* 15: 157–60.

Meier, M. (1998) *Aristokraten und Damoden: Untersuchungen zur inneren Entwicklung Spartas im 7. Jahrhundert v. Chr. und zur politischen Funktion der Dichtung des Tyrtaios*, Stuttgart.

Mersch, A. (1995) Archäologischer Kommentar zu den "Gräbern der Athener und Plataier" in der Marathonia, *Klio* 77: 55–64.

Mertens, N. (1999) Die Perïöken Spartas. Unpublished M.A. thesis, Freie Universität Berlin.

Meskell, L. (1996) The somatization of archaeology: institutions, discourses, corporeality, *Norwegian Archaeological Review* 29: 1–16.

(1999) *Archaeologies of Social Life*, Oxford.

Meyer, E. (1978) Messenien, *Real-Encyclopädie der klassischen Altertumswissenschaft* (Supplement 15), 155–289.

Mignolo, W. (1992) Misunderstanding and colonization: the reconfiguration of memory and space, *The South Atlantic Quarterly* 92: 209–60.

Millar, F. (1969) P. Herennius Dexippus: the Greek world and the third-century invasions, *JRS* 59: 12–29.

(1993) The Greek city in the Roman period, in M. H. Hansen, ed., *The Ancient Greek City-State* (Acts of the Copenhagen Polis Centre 1), 232–60. Copenhagen.

Miller, A. G. (1991) Transformations of time and space: Oaxaca, Mexico, circa 1500–1700, in S. Küchler and W. Melion, eds., *Images of Memory: On Remembering and Representation*, 141–75. Washington, DC.

Millett, P. (1998) Encounters in the Agora, in P. A. Cartledge, P. Millett, and S. von Reden, eds., *Kosmos: Essays in Order, Conflict and Community in Classical Athens*, Cambridge.

Mitchell, S. (1984) The Greek city in the Roman world: Pontus and Bithynia, in *Praktika of the Eighth International Congress of Greek and Latin Epigraphy (Athens 1982)*, 120–33. Athens.

(1990) Festivals, games and civic life in Roman Asia Minor, *JRS* 80: 183–93.

Moody, J., Nixon, L., Price, S., and Rackham, O. (1998) Surveying poleis and larger sites in Sphakia, in W. G. Cavanagh and M. Curtis, eds., with J. N. Coldstream and A. W. Johnston, co-eds., *Post-Minoan Crete. Proceedings of the First Colloquium on Post-Minoan Crete held by the British School at Athens and the Institute of Archaeology, University College London, 10–11 November 1995*, 87–95. (British School at Athens Studies 2), London.

Moreau, P. (1994) La mémoire fragile: falsification et destruction des documents publics au Ier siècle av. J.C., in S. Demougin, ed., *La mémoire perdue: à la recherche des archives oubliées, publiques et privées, de la Rome antique*, 121–47. Paris.

Morphy, H. (1993) Colonialism, history, and the construction of place: the politics of landscape in Northern Australia, in B. Bender, ed., *Landscape: Politics and Perspectives*, 205–43. Oxford.

Morris, I. (1988) Tomb cult and the "Greek Renaissance": the past in the present in the 8th century BC, *Antiquity* 63: 750–61.

(1994) Archaeologies of Greece, in I. Morris, ed., *Classical Greece: Ancient Histories and Modern Archaeologies*, 8–47. Cambridge.

(2000) *Archaeology as Cultural History: Words and Things in Iron Age Greece*, Malden, MA.

Morris, S. P. (1992) *Daidalos and the Origins of Greek Art*, Princeton.

Mossman, J., ed. (1997) *Plutarch and His Intellectual World: Essays on Plutarch*, London.

Müller, S. (1996) Prospection archéologique de la plaine de Malia, *BCH* 120: 921–28.

Murphy-O'Connor, J. (1998) *The Holy Land: An Oxford Archaeological Guide from Earliest Times to 1700*, Oxford and New York.

Murray, W. M. and Petsas, P. M. (1989) *Octavian's Campsite Memorial for the Actian War* (Transactions of the American Philosophical Society 79.4), Philadelphia.

Musti, D. (1996) La struttura del discorso storico in Pausania, in J. Bingen, ed., *Pausanias historien* (EntrHardt 41), 9–34. Vandœuvres.

Musti, D. and Torelli, M. (1991) *Pausania, Guida della Grecia. Libro IV: La Messenia*, Milan.

Myers, J. W., Myers, E. E., and Cadogan, G., eds. (1992) *The Aerial Atlas of Ancient Crete*, London.

Namer, G. (2000) *Halbwachs et la mémoire sociale*, Paris.

Neils, J. (1992) *Goddess and Polis: The Panathenaic Festival in Ancient Athens*, Princeton.

Neisser, U. (1989) Domains of memory, in P. R. Soloman, G. R. Goethals, C. M. Kelley, and B. R. Stephens, eds., *Memory: Interdisciplinary Approaches*, 67–83. New York.

Nicolet, C. (1988) *L'inventaire du monde: géographie et politique aux origines de l'empire romain*, Paris.

Nora, P. (1996) General introduction: between memory and history, in P. Nora, director, *Realms of Memory: Rethinking the French Past* I, trans. A. Goldhammer, English-language edition edited and with foreword by L. D. Kritzman, 1–20. New York. (Originally published 1984; reprinted 1986.)

    director (1996–98) *Realms of Memory: Rethinking the French Past* I–III, trans. A. Goldhammer, English-language edition edited and with foreword by L. D. Kritzman, New York.

    (1997) *Les lieux de mémoire I–III*, Paris. (Originally published 1984–92.)

North, J. A. (1993) Roman reactions to empire, *Scripta Classica Israelica* 12: 127–38.

Nylander, C. (1980) Earless in Nineveh: who mutilated "Sargon's" head? *AJA* 84: 329–33.

O'Brien, J. and Rosebery, W. (1991) *Golden Ages, Dark Ages: Imagining the Past in Anthropology and History*, Berkeley.

O'Bryhim, S. (1997) Hesiod and the Cretan cave, *Rheinisches Museum für Philologie* 140: 95–96.

Olick, J. K. and Levy, D. (1997) Collective memory and cultural constraint: Holocaust myth and nationality in German politics, *American Sociological Review* 62: 921–36.

Olick, J. K. and Robbins, J. (1998) Social memory studies: from "collective memory" to the historical sociology of mnemonic practices, *Annual Review of Sociology* 22: 105–40.

Oliva, P. (1971) *Sparta and her Social Problems*, Amsterdam and Prague.

Oliver, J. H. (1951) New evidence on the Attic Panhellenion, *Hesperia* 20: 31–33.

    (1965) Livia as Artemis Boulaia at Athens, *CP* 60: 179.

    (1970) *Marcus Aurelius: Aspects of Civil and Central Policy in the East* (*Hesperia* Supplement 13), Princeton.

    (1980) From Gennetai to Curiales, *Hesperia* 49: 30–56.

    (1982) Arrian in two roles, in *Studies in Attic Epigraphy, History and Topography Presented to E. Vanderpool* (*Hesperia* Supplement 19), 122–29. Princeton.

Ollier, F. (1973) *Le mirage spartiate*, New York. (First published 1933, 1943; two vols.)

Orlandos, A. K. (1976) Neoterai erevnai en Messene (1957–73), in U. Jantzen, ed., *Neue Forschungen in griechischen Heiligtümern*, 9–38. Tübingen.

Ortner, S. B. (1995) Resistance and ethnographic refusal, *Comparative Studies in Society and History* 37: 173–93.

Osborne, R. (1996) *Greece in the Making, 1200–479 BC*, London and New York.

Oster, R. E. (1990) Ephesus as a religion centre under the Principate, *ANRW* II.18.3: 1162–1728.

Parker, R. (1989) Spartan religion, in A. Powell, ed., *Classical Sparta: Techniques behind Her Success*, 142–72. London.

Paton, S. (1994) Roman Knossos and the Colonia Julia Nobilis Cnossus, in D. Evely, H. Hughes-Brock, and N. Momigliano, eds., *Knossos: A Labyrinth of History. Papers in Honour of Sinclair Hood*, 141–53. Oxford.

    (1998) The Villa Dionysos at Knossos and its predecessors, in W. G. Cavanagh and M. Curtis, eds., with J. N. Coldstream and A. W. Johnston, co-eds., *Post-Minoan Crete. Proceedings of the First Colloquium on Post-Minoan Crete held by the British School at Athens and the Institute of Archaeology, University College London, 10–11 November 1995*, 123–28. (British School at Athens Studies 2), London.

Payne, J. J. (1984) Aretas Eneken: Honors for Romans and Italians in Greece from 260 to 27 BC. Unpublished Ph.D. thesis, Michigan State University.

Paynter, R. and McGuire, R. H. (1991) The archaeology of inequality: material culture, domination and resistance, in R. H. McGuire and R. Paynter, eds., *The Archaeology of Inequality*, 1–27. Oxford.

Pearson, L. (1962) The pseudo-history of Messenia and its authors, *Historia* 11: 397–426.

Pelling, C. B. (1986) Plutarch and Roman politics, in I. S. Moxon, J. D. Smart, and A. J. Woodman, eds., *Past Perspectives: Studies in Greek and Roman Historical Writing*, 159–87. Cambridge.

Pendlebury, J. D. S. (1939) *The Archaeology of Crete: An Introduction*, London.

Perlman, P. (1992) One hundred-citied Crete and the "Cretan Politeia," *CP* 87: 193–205.

    (1995) Invocatio and imprecatio: the Hymn to the Greatest Kouros from Palaikastro and the oath in ancient Crete, *JHS* 115: 161–67.

    (1996) Polis upekoos. The dependent polis and Crete, in M. H. Hansen, ed., *Introduction to an Inventory of Poleis*, 233–85. Copenhagen.

Petrochilos, N. K. (1974) *Roman Attitudes to the Greeks*, Athens.

Photiou, K. (1982) *E Tetrapole tou Marathona*, Athens.

Piatkowski, A. (1981) La Crète sous l'empire romain jusqu'à l'époque de Néron, *Acts of the Fourth Cretological Congress*, vol. II, pp. 416–20.

Picard, G. C. (1957) *Les trophées romains: contribution à l'histoire de la religion et de l'art triomphal de Rome* (Bibliothèque des Ecoles Françaises d'Athènes et de Rome 187), Paris.

Piérart, M. (1999) Les puits de Danaos et les fontaines d'Hadrien. Eau, urbanisme et idéologie à Argos, in J. Renard, ed., *Le Péloponnèse: archéologie et histoire*, 243–68. Rennes.

Piérart, M. and Touchais, G. (1996) *Argos: un ville grecque de 6000 ans*, Paris.

Piolot, L. (1999) Pausanias et les Mystères d'Andanie: histoire d'une aporie, in J. Renard, ed., *Le Péloponnèse: archéologie et histoire*, 195–28. Rennes.

Pocock, J. (1962) The origins of the study of the past: a comparative approach, *Comparative Studies in Society and History* 4: 209–46.

Polignac, F. de (1984) *La naissance de la cité grecque*, Paris.

Pollitt, J. J. (1965) *The Art of Ancient Greece: Sources and Documents*, Englewood Cliffs, NJ.

    (1986) *Art in the Hellenistic Age*, Cambridge.

Powell, A. (1988) *Athens and Sparta: Constructing Greek Political and Social History from 478 BC*, London.

    ed. (1989a) *Classical Sparta: Techniques behind Her Success*, London.

    (1989b) Mendacity and Sparta's use of the visual, in A. Powell, ed., *Classical Sparta: Techniques behind Her Success*, 173–92. London.

Price, S. R. F. (1984) *Rituals and Power: The Roman Imperial Cult in Asia Minor*, Cambridge.

Pritchett, W. K. (1957) New light on Plataia, *AJA* 61: 9–28.

    (1958) New light on Thermopylai, *AJA* 62: 203–13.

    (1959) Toward a restudy of the Battle of Salamis, *AJA* 63: 251–62.

    (1960) *Marathon* (University of California Publications in Classical Archaeology 4), Berkeley.

(1965a) The Battle of Thermopylai in 191 B.C., in *Studies in Ancient Greek Topography, Part 1*, 71–82. Berkeley.

(1965b) Marathon revisited, in *Studies in Ancient Greek Topography, Part 1*, 83–93. Berkeley.

(1965c) Plataia revisited, in *Studies in Ancient Greek Topography, Part 1*, 103–21. Berkeley.

(1965d) Salamis revisited, in *Studies in Ancient Greek Topography, Part 1*, 94–102. Berkeley.

(1979) Plataiai, *American Journal of Philology* 100: 145–52.

(1980) The site of the Skolos near Plataiai, in *Studies in Ancient Greek Topography, Part 3*, 289–94. Berkeley.

(1985a) In defense of the Thermopylai pass, in *Studies in Ancient Greek Topography, Part 5*, 190–216. Berkeley.

(1985b) The strategy of the Plataiai campaign, in *Studies in Ancient Greek Topography, Part 5*, 92–137. Berkeley.

Purcell, N. (1987) The Nicopolitan synoecism and Roman urban policy, in E. Chrysos, ed., *Nicopolis I*, 71–90. Preveza.

(1990) The creation of provincial landscape: the Roman impact, in T. Blagg and M. Millett, eds., *The Early Roman Empire in the West*, 7–29. Oxford.

Quantrill, M. (1974) *Ritual and Response in Architecture*, London.

Quass, F. (1982) Zur politischen Tätigkeit der munizipalen Aristokratie des griechischen Ostens in der Kaiserzeit, *Historia* 31: 188–213.

Rackham, O. and Moody, J. (1996) *The Making of the Cretan Landscape*, Manchester.

Rappaport, J. (1998) *The Politics of Memory: Native Historical Interpretation in the Columbian Andes*, Durham, NC.

Rawson, E. (1985) *Intellectual Life in the Late Roman Republic*, Baltimore.

Reardon, B. P. (1984) The Second Sophistic, in W. Treadgold, ed., *Renaissances Before the Renaissance: Cultural Revivals of Late Antiquity and the Middle Ages*, 23–41. Stanford.

Reynolds, J. (1982) *Aphrodisias and Rome*, London.

Ricciardi, M. (1991) Il tempio di Apollo Pizio a Gortina, *ASAtene* 54–55 (1986–87): 7–131.

Richards, J. and Van Buren, M., eds. (2000) *Order, Legitimacy and Wealth in Early States*, Cambridge.

Richer, N. (1999) *Les Ephores: études sur l'histoire et l'image de Sparte (VIIIᵉ–IIIᵉ siècle avant Jésus-Christ)*, Paris.

Rife, J. (1999) Death, ritual and memory in Greek society during the early and middle Roman empire. Unpublished Ph.D. thesis, University of Michigan.

Rigsby, K. J. (1976) Cnossus and Capua, *TAPA* 106: 313–30.

(1986) Notes sur la Crète hellénistique, *Revue des Etudes Grecques* 99: 350–60.

Rizakis, A. (1997) Roman colonies in the province of Achaia: territories, land and population, in S. E. Alcock, ed., *The Early Roman Empire in the East*, 15–36. Oxford.

Robert, L. (1929) Recherches épigraphiques I, *Aristos Hellenon* et Addendum, in *Opera Minora Selecta II*, 758–67. Amsterdam.

(1949) Un athlète milésien, in *Hellenica. Recueil d'épigraphie, de numismatique et d'antiquités grecques*, VII, 117–25. Amsterdam.

(1968) Les épigrammes satiriques de Lucilius sur les athlètes. Parodies et réalités, in *L'épigramme grecque* (EntrHardt 14), 181–291. Geneva.

(1977a) Documents d'Asie Mineure, *BCH* 101: 43–132.

(1977b) La titulature de Nicée et de la Nicomédie: la gloire et la haine, *HSCP* 81: 1–39.

(1981) Une épigramme satirique d'Automédon et Athènes au début de l'empire (*Anthologie Palatine* xi.319), *Revue des études grecques* 94: 338–61.

Robertson, N. (1986) A point of precedence at Plataia: the dispute between Athens and Sparta over leading the procession, *Hesperia* 55: 88–102.

Rocchetti, L. (1969–70) Depositi sub-micenei e protogeometrici nei dintorni di Festòs, *ASAtene* 47–48 (n.s. 31–32): 41–70.

Rodman, M. C. (1992) Empowering place: multilocality and multivocality, *American Anthropologist* 94: 640–56.

Roebuck, C. A. (1941) *A History of Messenia from 369 to 146 B.C.*, Chicago.

(1945) A note on Messenian economy and population, *CP* 40: 149–65.

Rogers, G. (1991) *The Sacred Identity of Ephesos: Foundation Myths of a Roman City*, London.

Romano, D. G. (1994) Post-146 BC land use in Corinth, and planning of the Roman colony of 44 BC, in T. Gregory, ed., *The Corinthia in the Roman Period* (*JRA* Supplement 8), 9–30. Ann Arbor.

(2000) A tale of two cities: Roman colonies at Corinth, in E. Fentress, ed., *Romanization and the City: Creation, Transformations, and Failures* (*JRA* Supplement 38), 83–104. Ann Arbor.

Romeo, I. (forthcoming) Il Panhellenion, Gortina ed una nuova copia della Zeus di Dresda, *ASAtene*.

Romeo, I. and Portale, E. C. (1998) *Gortina III: Le Sculture* (Monografie della Scuola Archeologica di Atene e delle Missioni Italiane in Oriente 8), Padua.

Roobaert, A. (1977) Le danger hilote?, *Ktema* 2: 141–55.

Rosaldo, R. (1988) Ideology, place and people without culture, *Cultural Anthropology* 3: 77–96.

(1989a) *Culture and Truth: The Remaking of Social Analysis*, Boston.

(1989b) Imperialist nostalgia, *Representations* 26: 107–22.

Rose, C. B. (1997a) *Dynastic Commemoration and Imperial Portraiture in the Julio-Claudian Period*, Cambridge.

(1997b) The imperial image in the eastern Mediterranean, in S. E. Alcock, ed., *The Early Roman Empire in the East*, 108–20. Oxford.

Rose, H. J. (1970) Messenia (cults and myths), in N. G. L. Hammond and H. H. Scullard, eds., *The Oxford Classical Dictionary*, second edn, 676. Oxford.

Roth, M. S. (1994) We are what we remember (and forget), *Tikkun* 9.6: 41–42, 91.

(1995) *The Ironist's Cage: Memory, Trauma, and the Construction of History*, New York.

(1997) Irresistible decay: ruins reclaimed, in M. S. Roth (with C. Lyons and C. Merewether), *Irresistible Decay: Ruins Reclaimed*, 1–23. Los Angeles.

Roueché, C. and Erim, K., eds. (1990) *Aphrodisias Papers* (*JRA* Supplement 1), Ann Arbor.

Rowlands, M. (1993) The role of memory in the transmission of culture, *World Archaeology* 25: 141–51.

Rutkowski, B. and Nowicki, K. (1996) *The Psychro Cave and Other Sacred Grottoes in Crete* (Studies and Monographs in Mediterranean Archaeology and Civilization II.1), Warsaw.

Sackett, L. H., ed. (1992) *Knossos from Greek City to Roman Colony: Excavations at the Unexplored Mansion II*, Oxford.

Said, E. W. (1993) *Culture and Imperialism*, New York.

Saïd, S., ed. (1991) *HELLENISMOS: Quelques jalons pour une histoire de l'identité grecque*, Leiden.

Sakellarakis, Y. (1985a) L'antro Idea. Cento anni di attività archeologica (1894–1984), *Atti dei Convegni Lincei* 74: 19–48.

(1985b) E nea erevna sto Idaio Antro, *Archaiologia* 15: 14–22.

(1988) The Idaean cave: Minoan and Greek worship, *Kernos* 1: 207–14.

Sanders, I. F. (1976) Settlement in the Hellenistic and Roman periods on the plain of the Mesara, Crete, *BSA* 71: 131–37.

(1982) *Roman Crete: An Archaeological Survey and Gazetteer of Late Hellenistic, Roman and Early Byzantine Crete*, Warminster.

Sando, J. S. (1979) The Pueblo Revolt, in A. Ortiz, ed., *Handbook of North American Indians, IX: Southwest*, 194–97. Washington, DC.

Sapouna, P. (1998) *Die Bildlampen römischer Zeit aus der Idäischen Zeusgrotte auf Kreta* (British Archaeological Reports International Series 696), Oxford.

Sartre, M. (1979) Aspects économiques et aspects religieux de la frontière dans les cités grecques, *Ktema* 4: 213–24.

Schachter, A. (1994) *Cults of Boeotia 3: Potnia to Zeus, Cults of Deities Unspecified by Name*, London.

Schacter, D. L. (1996) *Searching for Memory: The Brain, the Mind, and the Past*, New York.

Schama, S. (1995) *Landscape and Memory*, New York.

Schmalz, G. (1994) Public building and civic identity in Augustan and Julio-Claudian Athens. Unpublished Ph.D. thesis, University of Michigan.

Schmitz, T. (1997) *Bildung und Macht: Zur sozialen und politischen Funktion der zweiten Sophistik in der griechischen Welt der Kaiserzeit* (Zetemata 97), Munich.

Schnapp, A. (1996) *The Discovery of the Past*, trans. I. Kinnes and G. Varndell, New York.

Schneider, L. and Höcker, C. (1990) *Die Akropolis von Athen: Antikes Heiligtum und modernes Reiseziel*, Cologne.

Schroeder, A. H. (1979) Pecos Pueblo, in A. Ortiz, ed., *Handbook of North American Indians, IX: Southwest*, 430–37. Washington, DC.

Schudson, M. (1992) *Watergate in American Memory: How We Remember, Forget, and Reconstruct the Past*, New York.

Schumacher, R. W. M. (1993) Three related sanctuaries of Poseidon: Geraistos, Kalaureia and Tainaron, in N. Marinatos and R. Hägg, eds., *Greek Sanctuaries: New Approaches*, 62–87. London and New York.

Schwartz, B. (1982) The social context of commemoration: a study in collective memory, *Social Forces* 61: 374–402.

Scott, J. C. (1985) *Weapons of the Weak: Everyday Forms of Peasant Resistance*, New Haven.

Sennett, R. (1998) Disturbing memories, in P. Fara and K. Patterson, eds., *Memory*, 10–26. Cambridge.

Shanks, M. (1996) *Classical Archaeology of Greece: Experiences of the Discipline*, London and New York.

Shaw, J. W. (1992) Kommos, in J. L. Myers, E. E. Myers and G. Cadogan, eds., *The Aerial Atlas of Ancient Crete*, 148–53. London.

Shayegan, R. M. (1999) Aspects of Early Sasanian history and historiography. Unpublished Ph.D. thesis, Harvard University.

Shear, J. P. (1936) Athenian imperial coinage, *Hesperia* 5: 285–332.

Shear, T. L., Jr. (1970) The monument of the Eponymous Heroes in the Athenian Agora, *Hesperia* 39: 145–222.

     (1971) The Athenian agora: excavations of 1970, *Hesperia* 40: 241–79.

     (1981) Athens: from city-state to provincial town, *Hesperia* 50: 356–77.

     (1984) The Athenian agora: excavations of 1980–82, *Hesperia* 53: 1–57.

     (1997) The Athenian agora: excavations of 1989–1993, *Hesperia* 66: 495–548.

Sheppard, A. R. R. (1984–86) Homonoia in the Greek cities of the Roman empire, *Ancient Society* 15–17: 229–52.

Shero, L. R. (1938) Aristomenes the Messenian, *TAPA* 69: 500–31.

Shipley, G. (1992) *Perioikos*: the discovery of Classical Lakonia, in J. M. Sanders, ed., *PHILOLAKON: Lakonian studies in honour of Hector Catling*, 211–26. London.

     (1997) "The other Lakedaimonians": the dependent perioikic poleis of Laconia and Messenia, in M. H. Hansen, ed., *The Polis as an Urban Centre and as a Political Community* (Acts of the Copenhagen Polis Centre 4), 189–281. Copenhagen.

Silverblatt, I. (1988) Political memories and colonizing symbols: Santiago and the mountain gods of colonial Peru, in J. D. Hill, ed., *Rethinking History and Myth: Indigenous South American Perspectives on the Past*, 174–94. Urbana.

Simmons, M. (1979) History of Pueblo–Spanish relations to 1821, in A. Ortiz, ed., *Handbook of North American Indians, IX: Southwest*, 178–93. Washington, DC.

Sines, G. and Sakellarakis, Y. A. (1987) Lenses in antiquity, *AJA* 91: 191–96.

Slyomovics, S. (1998) *The Object of Memory: Arab and Jew Narrate the Palestinian Village*, Philadelphia.

Small, J. P. (1997) *Wax Tablets of the Mind: Cognitive Studies of Memory and Literacy in Classical Antiquity*, London.

Small, J. P. and Tatum, J. (1995) Memory and the study of classical antiquity: introduction, *Helios* 22: 149–50.

Smith, R. R. R. (1987) The imperial reliefs from the Sebasteion at Aphrodisias, *JRS* 77: 88–138.

(1988) Simulacra gentium: the ethne from the Sebasteion at Aphrodisias, *JRS* 78: 50–77.

(1998) Cultural choice and political identity in honorific portrait statues in the Greek east in the second century A.D., *JRS* 88: 56–93.

Smith, R. R. R. and Erim, K., eds. (1991) *Aphrodisias Papers 2* (*JRA* Supplement 2), Ann Arbor.

Smith, R. R. R. and Ratté, C. (1995) Archaeological research at Aphrodisias in Caria, 1993, *AJA* 99: 33–58.

(1996) Archaeological research at Aphrodisias in Caria, 1994, *AJA* 100: 5–33.

(1997) Archaeological research at Aphrodisias in Caria, 1995, *AJA* 101: 10–14.

(1998) Archaeological research at Aphrodisias in Caria, 1996, *AJA* 102: 225–50.

Snodgrass, A. M. (1987) *An Archaeology of Greece: The Present State and Future Scope of a Discipline*, Berkeley.

(1990) Survey archaeology and the rural landscape of the Greek city, in O. Murray and S. Price, eds., *The Greek City: From Homer to Alexander*, 113–36. Oxford.

Souza, P. de (1998) Late Hellenistic Crete and the Roman conquest, in W. G. Cavanagh and M. Curtis, eds., with J. N. Coldstream and A. W. Johnston, co-eds., *Post-Minoan Crete. Proceedings of the First Colloquium on Post-Minoan Crete held by the British School at Athens and the Institute of Archaeology, University College London, 10–11 November 1995*, 112–16. (British School at Athens Studies 2), London.

Spawforth, A. J. S. (1978) Balbilla, the Euryclids and memorials for a Greek magnate, *BSA* 73: 249–60.

(1989) Agonistic festivals in Roman Greece, in S. Walker and A. Cameron, eds., *The Greek Renaissance in the Roman Empire*, 193–97. London.

(1992a) Review of G. Rogers, *The Sacred Identity of Ephesos: Foundation Myths of a Roman City*, *CR* 42: 383–84.

(1992b) Spartan cults under the Roman empire: some notes, in J. M. Sanders, ed., *PHILOLAKON: Lakonian studies in honour of Hector Catling*, 227–38. London.

(1994a) Corinth, Argos and the imperial cult: Pseudo-Julian, *Letters* 198, *Hesperia* 63: 211–32.

(1994b) Symbol of unity? The Persian-Wars tradition in the Roman empire, in S. Hornblower, ed., *Greek Historiography*, 233–47. Oxford.

(1996) Roman Corinth: the formation of a colonial elite, in A. D. Rizakis, ed., *Roman Onomastics in the Greek East: Social and Political Aspects* (*Meletemata* 21), 167–82. Athens.

(1997) The early development of the imperial cult in Athens, in M. Hoff and S. Rotroff, eds., *The Romanization of Athens*, 183–201. Oxford.

(1999) The Panhellenion again. *Chiron* 29: 339–52.

Spawforth, A. J. S. and Walker, S. (1985) The world of the Panhellenion: I. Athens and Eleusis, *JRS* 75: 78–104.

(1986) The world of the Panhellenion: II. Three Dorian cities, *JRS* 76: 88–105.

Spencer, N. (1995) Heroic time: monuments and the past in Messenia, southwest Greece, *Oxford Journal of Archaeology* 14: 277–92.

(1998) The history of archaeological investigations in Messenia, in J. L. Davis, ed., *Sandy Pylos: An Archaeological History from Nestor to Navarino*, 23–41. Austin.

Spencer, T. (1954) *Fair Greece, Sad Relic: Literary Philhellenism from Shakespeare to Byron*, Bath.

Spyridakis, S. (1970) *Ptolemaic Itanos and Hellenistic Crete* (University of California Publications in History 82), Berkeley.

(1992a) The Roman involvement in Crete, in *Cretica: Studies on Ancient Crete*, 129–40. New Rochelle, NY.

(1992b) Zeus is dead: Euhemerus and Crete, in *Cretica: Studies on Ancient Crete*, 1–7. New Rochelle, NY.

St. Clair, W. L. (1972) *That Greece Might Still be Free: The Philhellenes in the War of Independence*, London.

Stais, V. (1893) O en Marathoni Tymbos, *Mitteilungen des deutschen archöologischen Instituts, Athenische Abteilung*, 46–63.

Stambaugh, J. E. (1988) *The Ancient Roman City*, Baltimore and London.

Starr, C. G. (1983) Minoan flower lovers, in R. Hägg and N. Marinatos, eds., *The Minoan Thalassocracy: Myth and Reality* (Skrifter utgivna av Svenska Institutet i Athen 4°, 32), 9–12. Göteborg.

Ste. Croix, G. E. M. de (1972) *The Origins of the Peloponnesian War*, London and Ithaca.

(1981) *The Class Struggle in the Ancient World from the Archaic Age to the Arab Conquests*, London.

Stewart, K. (1988) Nostalgia – a polemic, *Cultural Anthropology* 3: 227–41.

Stewart, S. (1984) *On Longing: Narratives of the Miniature, the Gigantic, the Souvenir, the Collection*, Baltimore.

Stibbe, C. M. (1996) *Das Andere Sparta* (Kulturgeschichte der Antiken Welt 65), Mainz.

Stieglitz, R. R. (1976) The Eteocretan inscription from Psychro, *Kadmos* 15: 84–86.

Sutton, D. E. (1998) *Memories Cast in Stone: The Relevance of the Past in Everyday Life*, Oxford and New York.

Svoronos, J.-N. (1890) *Numismatique de la Crète ancienne* I, Macon, GA.

Swain, S. (1996) *Hellenism and Empire: Language, Classicism and Power in the Greek World, AD 50–250*, Oxford.

Syme, R. (1979) Problems about Janus, *AJP* 100: 188–212.

Tacitus (1956) *The Annals of Imperial Rome*, trans. Michael Grant, Harmondsworth.

Talbert, R. (1989) The role of the helots in the class struggle at Sparta, *Historia* 38: 22–40.

Tarditi, C. (1992) Lebena-Asklepieion, in J. W. Myers, E. E. Myers, and G. Cadogan, eds., *The Aerial Atlas of Ancient Crete*, 160–63. London.

Tarlow, S. (1997) An archaeology of remembering: death, bereavement and the First World War, *Cambridge Archaeological Journal* 7: 105–21.

Tatum, J. (1995a) Aunt Elvie's quilt on the bed of Odysseus: the role of artifacts in natural memory, in J. P. Small and J. Tatum, 'Memory and the Study of Classical Antiquity', *Helios* 22: 167–74.

(1995b) Memory in recent humanistic research, in J. P. Small and J. Tatum, 'Memory and the Study of Classical Antiquity', *Helios* 22: 151–55.

Taylor, A. C. (1993) Remembering to forget: identity, mourning and memory among the Jivaro, *Man* 28: 653–78.

Taylor, D. (1997) *Disappearing Acts: Spectacles of Gender and Nationalism in Argentina's 'Dirty War'*, Durham, NC.

Thelen, D. (1989) Memory and American history, *The Journal of American History* 75: 1117–29.

Themelis, P. (1969) Ieron Poseidonos eis Akovitika Kalamatas, *AAA* 2: 352–57.

    (1970) Archaïke Epigraphe ek tou Ierou tou Poseidonos eis Akovitika, *ArchDelt* 25: 109–25.

    (1974) Marathon, *ArchDelt* 29: 226–44.

    (1993) Damophon von Messene – Sein Werk im Lichte der Neuen Ausgrabungen, *Antike Kunst* 36: 24–40.

    (1994a) Artemis Ortheia at Messene: the epigraphical and archaeological evidence, in R. Hägg, ed., *Ancient Greek Cult Practice from the Epigraphical Evidence*, 101–22. Stockholm.

    (1994b) Damophon of Messene: new evidence, in K. A. Sheedy, ed., *Archaeology in the Peloponnese: New Excavations and Research*, 1–37. Oxford.

    (1998) The sanctuary of Demeter and the Dioscouri at Messene, in R. Hägg, ed., *Ancient Greek Cult Practice from the Archaeological Evidence*, 157–86. Stockholm.

Thomas, J. (1993) The politics of vision and the archaeologies of landscape, in B. Bender, ed., *Landscape: Politics and Perspectives*, 19–48. Oxford.

Thomas, R. (1989) *Oral Tradition and Written Record in Classical Athens*, Cambridge.

    (1992) *Literacy and Orality in Ancient Greece* (Key Themes in Ancient History), Cambridge.

Thompson, H. A. (1940) *The Tholos of Athens and its Predecessors* (Hesperia Supplement 4), Princeton.

    (1952) Excavations in the Athenian Agora: 1951, *Hesperia* 21: 83–113.

    (1960) Activities in the Athenian Agora: 1959, *Hesperia* 29: 327–68.

    (1966) The annex to the Stoa of Zeus in the Athenian Agora, *Hesperia* 35: 171–87.

    (1987) The impact of Roman architects and architecture on Athens, in S. Macready and F. H. Thompson, eds., *Roman Architecture in the Greek World*, 1–17. London.

Thompson, H. A. and Wycherley, R. E. (1972) *The Athenian Agora, XIV: The Agora of Athens: The History, Shape and Uses of an Ancient City Center*, Princeton.

Tilley, C. (1994) *A Phenomenology of Landscape: Places, Paths and Monuments*, Oxford.

    (1999) *Metaphor and Material Culture*, Oxford.

Tobin, J. (1997) *Herodes Attikos and the City of Athens: Patronage and Conflict under the Antonines*, Amsterdam.

Tod, M. N. (1905) Notes and inscriptions from southwestern Messenia, *JHS* 25: 32–55.

Tonkin, E. (1995) *Narrating Our Pasts: The Social Construction of Oral History* (Cambridge Studies in Oral and Literate Cultures 22), Cambridge and New York. (Originally published 1992.)

Torelli, M. and Musti, D. (1991a) Commento, in *Pausania, Guida della Grecia, IV: La Messenia*, 203–72. Milan.

    (1991b) Nota introduttiva al Libro IV, in *Pausania, Guida della Grecia, IV: La Messenia*, ix–xxviii. Milan.

Townsend, E. (1955) A Mycenaean chamber tomb under the Temple of Ares, *Hesperia* 24: 187–219.

Treves, P. (1944) The problem of a history of Messenia, *JHS* 64: 102–6.

Tsigakou, F.-M. (1981) *The Rediscovery of Greece: Travellers and Painters of the Romantic Era*, London.

Tsipopoulou, M. (1989) *Archaeological Survey at Aghia Photia, Siteia*, Partille.

Tyree, L. (1974) Cretan sacred caves: archaeological evidence. Unpublished Ph.D. thesis, University of Missouri-Columbia.

Valmin, M. N. (1927–28) Continued explorations in Eastern Triphylia, *Bulletin de la Société Royale de Lettres de Lund* 1927–28: 171–224.

(1929) Inscriptions de la Messénie, *Bulletin de la Société Royale de Lettres de Lund* 1928–29: 108–55.

(1930) *Etudes topographiques sur la Messénie ancienne*, Lund.

(1938) *The Swedish Messenia Expedition*, Lund.

(1941) Ein messenisches Kastell und die arkadische Grenzfrage, *Opuscula Archaeologica* 2: 59–76.

van der Veer, J. A. G. (1982) The battle of Marathon: a topographical survey, *Mnemosyne* 35: 290–321.

van Effenterre, H. (1942) Querelles crétoises, *Revue des études anciennes* 44: 31–51.

(1948) *La Crète et le monde grec de Platon à Polybe*, Paris.

(1982) Terminologie et formes de dépendance en Crète, in L. Hadermann-Misguich and G. Raepsaet, eds., *Rayonnement grec: hommages à Charles Delvoye*, 35–44. Brussels.

van Effenterre, H. and Bougrat, M. (1969) Les frontières de Lato, *Kretika Chronika* 21: 9–53.

Van Groningen, B. A. (1965) Literary tendencies in the second century A.D., *Mnemosyne* 18: 41–56.

Vanderpool, E. (1959) Athens honors the emperor Tiberius, *Hesperia* 28: 86–90.

(1966a) The deme of Marathon and the Herakleion, *AJA* 70: 319–23.

(1966b) A monument to the Battle of Marathon, *Hesperia* 35: 93–106.

(1967) The marble trophy from Marathon in the British Museum, *Hesperia* 36: 108–110.

Vansina, J. (1980) Memory and oral tradition, in J. C. Miller, ed., *The African Past Speaks: Essays on Oral Tradition and History*, 262–76. Folkstone.

(1985) *Oral Tradition as History*, London and Nairobi.

Vasaly, A. (1993) *Representations: Images of the World in Ciceronian Oratory*, Berkeley.

Verbruggen, H. (1981) *Le Zeus crétois*, Paris.

Versakis, F. (1916) To ieron tou Korynthou Apollonos, *ArchDelt* 2: 65–118.

Vidal-Naquet, P. (1986) *The Black Hunter: Forms of Thought and Forms of Society in the Greek World*, trans. A. Szegedy-Maszak, Baltimore. (Originally published 1981.)

(1992) *Assassins of Memory: Essays on the Denial of the Holocaust*, trans. J. Mehlman, New York. (Originally published 1987.)

Viviers, D. (1994) La cité de Dattalla et l'expansion territoriale de Lyktos en Crète centrale, *BCH* 118: 229–59.

(1999) Economy and territorial dynamics in Crete from the Archaic to the Hellenistic period, in A. Chaniotis, ed., *From Minoan Farmers to Roman Traders: Sidelights on the Economy of Ancient Crete*, 221–33. Stuttgart.

Wachtel, N. (1990) Introduction, in M.-N. Bourguet, L. Valensi, and N. Wachtel, eds., *Between Memory and History*, 1–18. London.

Walker, S. (1997) Athens under Augustus, in M. Hoff and S. Rotroff, eds., *The Romanization of Athens*, 67–80. Oxford.

Wallace, P. W. (1969) Psyttaleia and the trophies of the Battle of Salamis, *AJA* 73: 293–303.

(1982) The final battle at Plataia, in *Studies in Attic Epigraphy and Topography Presented to Eugene Vanderpool* (*Hesperia* Supplement 19), 183–92. Princeton.

Wallace-Hadrill, A. (1990) Roman arches and Greek honours: the language of power at Rome, *PCPS* 36: 143–81.

(1998) To be Roman, go Greek: thoughts on hellenization at Rome, in M. Austin, J. Harries, and C. Smith, eds., *Modus Operandi: Essays in Honour of Geoffrey Rickman* (Bulletin of the Institute of Classical Studies Supplement 71), 79–91. London.

Ward-Perkins, J. B. (1981) *Roman Imperial Architecture*, second edn, Harmondsworth.

Wardman, A. (1976) *Rome's Debt to Greece*, London.

Watrous, L. V. (1982) *Lasithi: A History of Settlement on a Highland Plain in Crete* (*Hesperia* Supplement 18), Princeton.

(1996) *The Cave Sanctuary of Zeus at Psychro: A Study of Extra-Urban Sanctuaries in Minoan and Early Iron Age Crete* (Aegaeum 15), Liège and Austin.

Watrous, L.V., Xatzi-Vallianou, D., Pope, K., Mourtzas, N., Shay, J., Shay, C.T., Bennet, J., Tsoungarakis, D., Angelomati-Tsoungarakis, E., Vallianos, C., and Blitzer, H. (1993) A survey of the Western Mesara plain in Crete: preliminary report of the 1984, 1986 and 1987 field seasons, *Hesperia* 62: 191–248.

Webster, J. (2001) Creolizing the Roman provinces, *AJA* 105: 209–25.

Weiss, P. (1984) Lebendiger Mythos: Gründerheroen und städtische Gründungstraditionen im griechisch-römischen Osten, *Würzburger Jahrbücher für die Altertumswissenschaft* 10: 179–208.

(2000) Eumeneia und das Panhellenion, *Chiron* 30: 618–39.

Welch, K. (1999) Negotiating Roman spectacle architecture in the Greek world: Athens and Corinth, in B. Bergmann and C. Kondoleon, eds., *The Art of Ancient Spectacle* (Studies in the History of Art 56; Center for Advanced Study in the Visual Arts Symposium Papers 34), 125–45. New Haven and London.

Welwei, K.-W. (1979) Das sog. grab der Plataier im Vranatal bei Marathon, *Historia* 28: 101–6.

West, W. C. (1969) The trophies of the Persian Wars, *CP* 64: 7–19.

Whitby, M. (1994) Two shadows: images of Spartans and helots, in A. Powell and S. Hodkinson, eds., *The Shadow of Sparta*, 87–126. London and New York.

Whitley, J. (1988) Early states and hero cults: a reappraisal, *JHS* 108: 173–82.

(1992) Praisos, in J. L. Myers, E. E. Myers and G. Cadogan, eds., *The Aerial Atlas of Ancient Crete*, 256–61. London.

(1994) The monuments that stood before Marathon: tomb cult and hero cult in Archaic Attica, *AJA* 98: 213–30.

(1998) From Minoans to Eteocretans: the Praisos region, 1200–500 BC, in W. G. Cavanagh and M. Curtis, eds., with J. N. Coldstream and A. W. Johnston, co-eds., *Post-Minoan Crete. Proceedings of the First Colloquium on Post-Minoan Crete held by the British School at Athens and the Institute of Archaeology, University College London, 10–11 November 1995*, 27–39. (British School at Athens Studies 2), London.

Whitley, J., O'Conor, K., and Mason, H. (1995) Praisos III: a report on the architectural survey undertaken in 1992, *BSA* 90: 405–28.

Whitmer, P. O. (1993) *When the Going Gets Weird: The Twisted Life and Times of Hunter S. Thompson*, New York.

Wickham, C. (1994) Lawyers' time: history and memory in tenth- and eleventh-century Italy, in *Land and Power: Studies in Italian and European Social History, 400–1200*, 275–93. London.

Wilcox, M. (2001) The archaeology of the Pueblo revolt in 1680. Unpublished Ph.D. thesis, Harvard University.

Wilhelm, A. (1891) Inschriften aus Messene, *Mitteilungen des deutschen archäologischen Instituts, Athenische Abteilung* 16: 345–55.

Willers, D. (1990) *Hadrians panhellenisches Programm: Archäologische Beiträge zur Neugestaltung Athens durch Hadrian*, Basel.

Willetts, R. F. (1962) *Cretan Cults and Festivals*, London.

(1965) *Ancient Crete: A Social History from Early Times until the Roman Occupation*, London.

(1977) *The Civilization of Ancient Crete*, Berkeley.

Williams, C. K. (1987) The refounding of Corinth: some Roman religious attitudes, in S. Macready and F. H. Thompson, eds., *Roman Architecture in the Greek World*, 26–37. London.

Wilson, J. (1966) *Emigration from Italy in the Republican Age*, Manchester.

Wilson, J. B. (1979) *Pylos 425 BC: A Historical and Topographical Study of Thucydides' Account of the Campaign*, Warminster.

Winter, J. (1995) *Sites of Memory, Sites of Mourning: The Great War in European Cultural History*, Cambridge.

Winter, J. and Sivan, E., eds. (1999) *War and Remembrance in the Twentieth Century*, Cambridge.

Wiseman, T. P. (1986) Monuments and the Roman annalists, in I. S. Moxon, J. D. Smart, and A. J. Woodman, eds., *Past Perspectives: Studies in Greek and Roman Historical Writing*, 87–101. Cambridge.

Woolf, G. (1994) Becoming Roman, staying Greek: culture, identity and the civilizing process in the Roman east, *PCPS* 40: 116–43.

   (1996) The uses of forgetfulness in Roman Gaul, in H.-J. Gehrke and A. Möller, eds., *Vergangenheit und Lebenswelt: Soziale Kommunikation, Traditionsbildung und historisches Bewusstsein*, 361–81. Tübingen.

   (2001) Inventing empire in ancient Rome, in S. E. Alcock, T. N. D'Altroy, K. D. Morrison, and C. M. Sinopoli, eds., *Empires: Perspectives from Archaeology and History*, 311–22. Cambridge.

Wörrle, M. (1988) *Stadt und Fest im kaiserzeitlichen Kleinasien: Studien zu einer agonistischen Stiftung aus Oinoanda*, Munich.

Yadin, Y. (1966) *Masada: Herod's Fortress and the Zealots' Last Stand*, New York.

Yates, F. A. (1966) *The Art of Memory*, Chicago.

Yates, R. (2001) Cosmos, central authority and communities in the early Chinese empire, in S. E. Alcock, T. N. D'Altroy, K. D. Morrison, and C. M. Sinopoli, eds., *Empires: Perspectives from Archaeology and History*, 351–68. Cambridge.

Yegül, F. Y. (2000) Memory, metaphor and meaning in the cities of Asia Minor, in E. Fentress, ed., *Romanization and the City: Creation, Transformations, and Failures* (*JRA* Supplement 38), 133–53. Ann Arbor.

Young, J. E. (1993) *The Texture of Memory: Holocaust Memorials and Meanings*, New Haven.

   (1994a) The art of memory: holocaust memories in history, in J. E. Young, ed., *The Art of Memory: Holocaust Memorials in History*, 19–38. Munich.

   ed. (1994b) *The Art of Memory: Holocaust Memorials in History*, Munich.

Young, R. J. C. (1995) *Colonial Desire: Hybridity in Theory, Culture and Race*, London and New York.

Zanker, P. (1988) *The Power of Images in the Age of Augustus*, Ann Arbor.

Zerubavel, Y. (1994) The death of memory and the memory of death: Masada and the Holocaust as historical metaphors, *Representations* 45: 72–100.

   (1995) *Recovered Roots: Collective Memory and the Making of Israeli National Tradition*, Chicago.

Ziolkowski, A. (1986) The plundering of Epirus in 167: economic considerations, *Papers of the British School at Rome* 54: 69–80.

Zunino, M. L. (1997) *Hiera Messeniaka: la storia religiosa della Messenia dall'età micenea all'età ellenistica*, Udine.

INDEX

CPSIA information can be obtained
at www.ICGtesting.com
Printed in the USA
LVHW051611060123
736517LV00005B/204

9 780521 890007